Immigration and Crime

New Perspectives in Crime, Deviance, and Law Series
Edited by John Hagan

*Clean Streets: Controlling Crime, Maintaining Order, and
Building Community Activism*
Patrick J. Carr

Gender and Crime: Patterns in Victimization and Offending
Edited by Karen Heimer and Candace Kruttschnitt

*The Many Colors of Crime: Inequalities of Race,
Ethnicity, and Crime in America*
Edited by Ruth D. Peterson, Lauren J. Krivo, and John Hagan

Immigration and Crime: Race, Ethnicity, and Violence
Edited by Ramiro Martinez Jr. and Abel Valenzuela Jr.

Immigration and Crime

Race, Ethnicity, and Violence

EDITED BY

*Ramiro Martinez Jr. and
Abel Valenzuela Jr.*

New York University Press

NEW YORK AND LONDON

NEW YORK UNIVERSITY PRESS
New York and London

Library of Congress Cataloging-in-Publication Data
Immigration and crime : race, ethnicity, and violence /
edited by Ramiro Martinez Jr. and Abel Valenzuela Jr.
p.   cm. — (New perspectives in crime, deviance, and law series)
Includes bibliographical references and index.
ISBN-13: 978-0-8147-5704-8 (cloth : alk. paper)
ISBN-10: 0-8147-5704-9 (cloth : alk. paper)
ISBN-13: 978-0-8147-5705-5 (pbk. : alk. paper)
ISBN-10: 0-8147-5705-7 (pbk. : alk. paper)
1. Crime—Sociological aspects—United States. 2. Alien criminals—
United States. 3. Immigrants—Crimes against—United States. 4. United
States—Emigration and immigration. 5. United States—Race relations.
6. Immigrants—United States—Social conditions.   I. Martinez, Ramiro.
II. Valenzuela, Abel. III. Series.
HV6181.I45   2006
364.3086'9120973—dc22   2006002281

New York University Press books are printed on acid-free paper,
and their binding materials are chosen for strength and durability.

Manufactured in the United States of America

c 10 9 8 7 6 5 4 3 2 1
p 10 9 8 7 6 5 4 3 2 1

In Memory of Eric Monkkonen
1943–2005

Contents

Acknowledgments

We would like to thank the contributors for participating in the activities of the November 2003 National Consortium on Violence Research (NCOVR) conference "Beyond Racial Dichotomies of Violence: Immigrants, Race, and Ethnicity," at the University of California, Los Angeles (UCLA), that culminated in the publication of this volume. Most of the authors spent a great deal of time preparing for the conference workshops, engaging in discussion of the presentations, and revising papers on the topic of immigration and crime. This book is the end result of these meetings and lays the foundation for future social inquiry on this neglected subject matter.

We also acknowledge the contributions of other workshop participants who provided comments and suggestions. Thanks to Alfred Blumstein, Robert Crutchfield, Garth Davies, Janet Lauritsen, Bryan Page, Richard Rosenfeld, Rogelio Saenz, Avelardo Valdez, and Diego Vigil. We also thank Matthew T. Lee, Cecilia Menjívar, and Amie Nielsen for taking the time to read and comment on some of the chapters.

Most importantly, we express deep gratitude to the NCOVR, headquartered at the H. John Heinz III School of Public Policy and Management at Carnegie Mellon University, especially its director, Alfred Blumstein, and staff. NCOVR provided financial and institutional support for the workshops and meetings that allowed us to discuss, present, and respond to the findings presented in this volume. Without this generous assistance, the exchange of ideas among scholars of immigration and scholars of crime and violence would never have culminated in the publication of this book. We also thank the UCLA Center for the Study of Urban Poverty for hosting the NCOVR workshop and providing logistical support.

We are indebted to the many faculty members and graduate and undergraduate students who helped push the book out the door. The various session audiences provided helpful and useful comments at the UCLA/ NCOVR conference. We were surprised at the faculty and students turnout during the daylong sessions and remain indebted to the anonymous professors, instructors, and teaching assistants who encouraged their students to attend the conference. We thank them all.

Other students shaped the finished product. Thanks to an NCOVR undergraduate research fund, Tanya Trewick and Tatiana Manriquez entered and coded most of the Miami and San Diego homicide data used in this book. Monique Hernandez also produced many of the figures and maps in the chapters. Sean Kilpatrick worked hard on putting the entire manuscript together, formatting the chapters, and placing them in some semblance of order while toiling in a disorderly environment. We thank them for those efforts. We also thank Ilene Kalish, executive editor, and Salwa Jabado, editorial assistant, at the NYU Press for supporting this project.

Finally, we dedicate this book to the memory and career of our friend and colleague Eric Monkkonen, Distinguished Professor of History and Public Policy at UCLA. The late Eric Monkkonen was one of the world's leading crime historians and wrote about the important variations in the race/ethnicity of homicide offenders and their victims over the past two hundred years in New York City and Los Angeles. Despite battling cancer, he attended the UCLA/NCOVR conference in good humor, brought along many of his graduate students, and eagerly participated in the discussions. We were touched by his presence. He will be missed by many.

Chapter 1

Coming to America
The Impact of the New Immigration on Crime

Ramiro Martinez Jr.

The latest wave of immigration[1] to the United States—mainly from Asia, the Caribbean, and Latin America—has permanently altered the racial and ethnic composition of the United States.[2] One consequence is that Latinos replaced African Americans as the largest ethnic minority group at the turn of the new century. Many communities, both inside and outside traditional destination points in the southwestern United States, also felt a larger immigrant presence as Latinos in particular expanded the boundaries of older urban communities, reached into suburban areas, and pushed into small towns and rural communities in regions of the country where few co-ethnics had previously resided.[3] Moreover, Asians—one of the fastest growing immigrant groups—are now proportionally more numerous than African Americans in some West Coast cities, and several communities are now dominated by this new population. On the other side of the country, large Haitian and Jamaican communities are emerging, while immigrants from Africa are a burgeoning presence in many East Coast neighborhoods. The increasing numbers and diversity of the newcomers, overwhelmingly non-European in composition, have sparked a heated public debate about the consequences of immigration, shifting discourse from concerns about race to concerns about immigrants.

For example, discussion of social problems stereotypically associated with racial minorities (e.g., blacks and Native Americans), such as high rates of male unemployment, substance abuse, and violent crime involvement, have now become important themes in the public immigration debate. At the same time, discussion has shifted to the "Latino problem" or the "immigrant dilemma," again raising time-honored fears and suspicions about the newcomers. Since at least 1980, studies of race in the traditional black-and-white framework have increasingly been supplanted by more nuanced scholarly explorations of ethnicity. Research has appeared with increasing frequency on "Latino," "Asian," and even "Afro-Caribbean" populations at the same time that foreign-born newcomers have been changing the racial and ethnic configuration of the United States. While studies of immigrants in many social science disciplines have proliferated, less attention has been paid to immigrant crime or the consequences of immigration on crime, despite an intensified public debate about this topic. The current volume is an attempt to help fill this void in the research literature.

The contributors to this volume were asked that to the degree possible they cover the extent of immigrant criminal activity or immigrant victimization. The latter topic—the criminal victimization of immigrants—in particular is an overlooked theme in the social science literature and certainly not an issue central to the public debate on crime.[4] Yet victimization among this group is an important social problem to explore, since it both contributes to crime in the United States and helps form immigrants' perception of the criminal justice system.[5] Over time, it also shapes the nature and extent of the immigrant experience with other racial/ethnic group members and with co-ethnics in new communities as they are incorporated into society.

In the following sections, I highlight current stereotypes about immigrant criminality and provide a brief overview of early theoretical and empirical work on the immigration and crime relationship. I then focus on more contemporary work in this area. In the last section of the chapter, I address the many contributions the current volume makes to the nascent immigration and crime literature.

Criminal Immigrant Stereotypes

The connection between immigration and crime is an important issue to consider. Debates on the topic date back more than a hundred years; some early twentieth-century writers alleged that immigrant groups were biologically deficient compared with nonimmigrants. Thus crime and disorder were among several harmful outcomes that could be expected as long as "inferior" immigrants were allowed to enter the country.[6] Reactions to the alleged link between immigration and crime were soon reflected in immigration policy. In fact, the growing fear of immigrants and crime helped facilitate the passage of the Emergency Immigration Act of 1921 and the Immigration Act of 1924, which substantially reduced the number of immigrants admitted to the United States.[7]

The public media and politicians are now again debating the costs and consequences of allowing immigrants into American society, and, in the new era of immigration, familiar fears about the potential criminal activities of the newcomers have risen. Without much empirical research to consider, this debate risks inaccuracies and exaggerations of the level of immigrant crime, while possibly inflaming unfounded public concerns that immigrants might become an underclass group of criminals. Such fears have also been fueled by some academicians and writers. To illustrate, I present three recent examples from pseudo–social scientists and self-styled public intellectuals, along with empirically based assessments of their claims. I focus on Latinos in particular and look at a range of "concerns" and "claims" about Latino "crime." The first example comes from Dr. Samuel P. Huntington, a professor of political science at Harvard University and author of the widely read and often contested book *The Clash of Civilizations and the Remaking of World Order.* More recently in his latest book, *Who Are We? The Challenges to America's National Identity,* he continues to perpetuate stereotypes of an immigrant group singled out by many as crime-prone decades ago:

> The Cubanization of Miami coincided with high levels of crime. For each year between 1985 and 1993, Miami ranked among the top three large cities (over 250,000 people) in violent crime. Much of this was related to the growing drug trade but also to the intensity of Cuban immigrant politics. . . . Political groups, race riots, and drug-related crime had made Miami a volatile and often dangerous place.[8]

There are several inaccuracies and ambiguities in this statement. First, in referring to a "Cubanization" of Miami that took place in the 1980s, Huntington seems to ignore the sizable Cuban population that already lived in Miami before that time. Since an estimated 125,000 Mariel Cubans arrived in South Florida between April and October 1980, it is important to distinguish between Cubans living in Miami before 1980 and those who immigrated during and after the Mariel boatlift. This omission is curious because Huntington does distinguish between Mariel and other Cuban immigrants in his chapter "Mexican Immigration and Hispanization" and

Mariels were often stereotyped as especially crime prone by the national and local media. Regardless, published research demonstrates that the Mariel Cuban homicide victim and offending rates rose in the early 1980s, approaching those of African Americans at one point, but then declined to levels of other Latinos and non-Latino whites by 1985, the starting date of Huntington's concerns about Cubanization.[9]

Huntington also claims that Miami ranked high in violent crime during a period (1990–93) when the Mariel Cubans were rarely arrested for any killings. In fact, there were so few Mariels engaging in homicide in the late 1980s that the Miami Police Department homicide detectives stopped distinguishing them from other ethnic groups by 1990.[10] Moreover, while Miami had its share of drug-related homicides, between 1980 and 1990 at least 83 percent of solved homicides were not related to drugs.[11] Last, violent crime rates rose nationally during this period, including in places with few immigrants.[12] The city of Miami, a place with high poverty rates, a factor known to be associated with higher crime and violence, was near the top of this list even before the 1980 Mariel boatlift or "Cubanization" more generally. For example, Marvin Wolfgang, in his classic *Patterns in Criminal Homicide,* lists ten cities with the highest rates of homicide using data from 1950, a point predating sizable immigration from Cuba. Miami is at the top of that list.[13]

A second example of an inaccurate statement on criminal immigrants is provided in a widely publicized memoir by Victor Davis Hanson, a Senior Fellow at the Hoover Institution in Stanford, California. The author focuses on the Central Valley area, another region that traditionally has experienced significant immigration:

> The Latino death rate—both citizens and aliens—from homicide is three times higher than for non-Hispanic whites. It is daily fare in our local papers to read of bodies dumped in peach orchards, the putrid remains of corpses fished out of irrigation canals, or the body parts and bones of the long-dead uncovered by the cultivators. These are the remains of hundreds of young men from central Mexico who simply disappeared—shot or stabbed and then dumped by thieves and murderers.[14]

Professor Hanson's sources, or rather the lack of them throughout the book, are not clear, at least from my reading of his information. First, according to a National Center for Health Statistics report published in 1998, the Latino homicide rate is three times higher than that for non-Latino whites. However, it is also half the homicide rate of non-Latino blacks at the national level.[15] The same CDC report also notes that the Latino homicide rate declined by 43 percent from 1990 to 1998.[16] It is unfortunate that Hanson neglects to mention the dramatic drop in the Latino homicide rate over a period of intense Mexican immigration into the United States or the fact that Latino homicide rates are generally much lower than expected given social conditions.[17]

Second, it is hard to envision any place could contain the remains of "hundreds of young Mexicans" without arousing suspicion from co-workers, neighbors, spouses, lovers, family members, and others. For a point of comparison, consider that the City of San Diego Police Department reported almost 1,000 ($N = 932$) Hispanic or Mexican total homicide victims between the years of 1960 through 2002.[18] Thus we are asked to believe that the total number of Latino killings in one of the largest cities in the United States, over a forty-two-year time period, is likely substantially lower than what allegedly occurred in the Central Valley orchards. Moreover, it is not clear how the author concluded these were all Mexican victims of violent crime. Perhaps a new type of DNA test, one that can distinguish Mexicans from non-Mexicans, was conducted on these remains. Finally, it is regrettable that Professor Hanson did not provide any citations in his book to substantiate any of his claims. This is a task that he claims "professional Latinos" or "race hustlers" neglect in chapter 5 of his book.

A final example of public hysteria over immigrant crime, in this case singling out young Latinos rather than the Latino population as a whole, is provided by Heather MacDonald. MacDonald is a nonpracticing attorney and a fellow at the Manhattan Institute, a conservative think tank in New York City. She is also a contributing editor to *City Journal,* a magazine published by the Manhattan Institute. MacDonald's claim follows:

Hispanic youths, whether recent arrivals or birthright American citizens, are developing an underclass culture. (By "Hispanic" here, I mean the population originating in Latin America—above all, in Mexico—as distinct from America's much smaller Puerto Rican and Dominican communities of Caribbean descent, which have themselves long shown elevated crime and welfare rates.) Hispanic school dropout rates and teen birthrates are now the highest in the nation. Gang crime is exploding nationally—rising 50 percent from 1999 to 2002—driven by the march of Hispanic immigration east and north across the country. Most worrisome, underclass indicators like crime and single parenthood do not improve over successive generations of Hispanics—they worsen.[19]

It is not difficult to confirm that there was a rise in gang-related homicide, not necessarily crime, between 1999 and 2002. It is extremely difficult, however, to make the connection to the "Hispanic march across the country" that MacDonald blends into one concern. First, we can cautiously estimate the number of gang-related homicides. In the Bureau of Justice Statistics report entitled "Homicide Trends in the United States,"[20] the homicide circumstance section notes that "[f]or gang related homicides, the number of victims begins at 129 in 1976 and gradually increases to a high of 1,362 in 1993. It drops to 834 in 1998 followed by an increase reaching 1,119 in 2002." According to my calculations this is a 34 percent increase from 1998 to 2002. Moreover, for some perspective, the Bureau of Justice Statistics reports that in 2002 there were 4,752 killings that began as some type of argument or fight. That same year 2,656 felony homicides were committed during a rape, robbery, burglary, theft, motor vehicle theft, or other crime. Most homicides are not gang related, and most homicides declined while immigration grew and immigrants spread across the nation.[21] In addition, the connection to Latino/Hispanic disproportionate involvement, especially over time and across generations, was not established, since ethnicity was not detailed in this report—or in most crime studies, for that matter. Ethnicity is also not typically available in national data, one impetus for the studies that follow in this book.

Finally, it is also unfortunate that MacDonald did not provide sources for her contention that Puerto Ricans and Dominicans have long had high crime rates or specify a time period. To the best of my knowledge few scholars have access to Latino-specific data of this type.[22] Given the concentration of Puerto Ricans and Dominicans in New York City, and the steep homicide decline in the city from 1990 to 2002, it is hard to imagine homicide rates for any group soaring during the period.

With these examples of the immigration-crime stereotype in mind, I turn to discuss the early work conducted on the topic.

The Reality of Immigrant Crime: Early Theoretical and Empirical Lessons

Public anxiety about crime-prone immigrants and immigrant communities is as old as the topic itself.[23] Rising immigration into the United States coincided with increased fear of crime in many areas—a presumed connection dating back to at least the early 1900s. At that time, massive waves of European immigration to the United States prompted the founders of American sociology in Chicago to concentrate on various consequences of immigration. Juvenile delinquency and other urban social problems were among their central concerns. Early scholars, especially Shaw and McKay,[24] wrote about the high concentration of juvenile delinquency in areas adjacent to the downtown business and industrial districts. These low-income areas contained high levels of recent immigrants and southern black migrants. As Shaw and McKay note:

> Thus the newer European immigrants are found concentrated in certain areas, while Negroes from the rural South and Mexicans occupy others of comparable status. Neither of these population categories, considered separately, however, is suitable for correlation with rates of delinquents, since some areas of high rates have a predominantly immigrant population and others are entirely or largely Negro. Both categories, however, refer to groups of low economic status, making their adjustment to a complex urban environment.[25]

The Chicago data, and similar figures collected in several other cities by the authors and associates, noted that youth crime was concentrated in specific types of areas, regardless of "nativity and nationality." They also noted that as immigrants or immigrant group members moved out of these areas and into better communities their juvenile crime rates declined. It was not immigrants or blacks per se but the conditions in which they settled that were important for juvenile crime.

The finding that the impact of immigration as a social process at the community level was linked to crime did not necessarily engender additional research on the characteristics of distinct immigrant groups and crime. This is telling because, as Roger Lane points out, around 1900 "[i]mmigrant status in itself was not significant . . . in that most foreign-born ethnic groups in Philadelphia were apparently less inclined to violence than native Americans."[26] This finding was echoed in a report issued by the 1911 U.S. Immigration Commission, which found that immigration had not increased the volume of crime and noted that the presence of newcomers might have buffered criminal activity.[27] Contrary to stereotypes, the few empirical studies at the time generally did not discover newcomers to be hyperviolent or crime prone. Some evidence emerged that children of immigrants had higher levels of criminal activity than their parents but not necessarily higher rates than their native-born counterparts. Nevertheless, these early studies found that immigrants remained less involved in crime than the native born.[28]

Most of the handful of early studies focused on European immigrants. A notable exception to this pattern, volume 2 of *Mexican Labor in the United States*, is perhaps the earliest quantitative study on Mexican immigration to the United States. In this study Paul S. Taylor described the labor market, educational, criminal justice, and fertility experiences of Mexican-origin persons in Chicago.[29] By explicitly linking arrest statistics (felonies and misdemeanors) to local population sizes, he was able to compare white and Mexican criminal activities. While Mexicans were arrested at a percentage two to three times their population size, most of the arrests were not related to violence; rather, they were for property and alcohol-related offenses, a finding that Taylor linked to the high number of single males in the population. Regarding violence, Taylor noted that

> [a]ssault of various kinds, and carrying weapons of various kinds comprise another 9.7 percent of the charges on which convictions were obtained against Mexicans. This percentage also is higher than similar percentages for American whites and all nationalities, which were 3.3 and 4.7, respectively. The offenses of Mexicans are concentrated much more than average in these two groups of charges, probably mainly because of the very abnormal age and sex composition of the Mexican population in Chicago.[30]

This is important to highlight because patterns of criminal involvement were shaped by social factors, including neighborhood poverty and the age and sex distributions of the immigrant population, not the inherent criminality of immigrant Latinos.

The Taylor study is significant because it was published during a time when the handful of existing immigrant crime studies largely compared European immigrants to southern black migrants in Chicago, Philadelphia, and New York City.[31] Few scholars acknowledged the presence of Latino or non-European immigrants. The passage of restrictionist national-origin quota laws in the 1920s and assimilation campaigns gradually rendered the study of the immigrant European experience obsolete and forced scholars to focus on race or "black versus white" comparisons after World War II. Without data (and with few immigrants), researchers soon shifted attention from immigrant crime research to other aspects of urban social problems. In fact, in chapter 3 of this book Jeffrey Morenoff and Avi Astor note that there are now ten times as many articles on race and crime as on immigration and crime.

Contemporary Crime and Immigration Contexts

After 1965 and the dismantling of laws establishing preferences for immigrant Europeans, newcomers once again began arriving in large numbers. As noted at the start of this chapter, the contemporary immigrant influx is vastly different, in terms of national origins, from the influx at the turn of the last century. Most immigrants who have arrived since 1980 are from Latin America and Asia, while the vast majority of foreign-born arrivals in the 1910s and 1920s were from Europe. Moreover, today's newcomers still live in the nation's largest urban regions, but these places have become very different from the old immigrant destinations.

Undoubtedly, New York and Chicago are still significant settlement places for the foreign born, much as they were over a hundred years ago. However, contemporary immigrant communities in many ways define Los Angeles, San Diego, and, at the other end of the country, Miami, Florida. Substantial movements into or at least through cities such as New Orleans and Phoenix are also relatively common. Many of these places, which figure prominently as research sites in this book, also have had a long history of high rates of crime. Though the roots of such long-standing crime patterns lay elsewhere, in many instances Latinos and other immigrant groups have served as convenient scapegoats for contemporary crime problems.

Even as high levels of immigration revived stereotypical concerns about letting newcomers into the country, they simultaneously renewed research on a host of topics related to immigration in almost every branch of the social sciences. The exception was in scholarship on immigrants and crime and violence. This is surprising because the founders of American sociology were concerned about the role of community disorganization in producing high crime rates and the disorganizing influences inherent in moving from rural Europe to urban areas of the United States.[32]

Despite the general lack of research on contemporary immigration and crime, some scholars have examined the impact of recent immigration on violence and crime and have compared the characteristics of immigrant to nonimmigrant victimization. These include national, metropolitan, and community-level studies that control for percentages of recent immigrants while examining other factors associated with crime, including economic deprivation and residential instability. Almost all such research has reported null or negative effects of immigration on lethal and nonlethal violence, findings that are consistent with prior studies.[33] That is, higher levels of immigrants either have no effect on or are associated with lower levels of crime and violence. These results may indicate that the areas or neighborhoods into which newcomers settle are revitalized or stabilized by the presence of immigrants, arguments consistent with the "immigration revitalization perspective" rather than with the premise that recent immigrants disrupt communities.[34] Contemporary scholars are now more open to the possibility that an influx of immigrants into disadvantaged and high-crime communities may encourage new forms of social organization and adaptive social structures. Such adaptations may mediate the negative effects of economic deprivation and various forms of demographic heterogeneity (ethnic, cultural, social) on formal and informal social control, thereby decreasing crime.

In recent years, a handful of examinations of the relationship between immigrants and crime can be found in the work of Hagan and Palloni,[35] Butcher and Piehl,[36] Aguirre, Saenz, and James,[37] and myself, including my research with Lee and Nielsen on the Mariel Cubans.[38] All have suggested that immigrant differences in violent crime or incarceration, relative to the native born, are rare or nonexistent. Although considered original, if not pioneering, work by other immigration and violence scholars, these findings have not found a wide audience among members of the general public, policy makers, or the anti-immigrant pundits discussed earlier in this chapter.

The above-mentioned authors have provided some preliminary data, research findings, and lines of argument that have succeeded in challenging the contention that immigrants usually engage in crime more than the native born. However, I would suggest that because of their methodological concerns, especially a focus on quantitative data, they fail to capture fully the array of violence and crime concerns by, for example, looking only at homicides or total violent crime rates. Most do not examine finer ethnic distinctions among groups, including underexamined groups such as Haitians, Asian subgroups, or Mexican border crossers, thus suggesting the need for additional studies on the topic. As we will see, the persistent problem of examining violence among immigrants—specifically the lack of original crime data—has been addressed in innovative ways by the contributors to this volume. Their results are informative and suggest that additional data collection efforts might produce even more fruitful studies on the notion that immigration begets crime.

As noted earlier, immigrants currently constitute a larger portion of the U.S. population than in the early 1900s. In fact, it is common to highlight this as one of the most profound and recent demographic transformations across the nation. The immigrant population currently numbers over thirty-three million (not counting an almost equal number of U.S.-born children of immigrants), with newcomers now composing almost 12 percent of the U.S. population. This percentage falls short of that a hundred years ago (about one-third of the population was immigrant or children of immigrants in 1910), but it could grow rapidly through immigrants' continued entry and higher fertility rates than native-born Americans.

To be sure, it is not clear that the increasing proportion of new immigrants across time is directly linked to any change in the annual rates of violent crime. What is clear is that the annual percentage of immigrants has more than doubled since 1980 and that it rose steadily at the same time as rates of both homicide (per hundred thousand) and robbery (per thousand) at first fluctuated widely (between 1980 and 1994) and then dropped (between 1994 and 2002) (see figure 1.1).[39] Robberies increased slightly from 1990 to 1994, the same period over which immigration was increasing. However, by 2003, while the percent of the total population that was immigrant had doubled compared with 1980, the homicide and robbery rates had fallen to levels at least half their previous rate in the same period. This of course does not suggest a causal relationship, but these data are contrary to popular wisdom suggesting that immigration is driving violence upwards. The trends reported in figure 1.1 show that two very different rates of violent crime—reported robberies (which are usually between strangers) and homicides (which typically do not involve strangers)—

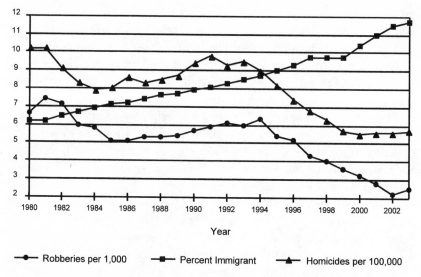

Fig. 1.1. Percent Immigrant in the United States by Violent Crime Rates, 1980–2003

both fluctuated dramatically during a period of steady increase in the proportion of the population that was composed of immigrants.[40]

Thus there is no clear evidence of increased violence over the last decade as the percentage of the nation's population increasingly became foreign born. The national trends shown in figure 1.1 counter the widespread belief that more violence was generated as more "aliens" entered the United States, spreading destruction, killing over drug markets, or increasing criminal activity. In fact, while the figure does not offer a definitive causal connection, it suggests that the opposite may be true—over time it appears that more immigrants means less violence. Studies of specific immigrant-destination cities show the same result as the national trend.[41]

However, the figure only shows national trends in immigration and violence over the last twenty-three years. As we will see in the following chapters, scholars who study this issue stress that the relationship between immigrants and violence is not always definitive but that when this connection is directly examined with empirical data there is typically a negative relationship or no association. The chapters that follow entail more detailed consideration of these issues.

Contributions of This Volume

Taking stock of the putative link between racial/ethnic/immigrant violence and crime is the aim of this book. To address this subject, the National Consortium on Violence Research (NCOVR)[42] funded a grant to commission the initial papers. The papers were presented and discussed at a conference held in November 2003 and hosted by the Center for the Study of Urban Poverty at the University of California, Los Angeles.

Building on this convergence on the topics, the chapters presented here broadly assess the state of immigration and crime research in a number of ways. Some, for example, revise traditional theoretical perspectives on immigration and crime, examine victimization among hard-to-find undocumented immigrant populations, or examine the consequences of delinquency for immigrants (versus nonimmigrants) while facing problems of absorption into American society. Others explore the longitudinal effects of violence within and among immigrant populations and the impact of local conditions on immigrant violence. By addressing the state of crime investigations in the field of immigration and criminological research, the contributors demonstrate the relevance of this area of social inquiry.

The contributors were asked to provide chapters that would explore the problem of violence from their own unique perspective. Of course, the primary strength and intellectual contribution of this volume is the diversity of approaches, qualitative and quantitative, to the theme of immigration and crime and the gamut of crime types that the authors explore. Much of the focus is on exposure to crime or violence, crime and serious delinquency, and the consequences of violence, broadly defined to include incarceration, deviance, and antisocial behavior. In some chapters, crime is not treated so much in relation to the justice system as in terms of how immigrants are victimized as they enter the United States, search for employment, avoid racial/ethnic conflict in the workplace, or are singled out by others in incidents that are not always reported to the police or captured in traditional surveys. Although diverse in focus, all of the chapters challenge stereotypes of immigrant criminality—that is, of immigrants as a criminally inclined group—and help fill some of the gaps in contemporary knowledge with research instead of rhetoric.

Few studies consider the impact of recent immigration on violence, crime, and deviance, and few compare the characteristics of immigrant and nonimmigrant crime. Still, as several of the contributors discuss, there are good theoretical reasons to expect that immigrants may be more likely to engage in crime than similarly situated native groups. Other researchers refer to the "immigration paradox": finding unexpectedly favorable social and health outcomes, such as infant health, for immigrants despite social and economic conditions that social scientists usually associate with "social disorganization." Scholars, especially some contributors to this book, are now expanding the notion of the immigrant paradox to include crime.

Of course, we are just beginning to understand the complex relationship between immigration and crime, especially at the community level. This issue will undoubtedly become increasingly influential for many of the new ethnic immigrant groups, in particular ones that are moving beyond traditional settlement places and into communities that were not affected in past decades. In many of these communities, residents have not been welcomed with open arms, and this new demographic shift and its implications should be examined in the future.

The chapters in this book do not cover everything about immigration, crime, and violence, but they do help us understand the importance of studying the topic. In many cases the contributors have had to grapple with racial/ethnic categories and definitions while compiling complete and reliable data. Because of these efforts, the authors have contributed important insights that make this book one of the first to explore the many dimensions of the relation between race/ethnicity/immigrant status and violence and crime. All of the authors are aware of the deep-rooted problems in this research area and have sought to overcome them in many ways. They should be thanked for completing this difficult task. The authors have many voices, differences in perspectives, interpretations, findings, and of course conclusions. Nevertheless, taken together the respective chapters should prompt much additional research.

Finally, the primary goal of this book is to assemble a diverse group of scholars who can offer innovative approaches to the study of ethnicity, immigration status, and crime, or the impact of immigration on violent events and crime. Taken together, they all extend this area of knowledge and offer guidance on much-needed future research efforts in this area of social inquiry. They also remind us that criminologists can no longer restrict studies of crime to whites and blacks. At the same time, immigration researchers can no longer ignore the study of violence or crime. Because the United States is increasingly multiethnic and immigrant communities are proliferating, the time has come to ask and answer more questions about immigration and crime than have been traditionally posed. Stereotypes surrounding this issue also need to be examined in light of empirical studies. This book will hopefully guide much needed future scholarly activity in this important area of research.

N O T E S

1. Due to restrictive legislation, most forms of legal immigration subsided in the 1920s and 1930s. The most recent immigration waves followed passage of the Hart-Celler Act of 1965.

2. Luke Larsen (2004) notes in *The Foreign-Born Population in the United States: 2003* that almost 12 percent of the population in the United States is foreign born. The majority originated in Latin America (53.3 percent) or Asia (25.0 percent). The remainder are from Europe (13.7 percent) or other regions of the world (8.0 percent).

3. For more on this topic, see Suro and Singer (2002).

4. See Menjívar and Bejarano (2004).

5. Again, see Menjívar and Bejarano (2004).

6. For more, see Martinez and Lee (2000: 488–97).

7. See Hagan and Palloni (1998: 369).

8. See Huntington (2004: 250–51).

9. See Martinez (2002: 106); Martinez and Lee (2000: 510).

10. Martinez (2002: 104).

11. See Martinez (2002: 127).

12. For more on national rates, see Fox and Zawitz (2004).

13. Wolfgang (1958: 25, table 1).

14. See Hanson (2003: 40).

15. See Keppel, Pearcy, and Wagener (2002). Local context in the form of homicide rates, especially the homicide rates in the Central Valley, would be more appropriate for reference points, but none were provided.

16. The homicide rate declined among all three racial/ethnic groups during this period, and Latinos/Hispanics had the steepest decline. See Keppel, Pearcy, and Wagener (2002: 5, table 1).

17. See Martinez (2002: 51).

18. These are from archival data stored in the City of San Diego Police Department Homicide Unit for a research project in progress. I retrieved each homicide callout sheet by hand for the entire period.

19. See MacDonald (2004: 30).

20. See Fox and Zawitz (2004).

21. MacDonald did not provide evidence that Hispanics were marching "east and north across the country." She should have provided evidence of this very specific temporal and spatial claim, but none exists.

22. For a recent study on ethnic variations and violence in New York City and the New York City homicide decline, see Fagan and Davies (2003). However, Latino groups are not disaggregated in this study.

23. For more on this topic, see Martinez and Lee (2000).

24. Shaw and McKay (1931, [1942] 1969).

25. Shaw and McKay ([1942] 1969: 146–47).

26. Lane (1979: 102).

27. See U.S. Immigration Commission (1911).

28. See Sutherland (1934: 112–17).

29. Taylor ([1932] 1970).

30. See Taylor ([1932] 1970: 147).

31. See Sutherland (1934); Lane (1979).

32. The most famous criminological examples of this research, of course, are the seminal publications of Clifford Shaw and Henry McKay (1931, [1942] 1969), but others would argue that Thomas and Znaniecki ([1918–20] 1984) played a role in conceptualizing the crime problems facing Polish immigrants. See chap. 2 of this volume.

33. For immigration and crime at the national level, see Butcher and Piehl (1998a); for the metropolitan level, see Hagan and Palloni (1998); for the census tract or community level, see Lee, Martinez, and Rosenfeld (2001); Martinez (2002); Morenoff, Sampson, and Raudenbush (2001); Sampson and Raudenbush (1999).

34. See Lee and Martinez (2002).

35. Hagan and Palloni (1998) report a tenuous link between immigrants and crime in El Paso and San Diego. Immigrants in both places are at greater risk of conviction and imprisonment, in part, because they are more vulnerable to pretrial detention. Thus immigrants are disproportionately represented among prison inmates because of biases in processes that lead from pretrial detention to sentencing. The authors also tested the effects of legal and illegal immigration on crime in forty-seven U.S. metropolitan areas on the southwestern border. There was little evidence at the metropolitan level that immigration influenced crime.

36. Butcher and Piehl (1998b) found that immigrants were less likely than the native born to be institutionalized and much less likely than males with similar demographic characteristics to be incarcerated. In another paper, Butcher and Piehl (1998a) found that recent immigrants had no significant effect either on crime rates or on changes in rates over time in several dozen U.S. metropolitan areas.

37. Aguirre, Saenz, and James (1997) discovered that Mariel Cubans were more likely to be incarcerated than older Cubans.

38. See Martinez and Lee (2000); Martinez, Lee, and Nielsen (2001); Martinez, Nielsen, and Lee (2003).

39. Annual data are gathered from three sources. First, for percentage of the

total population that is immigrant or foreign born, I used population estimates from published U.S. Census Bureau volumes. For example, see Larsen (2004). In some instances annual measures in the 1980s were not readily available from this source, so annual data were interpolated. I also used two distinct types of violent crime measures. Homicide rates were gathered from the FBI's Uniform Crime Reports for 1980–2003 (see Federal Bureau of Investigation 2003). Robbery rates for 1973–2003 were gathered from the National Crime Victimization Survey Violent Crime Trends data that are available on the Bureau of Justice Statistics Web site. Homicide rates are the number of homicides per hundred thousand persons. Robbery rates are number of robbery victimizations per thousand population age twelve and over. Readers should be aware that the robbery rates are substantially higher than the homicide rates but that they do not change the trajectory with the annual increase in percent foreign born.

40. The most numerous type of violent crime—aggravated assaults—also followed a similar trend over time. See National Crime Victimization Survey Violent Crime Trends data for 1973–2003.

41. Martinez (2002: 80).

42. Funding for this conference was provided through the National Consortium on Violence Research (NCOVR), Heinz School of Public Policy, Carnegie Mellon University. Special thanks to the director of NCOVR, Dr. Al Blumstein, for supporting the conference grant.

REFERENCES

Aguirre, B. E., Rogelio Saenz, and Brian Sinclair James. 1997. "Marielitos Ten Years Later: The Scarface Legacy." *Social Science Quarterly* 78:487–507.

Butcher, Kristin F., and Anna Morrison Piehl. 1998a. "Cross-City Evidence on the Relationship between Immigration and Crime." *Journal of Policy Analysis and Management* 17:457–93.

———. 1998b. "Recent Immigrants: Unexpected Implications for Crime and Incarceration." *Industrial and Labor Relations Review* 51:654–79.

Fagan, Jeffrey, and Garth Davies. 2003. "Policing Guns: Order Maintenance and Crime Control in New York." In *Guns, Crime, and Punishment in America,* edited by B. Harcourt. New York: New York University Press.

Federal Bureau of Investigation. 2003. "Crime in the United States—2003." Retrieved June 19, 2004, from www.fbi.gov/ucr/cius_03/pdf/03sec2.pdf.

Fox, James Alan, and Marianne W. Zawitz. 2004. "Homicide Trends in the United States." U.S. Department of Justice, Office of Justice Programs, Bureau of Justice Statistics. Retrieved September 28, 2004, from www.ojp.usdoj.gov/bjs/homicide/homtrnd.htm.

Hagan, John, and Alberto Palloni. 1998. "Immigration and Crime in the United

States." In *The Immigration Debate*, edited by J. P. Smith and B. Edmonston. Washington, DC: National Academy Press.

Hanson, Victor Davis. 2003. *Mexifornia: A State of Becoming*. San Francisco: Encounter Books.

Huntington, Samuel P. 2004. *Who Are We? The Challenges to America's National Identity*. New York: Simon and Schuster.

Keppel, Kenneth G., Jeffrey N. Pearcy, and Diane Wagener. 2002. "Trends in Racial and Ethnic-Specific Rates for the Health Status Indicators: United States, 1990–98." *Healthy People 2000 Statistical Notes*, no. 23 (January): 1–16.

Lane, Roger. 1979. *Violent Death in the City: Suicide, Accident, and Murder in Nineteenth-Century Philadelphia*. Cambridge, MA: Harvard University Press.

Larsen, Luke J. 2004. *The Foreign-Born Population in the United States: 2003*. Current Population Reports P20-551. Washington, DC: U.S. Census Bureau.

Lee, Matthew T., and Ramiro Martinez Jr. 2002. "Social Disorganization Revisited: Mapping the Recent Immigration and Black Homicide Relationship in Northern Miami." *Sociological Focus* 35: 363–80.

Lee, Matthew T., Ramiro Martinez Jr., and Richard Rosenfeld. 2001. "Does Immigration Increase Homicide? Negative Evidence from Three Border Cities." *Sociological Quarterly* 42:559–80.

MacDonald, Heather. 2004. "The Immigrant Gang Plague." *City Journal*, Summer, 30–43.

Martinez, Ramiro, Jr. 2002. *Latino Homicide: Immigration, Violence and Community*. New York: Routledge.

Martinez, Ramiro, and Matthew T. Lee. 2000. "On Immigration and Crime." In *The Nature of Crime: Continuity and Change*, vol. 2 of *Criminal Justice 2000*, edited by G. LaFree. Washington, DC: National Institute of Justice.

Martinez, Ramiro, Jr., Matthew T. Lee, and Amie L. Nielsen. 2001. "Revisiting the Scarface Legacy: The Victim/Offender Relationship and Mariel Homicides in Miami." *Hispanic Journal of Behavioral Sciences* 1 (February): 37–56.

Martinez, Ramiro, Jr., Amie L. Nielsen, and Matthew T. Lee. 2003. "Reconsidering the Marielito Legacy: Race/Ethnicity, Nativity and Homicide Motives." *Social Science Quarterly* 84 (June): 397–411.

Menjívar, Cecilia, and Cynthia L. Bejarano. 2004. "Latino Immigrants' Perceptions of Crime and Police Authorities in the United States: A Case Study from the Phoenix Metropolitan Area." *Ethnic and Racial Studies* 27:120–48.

Morenoff, Jeffrey D., Robert J. Sampson, and Stephen W. Raudenbush. 2001. "Neighborhood Inequality, Collective Efficacy, and the Spatial Dynamics of Urban Violence." *Criminology* 39:517–59.

Sampson, Robert J., and Stephen W. Raudenbush. 1999. "Systematic Social Observation of Public Spaces: A New Look at Disorder in Urban Neighborhoods." *American Journal of Sociology* 105:603–51.

Shaw, Clifford R., and Henry D. McKay. 1931. "Social Factors in Juvenile Delinquency." In *Report on the Causes of Crime,* no. 13, National Commission on Law Observance and Enforcement Report. Washington, DC: U.S. Government Printing Office.

———. [1942] 1969. *Juvenile Delinquency and Urban Areas.* Rev. ed. Chicago: University of Chicago Press.

Suro, Roberto, and Audrey Singer. 2002. *Latino Growth in Metropolitan America: Changing Patterns, New Locations.* Brookings Institution, Center on Urban and Metropolitan Policy and the Pew Hispanic Center, Survey Series, Census 2000. Retrieved October 21, 2005, from www.pewhispanic.org/site/docs/pdf/final_phc-brookings_paper-appendix-tables.pdf.

Sutherland, Edwin. 1934. *Principles of Criminology.* Chicago: J. B. Lippincott.

Taylor, Paul S. [1932] 1970. *Mexican Labor in the United States.* Vol. 2. New York: Arno Press and New York Times.

Thomas, William I., and Florian Znaniecki. [1918–20] 1984. *The Polish Peasant in Europe and America.* Abridged ed. Chicago: University of Illinois Press.

U.S. Immigration Commission. 1911. *Immigration and Crime.* Vol. 36. Washington, DC: U.S. Government Printing Office.

Wolfgang, Marvin E. 1958. *Patterns in Criminal Homicide.* Philadelphia: University of Pennsylvania Press.

Chapter 2

Rethinking the Chicago School of Criminology

A New Era of Immigration

Robert J. Bursik Jr.

The University of Chicago's Department of Sociology was established at a time, 1892, when the foreign born represented nearly 15 percent of the total population of the United States and one-third of Chicago's residents. In fact, Hull House, arguably the most famous settlement house in America, already had been founded by Jane Addams in 1889,[1] and by 1900 more than 75 percent of Chicago's population were of foreign stock.[2] Thus it is not surprising that immigration was a central theme in some of the most influential early publications of Chicago's faculty and that it shaped the perspective of many of the famous "urban laboratory" studies conducted by their students throughout the department's pre–World War II history.[3] The most famous criminological examples of this research, of course, are the classic publications of Clifford Shaw and Henry McKay.[4]

While sociologists and criminologists associated with the Chicago School continued to publish significant studies on immigration and crime after World War II,[5] the influence of the traditional Chicago model of urban sociology on research conducted outside the department waned significantly after Whyte's *Street Corner Society*[6] highlighted significant shortcomings of its perspective; this had a particularly devastating effect on the popularity of Shaw and McKay's social disorganization framework. Unfortunately, perhaps because these criticisms were first raised during a period characterized by steep declines in the number of immigrants (figure 2.1) and a major shift in disciplinary orientation,[7] it appears that the substantive interests of the early Chicago School also were perceived to be largely irrelevant to contemporary research; whatever the reason for its fall

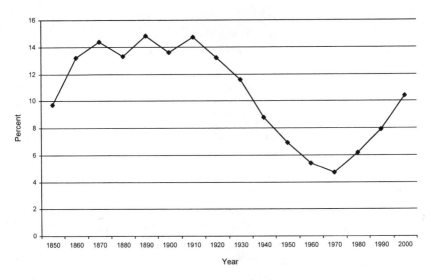

Fig. 2.1. Trends in the U.S. Foreign-Born Population

from grace, even a cursory review of the literature indicates that immigration was not a dominant criminological theme for many years after World War II.

Although criminologists lagged substantially behind the other social sciences in the amount of attention paid to the post-1970 surge in immigration, the differential criminal involvement of these groups once again has emerged as a major question.[8] At the same time, reformulations of the traditional Shaw and McKay framework have made a significant resurgence,[9] and a growing number of studies have examined the relevance of these models to the new immigrant populations.[10] Lacking, however, are extensive examinations of the relevance of the Chicago School's more general orientation to the adaptation of contemporary immigrants to U.S. society. This chapter is an attempt to begin to rectify that situation.

The Chicago School

Shaw and McKay's perspective on immigration and crime was deeply rooted in work generated by Robert Park and Ernest Burgess[11] and by William I. Thomas.[12] The hallmark of these studies was the assumption that the assimilation of immigrant ethnic groups was inevitable as well as desirable. As Park and Burgess noted, "As social contact initiates interaction, assimilation is its final perfect product."[13] Yet while in hindsight such a rosy "melting pot" argument is a bit naïve, Park and Burgess fully recognized that assimilation typically would be achieved only after a protracted period of conflict as groups competed for scarce economic resources within the context of a political or "moral" order that determined the manner in which individuals and groups "make the necessary internal adjustments to social situations created by competition and conflict."[14] Assimilation occurred when these modes of accommodation became "fixed in habit and custom,"[15] transmitted from generation to generation, and taken for granted—that is, "the product typically is unconscious."[16]

Importantly, Park and Burgess believed that assimilation depended critically on the development of primary group relationships that spanned group boundaries and that facilitated the mutual appreciation of cultural differences.[17] Unfortunately, these networks were extremely difficult to establish in communities in which the dominant culture of the host groups had little in common with those of the immigrant groups. However, Park and Burgess did not presume that only the hostility and suspicion expressed by the host group impeded the rate at which such linkages were developed. Rather, they also argued that since many immigrants realized that the personal characteristics that brought them respect in the old country often were regarded with contempt in the new homeland,[18] they typically were hesitant to initiate interactions that might result in personal degradation.

In addition, Park and Miller's research suggested that immigrants might become disillusioned when they discovered that America did not fully conform to the idealized version they hoped to find.[19] As a result, they tended to interact intimately only with those with whom they most closely identified, namely other similar immigrants. Finally, the development of primary out-group relationships depended a great deal on the individual motivations for relocation. Park and Miller,[20] for example, identified six basic settler types in this regard, ranging from the "colonist," who maintained strong emotional ties to the old country, to the "allrightnick," who sacrificed the cultural ideals of the homeland to fit in more fully with the established social order. Thus Park and Miller emphasized that substantial within-group variation existed in the way the assimilation process unfolded.

One might expect that these often acrimonious between-group dynamics spawned tightly knit, cohesive immigrant communities for the purposes of emotional and social support, and these were, in fact, some of the principal functions of the mutual aid societies, religious congregations, and other similar organizations that appeared in ethnic neighborhoods. However, Thomas and Znaniecki clearly demonstrated that this was a far different basis of organization from that found in the old country, which "centered around the family and the primary community and the fundamental principles of direct personal solidarity and conformity with public opinion."[21] For many of the immigrants they studied, preexisting primary group ties were either severed or greatly weakened by the relocation to the United States, and most immigrants were not able to enter into new relationships that were "as strong and coherent" as those left behind.[22] That is, immigrants were in a doubly weak position, unable to establish deep and meaningful associations with members of the host population or with the members of their own ethnicity that in the past had given them a sense of responsibility, security, and belonging. According to Thomas and Znaniecki, the resulting "passive demoralization" among many immigrants resulted in the condition to which they famously and controversially referred as "social disorganization," formally defined as a decrease in the influence of existing social rules of behavior upon individual members of the group.

Park and Burgess and Thomas and Znaniecki explicitly noted that immigrant communities characterized by disorganization would have relatively high rates of crime during the period of accommodation, and Thomas and Znaniecki provided detailed descriptions of several homicides that occurred among the Polish residents. However, since these sociologists were primarily interested in the urban structures and dynamics that facilitated assimilation, crime per se was a secondary consideration. The first well-known effort of the Chicago School to focus specifically on immigration and crime was Frederick Thrasher's landmark dissertation on gangs.[23] However, Clifford Shaw and Henry McKay produced by far the most influential examinations of this phenomenon.

Shaw and McKay

Given the many excellent summaries and critiques of Shaw and McKay's social disorganization model of delinquency, it is unnecessary to provide a detailed outline of their framework. Nevertheless, two aspects of their model are worth highlighting. First, given that they both had been students of Park and Burgess, it is not surprising that, with one notable exception, economic competition leading to eventual assimilation is central to their theory. That is, newly arrived immigrant groups were expected to initially settle in the most deteriorated high-crime sections of town because the costs of housing were minimal. Over time, as these groups became increasingly integrated into the occupational structure of the city and had more economic resources at their disposal, they would move into neighborhoods of progressively higher status and lower crime rates, being replaced in their former neighborhoods by more recent foreign-born arrivals.

Shaw and McKay supported these propositions by providing spot maps of the spatial distributions of African Americans, twelve European immigrant groups, and delinquency rates. On the basis of their examination of these data, they concluded that almost all immigrant groups took their turns living in areas with the highest rates of crime in the city and being perceived by the host population, at least in the short term, as unusually criminogenic. The one exception involved the residential movements of the African American population, about whom they stated: "[T]he same distribution among low-rent areas would probably characterize the Negroes were it not for the fact that racial barriers prevent their movement into many such areas."[24]

The second critical feature was the proposition that the observed relationship between economic deprivation and crime was not generated by a simple "poverty causes delinquency" process. Rather, Shaw and McKay argued that deprivation increased the rate of residential turnover and racial/ethnic heterogeneity, both of which heightened the likelihood of social disorganization. This aspect of their approach will be addressed in greater detail below, but the key point here is that Shaw and McKay assumed that any direct associations between immigrant status and crime or between economic deprivation and crime were largely spurious.

One of the shortcomings of their 1929, 1931, and 1942 publications is that the immigration and delinquency data are fairly cursory. Most notably, the actual delinquency rates are not provided on a group-specific basis, making their analysis more suggestive than definitive, and, whereas the authors had longitudinal data for delinquency rates, they had no such data for the spatial location of immigrants. However, McKay began to pursue this question in greater detail and actually produced a rough partial draft of a monograph entitled "Nationality and Delinquency," portions of which still existed in the files of the Institute for Juvenile Research when

TABLE 2.1
The Table of Contents of McKay and Kobrin's Nationality and Delinquency

I	Introduction
II	City Growth and Immigrant Groups
III	Area Rates of Delinquents in Sub-Groups of the Population
IV	The Effect of Change in Nationalities in Inner City Areas on Rates of Delinquency
V	Movement of Nationalities and Changes in the Nationality Composition of Juvenile Court Cases
VI	The Standardization of Rates of Delinquents
VII	Race and Rates of Delinquents
VIII	Conclusion

SOURCE: McKay and Kobrin (1965).

TABLE 2.2
Percentage Distribution of Delinquent Boys in the Cook County Juvenile Court by Country of Birth of Fathers, 1900–1940

	Year								
	1900	1905	1910	1915	1920	1925	1930	1935	1940
Germany	25.7	24.5	18.6	14.2	9.5	5.6	3.2	4.8	5.2
Ireland	23.5	20.3	15.7	13.9	9.1	5.1	2.2	3.0	2.9
England	4.3	3.9	3.4	3.4	1.2	1.3	1.0	0.9	1.3
Scandinavia	4.8	7.3	3.7	3.6	3.3	0.7	1.4	2.4	2.1
Italy	6.5	11.0	10.1	13.1	10.0	20.9	19.9	17.1	20.4
Poland	19.0	20.7	23.8	28.6	36.6	35.8	35.8	41.0	29.0
Russia	4.5	3.2	9.3	7.2	9.6	13.7	14.7	9.9	8.2
Other	11.7	9.1	15.4	16.0	11.6	16.9	21.8	20.9	30.9
Total	100	100	100	100	100	100	100	100	100

SOURCE: McKay and Kobrin (1965).

I took a job there in 1978 (Shaw and McKay were senior members of the institute's staff from 1927 until Shaw's death and McKay's retirement).[25] Table 2.1 presents the table of contents for this book, and the topics underscore how tragic it is that this material never became available to a general criminological audience, given the richly detailed group-specific data that were provided (see, for example, table 2.2, which is presented as an exemplar of these data rather than for substantive purposes).[26]

McKay summarized the major immigration-related conclusions in an internal memo as follows:

- The variations in the rates of delinquency for nativity, nationality, or racial groups correspond to types of community situations.
- In the same types of areas, boys of native parentage and boys of foreign parentage have similar rates of delinquency.
- Citywide rates of delinquency for nationality groups vary widely

from one another. In turn, the rates within nationality groups vary widely among types of areas, but in the same areas or types of areas the rates for nationality groups are not widely different.

- In the inner-city areas of Chicago where the rates of delinquency are high, there has been an almost complete turnover in the nationality composition of the population.
- In the inner-city areas of Chicago, changes in the nationality composition of the population are not accompanied by appreciable changes in relative rates of delinquency unless the changes in population are accompanied by changes in the general character of the area.
- As the older immigrant groups moved out of the inner-city areas in Chicago, their children disappeared from the juvenile court. Those children were replaced in the court by the children of new immigrant and migrant groups that took over the areas of first settlement.

Table 2.3 illustrates the statistical patterns that generated such conclusions. While there are some differences in prevalence among native white males and males of Polish and Italian stock, the similarities in the overall patterns are striking, lending strong support to the Shaw and McKay's arguments about the power of the neighborhood context and the relatively unimportant role of compositional effects.

Even so, "Nationality and Delinquency" can be criticized on several of the same grounds as Shaw and McKay's earlier work. Three are especially consequential: the strict reliance on Thomas and Znaniecki's conceptual-

TABLE 2.3
*Comparative Rates of Court Referrals by Ethnicity and Neighborhood
(per 100 Male Juveniles)*

Neighborhood Rates of Native White Court Referrals	Native Whites	Polish Stock	Italian Stock
A. 0.0–0.9	0.72	0.66	1.86
B. 1.0–1.9	1.50	2.34	3.45
C. 2.0–2.9	2.41	3.67	2.95
D. 3.0–3.9	3.37	3.82	4.18
E. 4.0–4.9	4.42	4.64	5.22
F. 5.0–5.9	5.40	6.85	7.97
G. 6.0–6.9	6.09	5.48	8.57
H. 7.0–7.9	7.15	6.73	10.55
I. 8 and above	9.97	9.73	11.30

SOURCE: McKay and Kobrin (1965).

ization of social disorganization,[27] the failure to examine the degree to which these dynamics were shaped by the political system of Chicago, and the unquestioned acceptance of the assumption of inevitable assimilation. Thus, despite the unique and important empirical insights produced by their analyses, the relevance of their general model to contemporary immigration research is limited.

The "New" Chicago School

Two closely related conceptual reformulations of the Shaw and McKay model have emerged in the last fifteen years, the systemic model of social disorganization[28] and the social capital/collective efficacy framework of Robert Sampson and his colleagues.[29] Although there are subtle but critical differences in these two approaches, both conceptualize disorganization in terms of the existence of interactional networks that tie community residents to one another and to institutions outside the area, the ability of these ties to effectively regulate the nature of the activities that occur within a neighborhood's boundaries, and the residents' willingness to use the networks for those purposes.

This orientation is similar to that of Thomas and Znaniecki in the sense that it also emphasizes the role of primary and secondary networks, although it does add linkages to external institutions. The basic difference is that the scope and relative effectiveness of these networks is an open question. That is, while secondary rather than primary ties predominated among the Polish immigrants studied by Thomas and Znaniecki in Chicago, this may not be the case for other ethnic groups and/or in other locations. For example, Whyte's study of Italian immigrants in Boston reached dramatically different conclusions in that rich primary ties bound the local residents into a highly cohesive community.[30] More recently, Wilson has argued that secondary and external ties are extremely weak in African American neighborhoods located in older industrial cities,[31] while Zatz and Portillos demonstrate, for a Phoenix Chicano community, the existence of strong primary and secondary associations but few external linkages.[32] Thus the variability in the scope and effectiveness of these three dimensions of social control, as well as the distal and proximate sources of that variability, are key empirical questions.

The most important departure of the new approaches from the traditional orientation of Shaw and McKay is found in their emphasis on the external (or public) networks through which neighborhoods potentially can solicit political, economic, and social resources controlled by persons or agencies located outside the local community. Unfortunately, this component of the systemic model has received relatively little empirical attention. An early exception is Bursik's analysis of public housing construction in Chicago, which showed that these facilities were built in areas that could not mobilize sufficient political support to locate them elsewhere.[33] The construction increased the residential instability of the affected areas, eventually leading to a subsequent rise in their delinquency rates.

More recently, Zatz and Portillos provided compelling evidence that many residents of a Chicano Phoenix neighborhood with a long tradition of gang activity were hesitant to ask the police to intercede on their behalf due to a long history of tense relationships with law enforcement agencies and the widespread perception that they could not be counted on to provide protective services.[34] This attitude was part of a more general belief that political decision makers who could make a difference in the community had abandoned the area. For example, many felt that state and local officials had reduced the community's resource base and given it a low priority for revitalization and that businesses took money from the area but did not reinvest in it. Frankly, we are just beginning to understand the complex relationship between politically based public networks and immigrant crime, but this will become an increasingly consequential issue for many of the new ethnic immigrant groups now that some of the Immigration and Naturalization Service law enforcement responsibilities have been folded into the Office of Homeland Security.

Unfortunately, there is an additional, albeit intentional, limitation of the traditional Shaw and McKay framework that characterizes all past and contemporary theoretical work in the social disorganization tradition: it is grounded explicitly in a model of urban dynamics. While this certainly is understandable given the intellectual context that shaped Shaw and McKay's focus and the urban environment in which that context evolved, it nevertheless is the case that 24.6, 20.8, and 20.0 percent of the immigrant population settled in rural areas (less than 2,500 residents) in 1920, 1930, and 1940 respectively.[35] Thus it is distinctly possible that these dynamics were irrelevant to a sizable minority of the immigrant population during the years reflected in the data analyzed in the original 1929, 1931, and 1942 publications.

It might be argued that this may no longer be a serious problem, for the March 2000 Current Population Survey estimated that only 5.4 percent of immigrants reside in rural areas.[36] Nevertheless, that relatively small percentage has had a dramatic impact on certain parts of the country. For example, during the 1990s, the residential composition of Schuyler, Nebraska, changed from one almost totally dominated by Czech, German, and Irish descendants to one in which Latinos accounted for almost half the population as immigrants were drawn to the employment opportunities provided by the meatpacking industry. Likewise, Taylor, Martin, and Fix document the significant changes that occurred as rural communities adapted to the settlement of poor Mexican migrant workers in neighborhoods *(colonias)* in the incorporated towns surrounding California farms, which they describe as "resembling overgrown labor camps."[37]

Although none of the few rural social disorganization studies published since 1990[38] have focused upon immigration per se, they do provide at least partial support for the viability of the social disorganization model in a rural setting; the evidence provided by Osgood and Chambers is especially strong. In addition, the review essay of Weisheit and Wells strongly suggests that the systemic/social capital/collective efficacy emphasis on the role of networks is especially relevant.[39] While the degree to which this may be the case for rural immigrant populations is not yet known, these studies indicate that it is a promising avenue of research.[40]

Final Observations

Despite the weaknesses of the Chicago School that have been outlined, it also had strengths that criminologists must do their best to maintain. In particular, unlike some modern studies that draw general inferences about the effects of membership in an unspecified Latino or Asian group on crime, there were very few references in the Chicago studies to a generic group of "European" migrants. Rather, the Chicago School researchers differentiated not only among the countries of origin but often even in terms of particular regions of those countries.[41] The aggregation of subgroups into global ethnic categories confounds cultural, structural, and political differences that may affect the adaptation of the ethnic group to its new locale. The field must try to recapture the rich racial and ethnic distinctions found in these earlier studies.[42]

In addition, Shaw and McKay had an intimate understanding of the dominant theories of urban sociology of their era. Likewise, when the "new" Chicago School models were first developed, they too were informed by contemporary perspectives on urban structure. Regrettably, that degree of familiarity seems to have disappeared from much of the recent immigration and crime literature, making it impossible to capitalize on the insights generated in other areas in the social sciences, particularly those found in the burgeoning literatures on segmented assimilation,[43] "second generation decline,"[44] the revisionist assimilation model,[45] or the roles of cross-country social networks.[46] Until we do so, our grasp of the immigration-crime association will be at best tenuous.

NOTES

This is a revision of a presentation made to the National Consortium on Violence Research conference, "Beyond Racial Dichotomies of Violence: Immigrants, Race, and Ethnicity," held at the University of California, Los Angeles, on November 6–8, 2003. The chapter has benefited substantially from comments on the earlier version by my colleagues at the University of Missouri, St. Louis (especially Eric Baumer, Jennifer Bursik, Scott Decker, Dave Klinger, and Rick Rosenfeld), Ramiro Martinez, Jim Short, and the conference attendees).

1. Deegan (1988).

2. Chicago Department of Development and Planning (1976).

3. It is telling that the *American Journal of Sociology,* which always has been sponsored by and housed in Chicago's Department of Sociology, published a five-part series of articles on social assimilation in 1901 and 1902 (Simons 1901). Likewise, George Herbert Mead served as vice president of the Immigrants' Protective League for several years (Deegan 1988).

4. See Shaw et al. (1929); Shaw and McKay (1931, 1942, 1969).

5. See Finestone (1967); Janowitz (1952); Kobrin (1951); McKay (1967); Shaw and McKay (1969: Part V); Short (1969); Suttles (1968).

6. Whyte (1943).

7. Bursik (1988).

8. Tonry (1997).

9. See Bursik and Grasmick (1993); Sampson and Groves (1989).

10. This chapter does not consider the voluminous literature on immigration and organized crime, for those studies tend not to focus upon the neighborhood dynamics emphasized by the Chicago School. See Martinez (2002); Zatz and Portillos (2000).

11. See Park and Burgess (1924); Park, Burgess, and McKenzie (1925); Park and Miller (1921).

12. It now is known that Park and Miller's *Old World Traits Transplanted* (1921) was primarily the work of Thomas (Coser 1977). The Carnegie Foundation, which

had commissioned the study, refused to allow the book's publication unless his name was removed as an author due to the scandal surrounding his tragic forced resignation from the University of Chicago in 1918. See Thomas and Znaniecki ([1918–20] 1984).

13. See Park and Burgess (1924: 736).

14. See Park and Burgess (1924: 509).

15. See Park and Burgess (1924: 510).

16. See Park and Burgess (1924: 736).

17. See Park and Burgess (1924: 737).

18. See also Park and Miller (1921: 48).

19. See Park and Miller (1921: 46).

20. See Park and Miller (1921: 81).

21. Thomas and Znaniecki ([1918–20] 1984: 241).

22. See Thomas and Znaniecki ([1918–20] 1984: 258).

23. Thrasher (1927).

24. See Shaw and McKay (1942: 37).

25. The history of this monograph is a bit mysterious, for there is evidence that as late as 1965 there was an oral agreement that the finished product would be published by the University of Chicago Press; that, of course, never happened. Although McKay appears to have written much (and perhaps all) of what exists of "Nationality and Delinquency," Solomon Kobrin, their colleague for many years at the institute (and another former Chicago graduate student), informed me in the early 1990s that they intended it to appear as written by Shaw, McKay and Kobrin. Yet the proper attribution is unclear, for the project memos and chapter drafts in my possession were written well after Shaw's death in 1957. Therefore, I will follow Short's lead (1969: xlvi) and assume that the authorship would have been McKay and Kobrin. Sadly, Sol Kobrin died in 1996, and we may never learn the full history of the piece. However, given that several of the internal memos expressed McKay's dismay that it was difficult for him to devote sufficient time to the project, I suspect that it never was completed. See McKay and Kobrin (1965).

26. For these patterns to be inferentially meaningful, controls must be imposed for the relative sizes of the foreign stock population, which is not the case here.

27. This problem was further compounded by the fact that they did not have access to any direct indicators of disorganization and therefore could only make educated guesses about its effects.

28. Bursik and Grasmick (1993).

29. Sampson, Raudenbush, and Earls (1997); Sampson, Morenoff, and Earls (1999).

30. Whyte (1943).

31. Wilson (1996).

32. Zatz and Portillos (2000).

33. Bursik (1989).

34. Zatz and Portillos (2000: 383).

35. Gibson and Lennon (1999).

36. Lollock (2001).

37. Taylor, Martin, and Fix (1997).

38. Barnett and Carson (2002); Kposowa and Breault (1993); Osgood and Chambers (2000); Vowell and Howell (1998).

39. Weisheit and Wells (1996).

40. However, the fact that the rapid influx of immigrant populations accounts for almost all of the population change in some communities will make it very difficult for future studies of the immigration/crime question to produce independent estimates of the effects of immigration and the effects of change in general.

41. See Park and Miller (1921).

42. Most of the important exceptions to this tendency are found in the body of gang research (see Vigil 1988, 2002); for a more general example, see Martinez (2002).

43. Portes and Zhou (1993).

44. Gans (1992).

45. Alba and Nee (1997).

46. Portes, Haller, and Guarnizo (2002).

REFERENCES

Alba, Richard, and Victor Nee. 1997. "Rethinking Assimilation Theory for a New Era of Immigration." *International Migration Review* 31:826–74.

Barnett, Cynthia, and F. Carson Mencken. 2002. "Social Disorganization Theory and the Contextual Nature of Crime in Nonmetropolitan Counties." *Rural Sociology* 67:362–93.

Bursik, Robert J., Jr. 1988. "Social Disorganization and Theories of Crime and Delinquency: Problems and Prospects." *Criminology* 26:519–51.

———. 1989. "Political Decision-Making and Ecological Models of Delinquency: Conflict and Consensus." In *Theoretical Integration in the Study of Deviance and Crime,* edited by S. F. Messner, M. D. Krohn, and A. E. Liska. Albany: State University of New York Press.

Bursik, Robert J., Jr., and Harold G. Grasmick. 1993. *Neighborhoods and Crime: The Dimensions of Effective Community Control.* New York: Lexington Books.

Chicago Department of Development and Planning. 1976. *The People of Chicago: Who We Are and Who We Have Been. Census Data on Foreign Born, Foreign Stock, and Race, 1837–1970.* MRC Cc P71. Chicago: Chicago Department of Development and Planning.

Coser, Lewis. 1977. *Masters of Sociological Thought.* New York: Harcourt, Brace, and Jovanovich.

Deegan, Mary Jo. 1988. *Jane Addams and the Men of the Chicago School, 1892–1918.* New Brunswick, NJ: Transaction Press.

Finestone, Harold. 1967. "Reformation and Recidivism among Italian and Polish Criminal Offenders." *American Journal of Sociology* 72:575–88.

Gans, Herbert J. 1992. "Second Generation Decline: Scenarios for the Economic and Ethnic Features of the Post-1965 American Immigrants." *Ethnic and Racial Studies* 15:173–92.

Gibson, Campbell J., and Emily Lennon. 1999. *Historical Census Statistics on the Foreign-Born Population of the U.S.: 1850–1990.* Population Division Working Paper no. 29.Washington, DC: U.S. Bureau of the Census.

Janowitz, Morris. 1952. *The Community Press in an Urban Setting.* Glencoe, IL: Free Press.

Kobrin, Solomon. 1951. "The Conflict of Values in Delinquency Areas." *American Sociological Review* 16:653–61.

Kposowa, Augustine J., and Kevin D. Breault. 1993. "Reassessing the Structural Co-variates of U.S. Homicide Rates: A County Level Study." *Sociological Focus* 26: 27–46.

Lollock, Lisa. 2001. *The Foreign-Born Population in the United States: Population Characteristics.* Current Population Reports, 20-534. Washington, DC: U.S. Bureau of the Census.

Martinez, Ramiro, Jr. 2002. *Latino Homicide: Immigration, Violence, and Community.* New York: Routledge.

McKay, Henry D. 1967. "A Note on Trends in Rates of Delinquency in Certain Areas of Chicago." In *Task Force Report: Juvenile Delinquency and Youth Crime,* 144–218. President's Commission on Law Enforcement and the Administration of Justice. Washington, DC: U.S. Government Printing Office.

McKay, Henry D., and Solomon Kobrin. Ca. 1965. "Nationality and Delinquency." Unpublished monograph, Institute for Juvenile Research, Chicago.

Osgood, D. Wayne, and Jeff M. Chambers. 2000. "Social Disorganization outside the Metropolis: An Analysis of Rural Youth Violence." *Criminology* 38:81–115.

Park, Robert E., and Ernest W. Burgess. 1924. *Introduction to the Science of Sociology.* Chicago: University of Chicago Press.

Park, Robert E., Ernest W. Burgess, and Roderick D. McKenzie. 1925. *The City.* Chicago: University of Chicago Press.

Park, Robert E., and Herbert A. Miller. 1921. *Old World Traits Transplanted.* New York: Harper and Barnes.

Portes, Alejandro, William Haller, and Luis Eduardo Guarnizo. 2002. "Transnational Entrepreneurs: An Alternative Form of Immigrant Economic Adaptation." *American Sociological Review* 67:278–98.

Portes, Alejandro, and Min Zhou. 1993. "The New Second Generation: Segmented

Assimilation and Its Variants." *Annals of the American Academy of Political and Social Science* 530:74–96.

Sampson, Robert J., and W. Byron Groves. 1989. "Community Structure and Crime: Testing Social-Disorganization Theory." *American Journal of Sociology* 94:774–802.

Sampson, Robert J., Jeffrey D. Morenoff, and Felton Earls. 1999. "Beyond Social Capital: Spatial Dynamics of Collective Efficacy of Children." *American Sociological Review* 64:633–60.

Sampson, Robert J., Stephen W. Raudenbush, and Felton Earls. 1997. "Neighborhoods and Violent Crime: A Multilevel Study of Collective Efficacy." *Science* 277:918–24.

Shaw, Clifford R., and Henry D. McKay. 1931. *Social Factors in Juvenile Delinquency.* National Commission on Law Observation and Enforcement, no. 13, Report on the Causes of Crime, vol. 2. Washington, DC: U.S. Government Printing Office.

———. 1942. *Juvenile Delinquency and Urban Areas.* Chicago: University of Chicago Press.

———. 1969. *Juvenile Delinquency and Urban Areas.* Rev. ed. Chicago: University of Chicago Press.

Shaw, Clifford R., Frederick M. Zorbaugh, Henry D. McKay, and Leonard S. Cottrell. 1929. *Delinquency Areas.* Chicago: University of Chicago Press.

Short, James F., Jr. 1969. "Introduction to the Revised Edition." In *Juvenile Delinquency and Urban Areas,* rev. ed., edited by Clifford R. Shaw and Henry D. McKay, xxv–liv. Chicago: University of Chicago Press.

Simons, Sarah E. 1901. "Social Assimilation. I." *American Journal of Sociology* 6:790–822.

Suttles, Gerald D. 1968. *The Social Order of the Slum: Ethnicity and Territory in the Inner City.* Chicago: University of Chicago Press.

Taylor, J. Edward, Philip L. Martin, and Michael Fix. 1997. *Poverty and Prosperity: Immigration and the Changing Face of Rural California.* Washington, DC: Urban Institute.

Thomas, William I., and Florian Znaniecki. [1918–20] 1984. *The Polish Peasant in Europe and America.* Abridged and abbreviated by Eli Zaretsky. Urbana: University of Illinois Press.

Thrasher, Frederic M. 1927. *The Gang.* Chicago: University of Chicago Press.

Tonry, Michael H., ed. 1997. *Ethnicity, Crime, and Immigration: Comparative and Cross-National Perspectives.* Chicago: University Chicago Press.

Vigil, James D. 1988. *Barrio Gangs: Street Life and Identity in Southern California.* Austin: University of Texas Press.

———. 2002. *A Rainbow of Gangs: Street Culture in the Mega-City.* Austin: University of Texas Press.

Vowell, Paul R., and Frank M. Howell. 1998. "Modeling Delinquent Behavior:

Social Disorganization, Perceived Blocked Opportunity, and Social Control." *Deviant Behavior* 19:361–95.

Weisheit, Ralph A., and L. Edward Wells. 1996. "Rural Crime and Justice: Implications for Theory and Research." *Crime and Delinquency* 42:379–97.

Whyte, William F., Jr. 1943. *Street Corner Society: The Social Structure of an Italian Slum.* Chicago: University of Chicago Press.

Wilson, William J. 1996. *When Work Disappears: The World of the New Urban Poor.* New York: Knopf.

Zatz, Marjorie S., and Edwardo L. Portillos. 2000. "Voices from the Barrio: Chicano/a Gangs, Families, and Communities." *Criminology* 38:369–401.

Chapter 3

Immigrant Assimilation and Crime
Generational Differences in
Youth Violence in Chicago

Jeffrey D. Morenoff and Avraham Astor

During the first half of the twentieth century, criminologists scrutinized the publicly popular view that immigrants from southern and eastern Europe, who came to the United States in large numbers between 1890 and 1924, were responsible for more crimes than the native-born population.[1] One of the central findings from this early research was that, contrary to popular belief, immigrants actually had lower rates of arrest and incarceration than nonimmigrants.[2] This early research also revealed that crime rates were alarmingly high among the children of immigrants—also known as "second-generation" immigrants—compared to the children of native-born parents.[3] Thus criminologists have long been interested in understanding how crime rates differ across generations of immigrants and why the children of immigrants appear to be particularly drawn to crime.

Unfortunately, contemporary scholarship has paid scant attention to the issue of immigration and crime, despite the massive influx of new immigrants to the United States—mostly from Latin America and Asia—beginning with the passage of the 1965 Immigration Act and continuing to the present. As a result, criminologists know relatively little about how crime in the United States might be affected by recent waves of immigrants and their descendants. In contrast, there has been a considerable amount of research in other fields (e.g., sociology, economics, and public health) on new immigrants' prospects for economic advancement and the implications that this may have for their health and well-being, as well as that of their descendants.

In this chapter, we review briefly the existing criminological literature on the immigration-crime nexus and the wider literature on immigrant assimilation. We also discuss theories of immigrant assimilation—both classic assimilation theory and the more recent segmented assimilation theory—and consider their applicability to criminological inquiry on immigration. We then present results from an analysis of self-reported offending among immigrant and nonimmigrant youth in Chicago that lays out some of the basic contours of the immigration-crime nexus, including how involvement in violent crime varies across (1) generations of immigrants, (2) the length of stay of first-generation immigrants in the United States, (3) level of linguistic acculturation, and (4) neighborhood context. We conclude by reassessing theories of immigrant assimilation and recommending directions for future research on immigration and crime.

Immigration and Crime: A Review of the Literature

Despite the massive influx of immigrants to the United States in recent decades and the continuing tendency of the media and politicians to portray immigrants as responsible for a disproportionate amount of crime, there is less empirical research on the connection between immigration and crime today than there was in the early decades of the twentieth century. To document just how little contemporary research there is on immigration and crime, we conducted an online search for articles listed in the Social Science Citation Index (SSCI), published between 1970 and 2004, that list "immigration" and "crime or delinquency" as keywords and found that there have been only 77 articles published on immigration and crime over this thirty-four-year time period.[4] By comparison, a search for articles on "race" and "crime or delinquency" yielded 750 articles over the same time period. One reason that there has been so little research is that many sources of crime data, such as the Uniform Crime Reports and the National Victimization Survey, do not include information on immigrant status of offenders or victims.

In the absence of such data, research on immigration and crime has proceeded in two directions. The first is ecological analysis that examines the association between aggregate arrest rates for geographic areas (e.g., counties, census tracts) and the proportion of the area population that is foreign born.[5] The results from such ecological studies show little evidence of a systematic relationship between immigrant composition of areas and crime, which casts doubt on the popular belief that immigrants are more involved in crime. Other studies have analyzed disparities in delinquent behavior between foreign-born and non-foreign-born youth using survey data and have found that foreign-born youth are significantly less likely than their native-born counterparts to engage in crime and other forms of risky behavior (e.g., substance use and early sexual initiation) or to have been stopped, booked, charged, or convicted for a crime.[6] Research conducted in other countries suggests that these findings are not unique to the United States. Cross-national and national studies of immigrant crime abroad find, with few exceptions, that the crime rates of second-generation immigrants surpass those of first-generation immigrants.[7] Thus, although there have been very few individual-level assessments of how crime differs by immigrant status, prior studies suggest that crime is relatively low among first-generation immigrants but higher among the descendants of immigrants.

The Fate of New Immigrants in the United States

The finding that children of immigrants appear to be more involved in crime than the foreign born is one piece of a larger debate about whether contemporary immigrants will follow a path of assimilation similar to that of their southern and eastern European predecessors, who achieved widespread integration into mainstream institutions by the middle decades of the twentieth century.[8] On one side of this debate are scholars who are pessimistic about the socioeconomic opportunities available to new immigrants. These scholars argue that whereas earlier European immigrants entered American cities at a time when manufacturing jobs were plentiful and provided a means of upward mobility, new immigrants must confront an "hourglass economy" that bifurcates opportunities for employment between menial low-wage jobs at the bottom and high-skill professional and technical jobs at the top and provides very limited opportunities for immigrants to advance beyond the bottom rung of the economic ladder without substantial investments in human capital and acquisition of requisite social networks.[9] As a consequence, some scholars argue, new immigrants are experiencing "second-generation decline" or "downward assimilation," as evidenced by their lack of socioeconomic advancement across generations, worsening health (e.g., higher prevalence of low birthweight, infant mortality, and adult mortality), and increasing involvement in crime and substance use.[10] On the other side of the debate are scholars who argue that new immigrants are experiencing gains across generations in wages, educational outcomes, and occupational status, much as their European predecessors did.[11] Both sides recognize that generational progress varies considerably across ethnic groups, with Asians generally experiencing the most upward mobility and Mexicans the least,[12] and that it is still too early to compare the descendants of post-1965 immigrants to those of earlier European immigrants, many of whom did not fully assimilate until the third or fourth generation. As one observer of this debate notes, "It is as if we were trying to measure the progress of the immigrants from southern and eastern Europe in 1910: some tentative patterns can be observed, but the full picture will not be evident for several decades."[13]

Classic Assimilation Theory

The empirical debate over the assimilation outcomes of post-1965 immigrants is grounded in a theoretical debate over the causal mechanisms associated with assimilation. Scholars who are more pessimistic about new immigrants' prospects for advancement take issue with classical assimilation theory for suggesting that contemporary immigrants would follow a "straight line" toward greater assimilation, as did earlier European immigrants. Other scholars argue that although some criticisms of classic assimilation theory are justified, the theory should be amended rather than rejected out of hand.[14]

Classic assimilation theory is rooted in the work of Robert Park and Ernest Burgess, who viewed assimilation as the process through which ethnic minorities became incorporated into the mainstream culture.[15] Park and Burgess emphasized that for ethnic minorities to assimilate they had to enter into intense and intimate "primary group" relations with members of the majority and that such interactions would become more common as ethnic minorities and native-born members of the dominant group began to share the same neighborhoods and schools. Milton Gordon later extended this framework by describing the multiple dimensions along which individuals and groups assimilate.[16] Like Park and Burgess, he viewed the entry of ethnic minorities into primary group relationships with members of the dominant group—which he called "structural assimilation"—as the key to attaining full assimilation. Gordon also argued that acculturation, which he defined as the minority group's adoption of the cultural patterns of the host society (including language, dress, modes of emotional expression, and personal values), was more or less inevitable as a group spent more time in the host society but that it was ultimately not as important as structural assimilation for ensuring ethnic incorporation into the American mainstream. Thus a key hypothesis from both Park and Burgess's and Gordon's theories is that the integration of ethnic minorities into the primary social groups in which members of the dominant group participate is a catalyst for full assimilation and the economic advancement of ethnic minority groups.

Unfortunately, neither Park and Burgess nor Gordon laid out a systematic theory about the causal mechanisms through which assimilation occurs or what its consequences are for understanding crime and other outcomes. Instead, the major legacy of classic assimilation theory is the idea that once assimilation begins it proceeds in more or less a "straight-line" fashion, with a steady progression toward more positive socioeconomic outcomes. Another legacy is the idea that assimilation is fueled by intergenerational change, whereby each new generation of immigrants is thought to represent not only the passage of time in the United States but also a new stage of adjustment to the host society.[17]

Segmented Assimilation Theory

Classic assimilation theory has become something of a lightning rod in the immigration literature, as many critics have taken issue with the straight-line model, arguing that it presents an oversimplified and empirically outdated view of assimilation. Perhaps the most influential alternative to classical assimilation theory is Portes and Zhou's theory of "segmented assimilation."[18] The theory attempts to explain how new immigrant groups may depart from the straight-line model by reframing the question of *whether* the second generation will assimilate as a question of *to what segment* of society it will assimilate. The answer to this question, according to segmented assimilation theory, depends on a complex set of factors that include the timing of an immigrant group's arrival, government policies toward immigrants, the degree of discrimination against the ethnic group, and the community context into which they settle.

Segmented assimilation theory identifies two important alternatives to straight-line assimilation. First, the theory predicts that immigrant youth who assimilate into disadvantaged neighborhood contexts, and who do not have strong family and community support from co-ethnics, are likely to adopt the norms and values of inner-city youth subcultures (particularly those that devalue education as a vehicle for advancement) and are at risk for experiencing downward assimilation and hence more involvement in crime.[19] This prediction challenges one of the tenets of classical assimilation theory, that social integration into primary groups with native-born members of the dominant group will inevitably lead to advancement.

Another important departure from straight-line assimilation occurs when immigrant youth maintain strong attachments to the values and tight solidarity of their co-ethnic community and purposefully resist the acculturation process. Portes and Rumbaut argue that communities of co-ethnics can supply social capital to immigrant families by (1) increasing the economic opportunities available to immigrant parents through assisting with their job searches and helping with other living needs such as housing, places to shop, and schools for children; (2) enforcing norms against divorce and family disruption, thereby preserving intact families; and (3) reinforcing parental authority over children.[20] Thus segmented assimilation theory implies that living in a tightly knit ethnic community with dense social ties provides social resources that should ultimately be protective against youth involvement in crime.

Criticism of segmented assimilation theory has come from three main directions. First, some scholars are skeptical of its emphasis on cultural transmission of norms that devalue education and condone crime as a key mechanism for downward assimilation. For example, Alba and Nee criticize segmented assimilation theory for suggesting that the urban underclass is a source of oppositional youth culture and for using the image of the underclass to essentialize African American culture.[21] They argue that in neighborhoods where African Americans are the dominant group immigrant youth are more likely to assimilate toward the norms of middle-class African Americans than toward those of the underclass. Similarly, Perlmann and Waldinger are critical of segmented assimilation theory's claim that downward assimilation is a result of an oppositional youth culture because, they argue, such oppositional norms were equally common among European second-generation youth in the mid-twentieth century and did not prevent their ultimate incorporation into the American mainstream. A second criticism targets the claim that ethnic neighborhoods protect immigrant families from downward assimilation.[22] Some researchers argue that living in an ethnic enclave may have a net negative impact on immigrants' economic opportunities because it restricts their labor market options and discourages them from developing English-language skills, both of which could lead to economic marginalization.[23]

Still others have criticized segmented assimilation theory for not offering a coherent account of the causes of upward and downward assimilation or a testable set of propositions. In a recent reformulation of segmented assimilation theory, Xie and Greenman argue that the theory can be operationalized as a set of propositions about the interaction between an individual's degree of assimilation and the social context in which assimilation occurs.[24] For example, if immigrant generation is taken as an indicator of individual-level assimilation, the theory generates a set of predictions about how immigrant generation structures the way crime should vary across neighborhood contexts. The theory predicts that youth who are more assimilated (e.g., the third generation) will be at a higher risk of involvement in crime when they live in more disadvantaged neighborhoods. However, youth who are less assimilated (e.g., the first generation) have stronger family and community supports that buffer them from the deleterious influences of youth subcultures, so living in a disadvantaged neighborhood should not substantially increase their risk of committing crime. The theory also predicts that living in neighborhoods with high concentrations of immigrants and co-ethnics should be protective against violence for unassimilated or partially assimilated youth, who are more closely tied to ethnic customs and more reliant on ethnic networks, but that fully assimilated youth (e.g., the third generation) may not derive such protective benefits from living in immigrant neighborhoods.

Immigration and Crime in Chicago Neighborhoods

In the analysis that follows, our goal is to illustrate how involvement in violent offenses varies across (1) generations of immigrants, (2) length of time that first-generation immigrants have lived in the United States, (3) level of linguistic acculturation, and (4) two key dimensions of neighborhood context, the level of concentrated disadvantage and the percentage of immigrants in the neighborhood. We analyze data from the Project on Human Development in Chicago Neighborhoods (PHDCN) Longitudinal Cohort Study, which contains sizable representations of first-, second-, and third-generation immigrants. The PHDCN sample was selected through a multistage procedure involving the selection of neighborhoods, households, and children.[25] To be age eligible, a household member must have been within twelve months of the following target ages: zero (or pre-natal), three, six, nine, twelve, fifteen, and eighteen years. Respondents and caregivers were interviewed in person up to three times from 1995 to 2002 in intervals of about 2.5 years.[26]

Subjects in the nine-, twelve-, fifteen-, and eighteen-year-old cohorts of PHDCN were asked about violent offenses at all three waves of the survey, and subjects in the six-year-old cohort were also asked these questions at wave 3 (at which time their average age was 10.8 years). We include all of these cases in our analysis, yielding a sample size of 3,675 subjects living in 186 of Chicago's census tracts. We construct outcome measures from self-reports of eight violent behaviors derived from questions that ask subjects at each interview whether, during the last year, they (1) hit someone out-side of the house; (2) threw objects such as rocks or bottles at people; (3) carried a hidden weapon; (4) were in a gang fight; (5) attacked someone with a weapon; (6) snatched a purse or picked a pocket; (7) maliciously set fire to a building, property, or car; or (8) used a weapon to rob someone. Previous research using this data set has shown that measures of these behaviors load onto a common dimension of violent crime, albeit with different degrees of severity.[27]

To conduct the analysis of immigrant generation, age at time of arrival to the United States, and linguistic acculturation, we pooled the data across all three waves of the study and used logistic regression models to estimate their associations with each of the eight violent behaviors.[28] All models control for *age* (categorized as less than twelve years, twelve to thirteen years, fourteen to fifteen years, sixteen to seventeen years, eighteen to nineteen years, and twenty years and over), *sex*, *race/ethnicity* (non-Latino white, non-Latino black, Mexican American, Puerto Rican/other Latino, non-Latino other race), *primary caregiver's educational attainment* (less than high school, high school, some college, college degree and higher), *household income* (less than $10,000, $10,000–19,999, $20,000–29,999, $30,000–39,999, $40,000–49,999, $50,000 or more), and *change over time* (using dummy variables to index the survey wave at which the outcome is being measured).

We began the analysis by considering differences in violent crime across immigrant generations. In our sample of adolescents, 13.6 percent ($n = 500$) were first-generation, 30.8 percent ($n = 1,130$) were second-generation, and 55.7 percent ($n = 2,045$) were third-generation immigrants.[29] We estimated the association between immigrant generational status and the log odds of engaging in each type of violent behavior using logistic

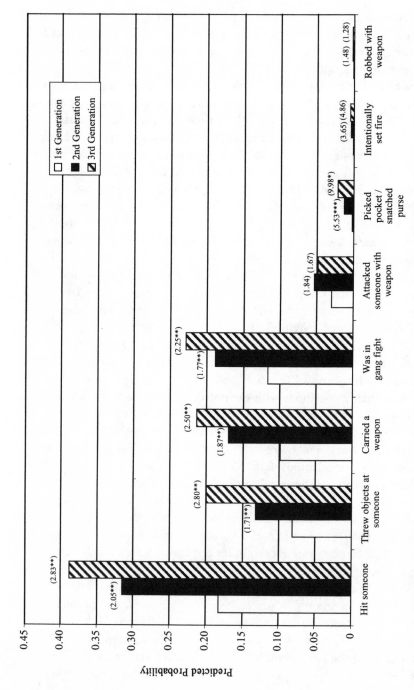

Fig. 3.1. Probability of Violent Behavior by Immigrant Generation: PHDCN Cohort Data, Waves 1 through 3. *Note:* Odds ratios in parentheses; reference category is first generation. * $p \leq .01$; ** $p < .05$; *** $p < .10$.

regressions, and we graphed the predicted probabilities for each immigrant generation in figure 3.1.[30] The results show that the acts of hitting someone, throwing objects at someone, carrying a weapon, being involved in a gang fight, and picking pockets/snatching purses are all significantly more prevalent in the second and third generations than in the first generation. We do not find significant differences across generations on the probability of attacking someone with a weapon, robbing someone with a weapon, or committing arson, which may in part be due to the low frequencies of these events.

Although the finding that most violent behaviors tend to increase across immigrant generations is consistent with the idea of downward assimilation, it is also possible that these differences are confounded by selection processes that make people who decide to migrate to the United States distinctively less crime prone than the general population from their countries of origin.[31] In other words, if first-generation immigrants possessed certain characteristics that made them selectively less crime prone and if these characteristics became less pronounced in subsequent generations, then we could observe increasing crime across generations even if there were no causal relation between assimilation and crime.

Another approach to analyzing the association between exposure to the United States and violent behavior is to consider variation in levels of violence among first-generation immigrant youth who have been living in the United States for different lengths of time. This approach has the merit of not being affected by selection factors that determine one's propensity both to migrate and to be involved in violence (although other forms of selection may still operate, as we discuss below). We used logistic regression models to estimate the relationship between the age at which first-generation subjects arrived in the United States and their probability of engaging in violent behavior (we omit from this analysis acts of pickpocketing, arson, and armed robbery because of their extremely low frequencies). For the purposes of this analysis, we grouped immigrant youth into three categories of age at time of arrival to the United States: before age six ($n = 243$), between ages six and nine ($n = 124$), and at ages ten and older ($n = 133$). The results, displayed in figure 3.2, show that subjects who immigrated to the United States at younger ages were more likely to engage in most acts of violence during adolescence than those who arrived at later ages. Specifically, subjects who were under age six when they arrived in the United States were significantly more likely to engage in all types of violence than were those who arrived at age ten or older; and subjects who

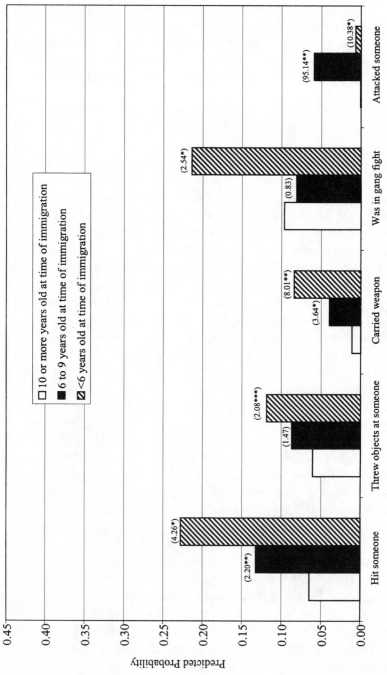

Fig. 3.2. Probability of Violent Behavior by Time in the United States for First Generation: PHDCN Cohort Data, Waves 1 through 3. *Note:* Odds ratios in parentheses; reference category is 10 or more years old at time of immigration. * $p \leq .01$; ** $p < .05$; *** $p < .10$.

were six to nine years old when they arrived were significantly more likely to hit someone, carry a weapon, or attack someone than were those who arrived at age ten or older. The magnitude of these associations is quite large, as evidenced by the odds ratios displayed in figure 3.2. For example, the odds that a first-generation immigrant youth who was less than six years old when he arrived in the United States will hit someone are 4.26 times larger than the odds of a similar immigrant youth who arrived at age ten or older. Comparable odds ratios for carrying a weapon and being in a gang fight are 8.01 and 2.54, respectively.

Our next set of comparisons focuses on how linguistic acculturation is related to crime. We constructed a scale of linguistic acculturation based on survey questions that asked primary caregivers what language they spoke the most (English, a language other than English, or both), how good their English was, and how often they used English in the following situations: speaking with their children, speaking with their partner, speaking with friends, speaking at work, watching television, and listening to the radio.[32] We divided this scale into three categories of acculturation: *not acculturated* (values less than 3, $n = 2,226$), which included households in which the primary caregiver used English infrequently; *partially acculturated* (values of greater than or equal to 3 and less than 5, $n = 1,283$), for households where the primary caregiver used a mixture of English and another language; and *fully acculturated* (values of 5, $n = 4,499$), for households in which the primary caregiver used English exclusively. We estimated the relationship between linguistic acculturation and violent offending using logistic regression. The results, displayed in figure 3.3, show that increasing acculturation is associated with significantly higher probabilities of many types of violence: Youth who live in fully acculturated households are significantly more likely to hit someone, throw objects at someone, and be in a gang fight than those from nonacculturated households; while youth from partially acculturated households are significantly more likely to hit someone and be in a gang fight than those from nonacculturated households. However, the associations between acculturation and acts of violence are generally not as strong or significant as those between age at time of arrival to the United States and violence; in fact, only one of the estimated odds ratios in the linguistic acculturation analysis is greater than 2.0. It is also important to note that although we control for age, sex, race/ethnicity, immigrant generation, and family socioeconomic status, the relationships we estimate between linguistic acculturation and violent behaviors may be confounded by unobserved factors that

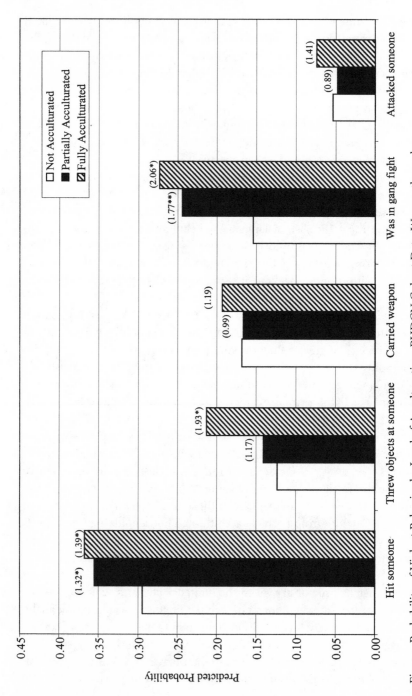

Fig. 3.3. Probability of Violent Behavior by Level of Acculturation: PHDCN Cohort Data, Waves 1 through 3.

Note: Odds ratios in parentheses; reference category is "not acculturated." * $p \leq .01$; ** $p < .05$.

predict both the language use of the primary caregiver and youth violence. For example, peer networks could motivate immigrant youth to use English more frequently, and their use of English could in turn motivate their primary caregivers to use it more often as well. At the same time, peer networks may also increase an adolescent's propensity to participate in violence. Thus the association between linguistic acculturation and violence is not only weak but also potentially spurious. Nonetheless, the results are at least consistent with the downward assimilation thesis, even if they do not constitute strong supporting evidence.

In the final stage of our analysis, we investigated hypotheses from segmented assimilation theory by examining whether involvement in violence varies by neighborhood context and, if so, whether these associations vary by immigrant generation in ways consistent with the theory. Segmented assimilation theory predicts that youth who assimilate into neighborhoods marked by high levels of disadvantage will become more involved in violence as they assimilate, and it also suggests that neighborhoods with high concentrations of immigrants should be protective environments, especially for less assimilated youth. We used the census tract where the subject lived at wave 1 (in 1995) as an operating definition of "neighborhood" and constructed measures of both concentrated disadvantage and immigrant concentration circa 1995, interpolating data from the 1990 and 2000 censuses.[33] In the interest of parsimony, rather than analyzing each violent behavior separately, we used a multilevel modeling approach that combined all of the items into a scale of violence and allowed us to account for the hierarchical nature of our data: scale items measured at a given time period were nested within persons (i.e., each person had repeated measures across items and over time), and persons were nested within census tracts. At level 1 we predicted the log-odds that an individual would endorse a given scale item (i.e., answer "yes" to a question about engaging in a particular type of violent behavior) at a given time period. This model produced an estimate of an individual's average propensity to engage in violence, which we modeled as a function of individual-level background characteristics (age, sex, race/ethnicity, immigrant generation, primary caregiver's education, and household income) at level 2, and tract-level neighborhood characteristics (concentrated disadvantage and the percent foreign born) at level 3. We also estimated cross-level interactions between immigrant generation and both concentrated disadvantage and percent foreign born so that we could estimate the neighborhood effects separately for each immigrant

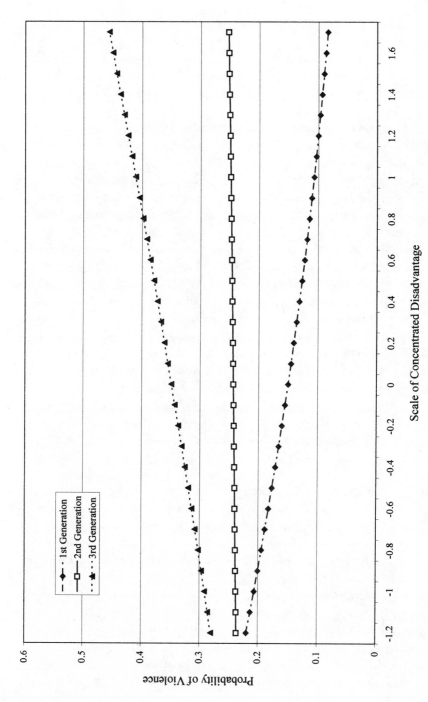

Fig. 3.4. Probability of Crime by Neighborhood Disadvantage: PHDCN Cohort Dat, Waves 1 through 3

generation. The modeling strategy is described in more detail in the Appendix.[34]

Figure 3.4 graphs the predicted probabilities of violent crime across levels of concentrated disadvantage. The guiding hypothesis, based on segmented assimilation theory, is that among more assimilated youth neighborhood disadvantage should be associated with a higher risk of criminal behavior but that nonassimilated or partially assimilated youth should be buffered from the deleterious effects of neighborhood disadvantage. Thus segmented assimilation implies that we should see a positive relationship between disadvantage and crime in the third generation but not necessarily in the second or first generation. The results are consistent with this hypothesis. Indeed, neighborhood disadvantage was associated with higher levels of violence only among third-generation youth; it was not significantly related to violence in the second generation, and it was associated with significantly *lower* odds of violence in the first generation—a counterintuitive finding that does not contradict segmented assimilation theory but was also not anticipated by the theory.

One possible explanation for the finding that concentrated disadvantage is a risk factor only for third-generation youth is that since most third-generation adolescents in Chicago are native-born whites and African Americans—many of whom are actually in the fourth and higher generations—the results may be driven by these racial groups and may not apply to any of major post-1965 immigrant groups. To examine this possibility, we re-ran the analysis on Mexican Americans, the only group with significant representation of all three generations in the PHDCN sample, and found a similar pattern of results: concentrated disadvantage was still associated with a significantly higher risk of violence in the third generation, but it had no significant effect in either the first or the second generation. Thus the findings for Mexicans—the only group on which the hypothesis could be fully tested—support the segmented assimilation hypothesis.

Segmented assimilation theory also predicts that immigrant neighborhoods should be protective against crime, mainly for youth who have not fully assimilated and not necessarily for those who have. Figure 3.5 shows that higher levels of neighborhood immigrant concentration are associated with lower levels of violence, but the effect is significant only for second-generation youth and is weakest for the third generation. Although these results are not entirely consistent with segmented assimilation theory—which did not predict that the protective effects of immigrant

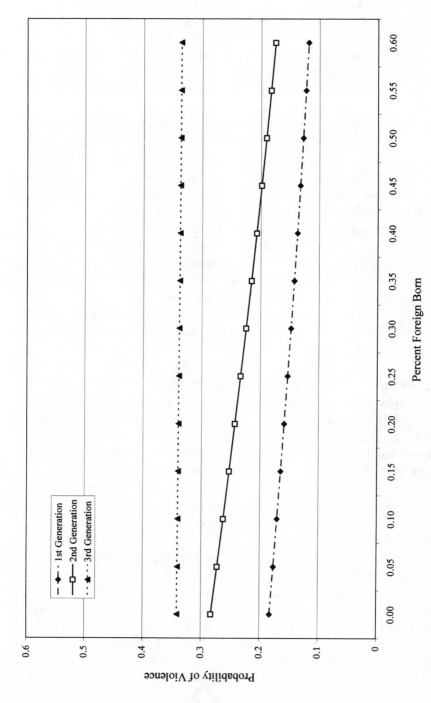

Fig. 3-5. Probability of Crime by Neighborhood Percent Foreign Born: PHDCN Cohort Data, Waves 1 through 3

neighborhoods would be stronger in the second generation than they were in the first—the effect is weakest among the most assimilated youth (those in the third generation) and stronger among less assimilated youth.

It is important to note as a caveat that the associations between neighborhood context and violence may be confounded by factors that predict both how individuals and families sort themselves into neighborhoods and whether youth participate in acts of violence. It is possible, for example, that most youth who live in disadvantaged neighborhoods also have more personal and family risk factors for crime than those who live in nondisadvantaged neighborhoods, which would make it difficult to separate the contextual effect of living in disadvantaged neighborhoods from confounding risk factors.[35] Although such selection is certainly plausible, unmeasured selection factors can only confound the associations between neighborhood context and violence that we estimate if they are uncorrelated with the measured characteristics we control for in our models (e.g., age, sex, race/ethnicity, immigrant generation, parents' education, and household income).

Conclusion

In our analysis we addressed four questions about immigration and crime with data on self-reported violent offending among adolescents living in Chicago neighborhoods. First, does violent crime vary across immigrant generations? We found that most types of violent behavior tend to become more prevalent across immigrant generations, which, taken at face value, suggests that as immigrants assimilate they become more involved in crime—a finding consistent with the idea of downward assimilation. An alternative interpretation is that intergenerational disparities in violence are a statistical artifact of selection processes that affect both who migrates and who commits crime. For example, people who decide to migrate to the United States could be selectively less crime prone than the general population from their country of origin, and the finding of increasing crime across generations of immigrants in the United States could simply reflect a shift in the composition of successive immigrant generations rather than a true contextual effect of being exposed to criminogenic influences through assimilation.

An empirical test of the immigrant selection hypothesis could be done only with a cross-national research design that sampled both immigrants in the United States and comparable nonmigrants who remained in the country of origin (e.g., Mexico). Few researchers have collected this type of cross-national data, and we are not aware of any such data on self-reported offending. However, simulations have shown that immigrant selection can potentially introduce large bias into intergenerational comparisons of the kind we present in this chapter.[36]

An additional source of selection bias is the geographic restriction of the PHDCN sample to youth from families that lived in the city of Chicago in 1995. If migration from the city to the suburbs is selective in ways related to crime, and if the relationship between out-migration to the suburbs and propensity to commit crime varies across immigrant generations, then these selection processes may distort our intergenerational comparisons of violence. More research on how out-migration from the city to the suburbs is related to crime and how it may affect the composition of immigrant generations could shed more light on this potential source of selection.

A second question is whether immigrant youth who migrated to the United States at younger ages are more likely to be involved in crime than immigrants of the same birth cohort who arrived in the United States at older ages. Our results indicate that longer spells of residence in the United States are associated with significantly higher odds of many types of violent behavior, in keeping with the downward assimilation thesis. Although this type of analysis circumvents some of the selection problems that plague comparisons of crime across immigrant generations, selection bias is still a threat if factors that predispose youth to crime also determine the age at which they migrate to the United States. For example, Mexican parents with older adolescent children who contemplate migration to the United States could be less likely to immigrate if their children are already involved in crime or other antisocial behaviors in Mexico. However, parents with younger children may be less able to detect and interpret signs of antisocial behavior in younger children, in which case their children's problem behavior would not influence their migration decision. This could result in more "weeding out" of crime-prone youth among immigrants who arrive at later ages compared to younger ages and could thus create the appearance of a relationship between greater exposure to the United States and more involvement in crime.

Our third question is whether the level of linguistic acculturation in the family, net of immigrant generation, is related to violent crime. We found that youth from fully acculturated families tended to be more involved in violence than those from partially or nonacculturated families but that the relationship was generally not as strong as that between age at arrival to the United States and violence. Once again, these findings do not suggest that linguistic acculturation is causally related to crime, and future research should scrutinize potential confounders of the association between linguistic acculturation and crime as well as possible mediators of the relationship.

Our final question is whether there is an association between neighborhood context and violent crime and, if so, whether the association varies by immigrant generation in ways consistent with segmented assimilation theory. Segmented assimilation theory predicts that immigrants who assimilate into neighborhood contexts marked by high levels of socioeconomic disadvantage, especially those who do not have strong attachment to their family or immigrant communities, will be at risk of becoming involved in criminal behavior. To operationalize this idea, we used immigrant generation as a marker for degree of assimilation and hypothesized that the risk to involvement in crime associated with living in a more disadvantaged neighborhood should be greatest among youth in the third generation, in which most youth presumably are fully assimilated. Indeed, we found that concentrated disadvantage is positively associated with the odds of violence in the third generation but not in the first or second. Interestingly, among first-generation immigrants, neighborhood disadvantage was associated with *lower* odds of violence and property offending, while there was no significant association between neighborhood disadvantage and crime in the second generation.

Segmented assimilation theory also predicts that neighborhoods with high concentrations of immigrants should be protective environments for immigrant youth who have not fully assimilated. Following the theory, we hypothesized that immigrant concentration should be protective environments for first- and second-generation youth, who may be only partially assimilated, but not as much for the third generation, most of whom have already assimilated. We found that the neighborhood concentration of immigrants was associated with lower odds of violence, but the effect was only significant for second-generation youth, a result partially consistent with segmented assimilation theory.

In sum, the neighborhood analysis suggests that the associations between neighborhood context and participation in acts of violence differ across immigrant generations. First-generation youth appear to be protected against violence when living either in more disadvantaged or more immigrant neighborhoods, although only the disadvantage effect is statistically significant. For second-generation youth, there is no significant association between neighborhood disadvantage and participation in violence, but they appear to be protected against violence when living in neighborhoods with greater concentrations of immigrants. Third-generation youth experience the greatest risk from living in disadvantaged neighborhoods and derive the least protection from living in immigrant neighborhoods. Here too, the results are potentially confounded by selection mechanisms, in this case relating to the factors that sort families into neighborhoods and possibly also influence the violent behavior of adolescents.

If criminologists are to gain a better understanding of how immigrant assimilation processes are related to crime, they must address the challenges presented by the various selection issues, including immigrant self-selection and selection into neighborhoods, with innovative research designs (e.g., sibling comparisons, natural experiments, and regression discontinuity designs) and methods for strengthening causal inferences when analyzing observational data (e.g., propensity score matching or stratification). Perhaps even more important, criminologists need to develop better theories of immigrant assimilation and crime. Segmented assimilation theory improves upon some of the outdated assumptions of classic assimilation theory, but critics are right to point out that it relies on a rather simplistic and perhaps unrealistic understanding of cultural transmission in inner-city neighborhoods.

Recent formulations of segmented assimilation theory rely less on a "cultural deviance" model of crime—one that assumes the causes of delinquency lie in a person's socialization into a subcultural value system that condones modes of conduct opposed to conventional norms and the law—than on the link between downward assimilation and the loosening of social controls within the family and the community.[37] Rather than locating the cause of crime in the influence of oppositional value systems, this offshoot of segmented assimilation theory suggests that assimilation can lead to crime when it reduces one's commitment to any value system and weakens familial bonds that diminish parents' capacity to supervise or in other ways influence the behavior of their children. These threats to parental authority emerge most strongly in what Portes and Rumbaut call cases of "dissonant acculturation," when children learn the English language and American customs, and/or abandon immigrant culture, at a pace that outstrips or conflicts with that of their parents.

Perhaps the risk of dissonant acculturation varies across spatial contexts in a way that has not been anticipated by prior theory. For example, the propensity for immigrant youth to adopt American customs and distance themselves from their parents and from the immigrant community may be higher in more affluent communities, and thus the threat of dissonant acculturation could vary inversely with neighborhood disadvantage. In other words, it is possible that new immigrants assimilating into white affluent neighborhoods are at greater risk of criminal involvement than those assimilating into minority disadvantaged neighborhoods. This idea is consistent with our finding that participation in acts of violence diminishes at higher levels of neighborhood disadvantage for first-generation immigrant youth. Such provocative theoretical issues deserve further consideration as criminologists return to the study of immigrant assimilation and crime.

Appendix: Methodology for Modeling Violent Crime

Let t denote the wave of data collection ($t = 1, 2, 3$), and let i denote the specific violent offense of interest, where $i = 0, 1, 2, \ldots 7$, with item 0 denoted as the "reference item." Define $Y_{tijk} = 1$ if participant j living in neighborhood k reported committing offense i at wave t, while $Y_{tijk} = 0$ if participant did not. We are interested in the probability of such an offense, $\text{Prob}(Y_{tijk} = 1) = \phi_{tijk}$. Rather than working directly with these probabilities, we work with the natural logarithm of the odds ratio, $\eta_{tijk} = \log[\phi_{tijk}/(1 - \phi_{tijk})]$. Our model views η_{tijk} as depending on the underlying propensity of the participant to commit violence at a given time. We formulate a model for variations in propensity to violence over time within participants (level 1), between participants within neighborhoods (level 2), and between neighborhoods (level 3).

At level 1 we model change over time within persons as follows:

$$(1) \quad \eta_{tijk} = \pi_{ojk} + \pi_{1jk} d_{tjk} + \pi_{2jk} d^2_{tjk} + \alpha_i$$

where π_{0jk} is the average violent propensity of a participant over the course of the study; d_{tjk} is the deviation of the age of person jk at wave t from that person's mean age over the three waves of data collection; π_{1jk} is the linear rate of change in propensity at the mean age; π_{2jk} captures the extent to which criminal propensity is accelerating or decelerating over time; and α_i is a fixed effect for each item i that captures the "severity" of that item.

According to equation 1, the log-odds that a participant will commit a given offense changes as a quadratic function of age, controlling for the severity of the offense.

Next, we model each individual's propensity to violence as follows:

$$(2) \quad \pi_{0jk} = \mu + X_{jk}\beta + W_k\gamma$$

where X_{jk} is a vector of background characteristics of participant j in neighborhood k and W_k is a vector of tract-level neighborhood characteristics. The components of β characterize partial associations between person or family characteristics and the propensity to offend, while the components of γ characterize partial associations between neighborhood characteristics and the propensity to offend; μ is a model intercept. We also test a similar model for π_{1jk}, which captures within-person change in the log-odds of violent offending, but this portion of the model was not used to generate the graphs presented above, which focus instead on the model for violence propensity. Taken together, equations 1 and 2 constitute a multilevel logistic regression model with covariates and random effects at the person and neighborhood levels, estimated simultaneously by means of generalized estimating equations with robust standard errors.

NOTES

1. For examples of early research on immigration and crime, see studies by Hart (1896); Hourwich (1912); Stofflet (1941); Taft (1933, 1936); Van Vechton (1941); von Hentig (1945).

2. This finding was most famously articulated by the Wickersham Commission (1931).

3. In this chapter we define the first generation of immigrants as people who were born abroad, the second generation as those with at least one parent born abroad, and the third generation as those with at least one grandparent born abroad.

4. The search was conducted on August 12, 2004.

5. For examples of such research, see studies by Butcher and Piehl (1999); Hagan and Palloni (1998); and Lee, Martinez, and Rosenfeld (2001).

6. See Butcher and Piehl's (1999) study of self-reported criminal offending among fifteen- to twenty-three-year-olds from the National Longitudinal Survey of Youth and Harris's (1999) analysis of delinquency and other risky behaviors using data from the National Longitudinal Study of Adolescent Health.

7. For research on immigration and crime in other countries, see studies by

Killias (1989); Sun and Reed (1995); and the collection of studies in the book *Ethnicity, Crime, and Immigration: Comparative and Cross- National Perspectives* (Tonry 1997). The only country where this trend does not seem to hold is Sweden (Martens 1997).

8. New immigrants are generally referred to as those who arrived in the United States following the Immigration and Nationality Act Amendments of 1965, which reopened the door to immigration.

9. Scholars who are pessimistic about the socioeconomic prospects for the new second generation include Alejandro Portes and his colleagues (Portes and Rumbaut 2001; Portes and Zhou 1993) and Herbert Gans (1992).

10. For an overview of the evidence on downward assimilation, see Rubén Rumbaut's (1997) article "Assimilation and Its Discontents."

11. Some examples of scholars who are more optimistic about the prospects for the new second generation are Farely and Alba (2002); Perlmann and Waldinger (1997).

12. See the review of this literature by Zhou (2001).

13. See Hirschman (2001: 317).

14. For an articulation of this position, see the interesting discussion of classical assimilation theory by Alba and Nee (1997).

15. For example, see Park and Burgess (1924).

16. See Gordon (1964).

17. This point is made by Alba and Nee (1997) in their review of classic assimilation theory.

18. Portes and Zhou originally formulated the theory of segmented assimilation in a 1993 article (Portes and Zhou 1993). For more recent work on segmented assimilation theory see Zhou (1997); Portes and Rumbaut (2001).

19. Deviant subcultures are an important part of the assimilation theories of both Portes and Zhou (1993) and Suarez-Orozco and Suarez-Orozco (1995).

20. See Portes and Rumbaut (2001).

21. See Alba and Nee (1997).

22. See Perlmann and Waldinger (1997).

23. For examples of research on ethnic enclaves, see Borjas (2000) and the work of Sanders, Nee, and colleagues (Nee, Sanders, and Sernau 1994; Sanders and Nee 1987).

24. See the recent paper by Xie and Greenman (2005).

25. In the first stage, all 825 Chicago census tracts were stratified by racial/ethnic composition (seven categories) and socioeconomic status (high, medium, and low), producing twenty-one strata. A total of 180 tracts were selected randomly within strata. At the second stage, over thirty-five thousand dwelling units were enumerated (or "listed") in person by the PHDCN research team within each area. Within each listed block, dwelling units were selected systematically (every nth unit) after an initial random draw, and all households were then enumerated

within selected dwelling units. Within each sampled household, all age-eligible participants were selected with certainty. For more details, see the recent study by Sampson, Morenoff, and Raudenbush (2005).

26. For convenience, we refer to each interview as a survey "wave." We refer to the baseline interview as wave 1 and the two follow-up interviews as waves 2 and 3, respectively.

27. Raudenbush, Johnson, and Sampson (2003) show that these eight items can be used to model a person's latent propensity to engage in violent crime, and Sampson, Morenoff, and Raudenbush (2005) use the same items in their analysis of racial/ethnic disparities in violence.

28. We run these models on a stacked data set, such that each observation represents a time period–specific observation for each person.

29. Due to limited sample sizes within some groups, we do not estimate immigrant generational differences separately for each racial/ethnic group, but we have replicated the analysis on Mexican Americans, the only group to contain sizable representations of all three immigrant generations, and the results do not change substantially.

30. In figure 3.1, the probability of violence is predicted for a hypothetical Mexican American male, aged sixteen to seventeen, at wave 1, with a primary caregiver who has less than a high school education and who has a household income of $20,000 to 29,999. For each of the eight violent outcomes in figure 3.1, we also present the odds ratios that compare the prevalence of violence in (1) the second generation versus the first and (2) the third generation versus the first. The odds ratios and their statistical significance are displayed above each bar on the graph.

31. One mechanism that could contribute to such selection is criminal background checks conducted by immigration officials to screen potential migrants with criminal backgrounds from entering the United States.

32. This scale has a range of 0 to 5, a mean of 3.9, and a Cronbach's alpha of .98. Because of the large number of people who use only English, the distribution of the linguistic acculturation scale is highly skewed, which is one reason that we treat it as a categorical rather than a continuous variable in the analysis.

33. To construct a tract-level scale of concentrated disadvantage, we factor-analyzed the following four census variables: the percentage of families with incomes below the poverty line, the percentage of families on public assistance, the percentage of female-headed families, and the unemployment rate. To measure immigrant concentration we used the percentage of people in a census tract who were foreign born. To obtain measures of neighborhood context circa 1995, we interpolated across the 1990 and 2000 census observations by taking the mean of the two observations on each variable.

34. For additional details on this multilevel modeling strategy and its application to the case of adolescent violence, see recent articles by Raudenbush, Johnson, and Sampson (2003); Sampson, Morenoff, and Raudenbush (2005).

35. It is also possible that such selection processes could explain why our results show that neighborhood disadvantage is a risk factor for crime only in the third generation. Third-generation youth are, perhaps, most likely to spatially assimilate by moving to more affluent neighborhoods in the city and suburbs, and, as a result, the selection processes that exclude low-risk youth from disadvantaged neighborhoods could be stronger in the third generation than in the first and second generations.

36. Palloni and Morenoff (2001) conduct simulations to show that even slight amounts of self-selection among immigrants on characteristics related to health can result in the appearance of large health disparities across immigrant and ethnic groups, and this same logic can be applied to crime.

37. For more on the distinction between theories of cultural deviance and social control, see Kornhauser (1978). For more on the consequences of immigrant assimilation for parental social control, see Portes and Rumbaut (2001).

REFERENCES

Alba, Richard, and Victor Nee. 1997. "Rethinking Assimilation Theory for a New Era of Immigration." *International Migration Review* 31:826–74.

Borjas, George. 2000. "Ethnic Enclaves and Assimilation." *Swedish Economic Policy Review* 7:89–122.

Butcher, Kristin F., and Anne Morrison Piehl. 1999. "Cross-City Evidence on the Relationship between Immigration and Crime." *Journal of Policy Analysis and Management* 17:457–93.

Farely, Reynolds, and Richard Alba. 2002. "The New Second Generation in the United States." *International Migration Review* 36:669–701.

Gans, Herbert J. 1992. "Second-Generation Decline: Scenarios for the Economic and Ethnic Futures of the Post-1965 American Immigrants." *Ethnic and Racial Studies* 15:173–92.

Gordon, Milton. 1964. *Assimilation in American Life: The Role of Race, Religion, and National Origins.* New York: Oxford University Press.

Hagan, John, and Alberto Palloni. 1998. "Immigration and Crime in the United States." In *The Immigration Debate: Studies on the Economic, Demographic, and Fiscal Effects of Immigration,* edited by J. P. Smith and B. Edmonston, 367–87. Washington, DC: National Academy Press.

Harris, Kathleen Mullan. 1999. "The Health Status and Risk Behavior of Adolescents in Immigrant Families." In *Children of Immigrants: Health, Adjustment, and Public Assistance,* edited by D. J. Hernandez, 286–347. Washington, DC: National Academy Press.

Hart, Hastings H. 1896. "Immigration and Crime." *American Journal of Sociology* 2:369–77.

Hirschman, Charles. 2001. "The Educational Enrollment of Immigrant Youth: A Test of the Segmented-Assimilation Hypothesis." *Demography* 38:317–36.

Hourwich, I. A. 1912. "Immigration and Crime." *American Journal of Sociology* 17: 478–90.

Killias, Martin. 1989. "Criminality among Second-Generation Immigrants in Western Europe: A Review of the Evidence." *Criminal Justice Review* 14:13–42.

Kornhauser, Ruth. 1978. *Social Sources of Delinquency: An Appraisal of Analytic Models.* Chicago: University of Chicago Press.

Lee, Matthew T., Ramiro Martinez Jr., and Richard Rosenfeld. 2001. "Does Immigration Increase Homicide? Negative Evidence from Three Border Cities." *Sociological Quarterly* 42:559–80.

Martens, Peter L. 1997. "Immigrants, Crime, and Criminal Justice in Sweden." In *Ethnicity, Crime and Immigration: Comparative and Cross-National Perspectives,* edited by Michael Tonry, 183–255. Chicago: University of Chicago Press.

Nee, Victor, Jimy M. Sanders, and Scott Sernau. 1994. "Job Transitions in an Immigrant Metropolis: Ethnic Boundaries and the Mixed Economy." *American Sociological Review* 59:849–72.

Palloni, Alberto, and Jeffrey D. Morenoff. 2001. "Interpreting the Paradoxical in the Hispanic Paradox: Demographic and Epidemiologic Approaches." *Annals of the New York Academy of Sciences* 954:140–74.

Park, Robert E., and Ernest W. Burgess. 1924. *Introduction to the Science of Sociology.* Chicago: University of Chicago Press.

Perlmann, Joel, and Roger Waldinger. 1997. "Second Generation Decline? Children of Immigrants, Past and Present: A Reconsideration." *International Migration Review* 31:893–922.

Portes, Alejandro, and Rubén G. Rumbaut. 2001. *Legacies: The Story of the Immigrant Second Generation.* Berkeley: University of California Press.

Portes, Alejandro, and Min Zhou. 1993. "The New Second Generation: Segmented Assimilation and Its Variants." *Annals of the American Academy of Political and Social Science* 530:74–96.

Raudenbush, Stephen W., Christopher Johnson, and Robert J. Sampson. 2003. "A Multivariate, Multilevel Rasch Model for Self-Reported Criminal Behavior." *Sociological Methodology* 33:169–211.

Rumbaut, Rubén G. 1997. "Assimilation and Its Discontents: Between Rhetoric and Reality." *International Migration Review* 31:923–60.

Sampson, Robert J., Jeffrey D. Morenoff, and Stephen W. Raudenbush. 2005. "Social Anatomy of Racial and Ethnic Disparities in Violence." *American Journal of Public Health* 95:224–32.

Sanders, Jimy M., and Victor Nee. 1987. "Limits of Ethnic Solidarity in the Enclave Economy." *American Sociological Review* 52:745–73.

Stofflet, E. H. 1941. "The European Immigrant and His Children." *Annals of the American Academy of Political and Social Science* 217:84–92.

Suarez-Orozco, Carola, and Marcelo Suarez-Orozco. 1995. *Transformations: Immigration, Family Life, and Achievement Motivation among Latino Adolescents.* Stanford: Stanford University Press.

Sun, H. E., and J. Reed. 1995. "Migration and Crime in Europe." *Social Pathology* 1:228–52.

Taft, Donald R. 1933. "Does Immigration Increase Crime?" *Social Forces* 12:69–77.

———. 1936. "Nationality and Crime." *American Sociological Review* 1:724–36.

Tonry, Michael. 1997. *Ethnicity, Crime, and Immigration: Comparative and Cross-National Perspectives.* Chicago: University of Chicago Press.

Van Vechton, C. C. 1941. "The Criminality of the Foreign Born." *Journal of Criminal Law and Criminology* 32:139–47.

von Hentig, Hans. 1945. "The First Generation and a Half: Notes on the Delinquency of the Native White of Mixed Parentage." *American Sociological Review* 10:792–98.

Wickersham Commission. 1931. *National Commission on Law Observance and Enforcement: Crime and the Foreign Born.* Washington, DC: U.S. Government Printing Office.

Xie, Yu, and Emily Greenman. 2005. "Testing Segmented Assimilation Theory: Evidence from the Add Health Study." Paper presented at the annual meeting of the Population Association of America, Philadelphia, March.

Zhou, Min. 1997. "Segmented Assimilation: Issues, Controversies, and Recent Research on the New Second Generation." *International Migration Review* 31:975–1008.

———. 2001. "Progress, Decline, Stagnation? The New Second Generation Comes of Age." In *Strangers at the Gates: New Immigrants in Urban America,* edited by Roger Waldinger. Berkeley: University of California Press.

Chapter 4

Immigration and Incarceration

Patterns and Predictors of Imprisonment among First- and Second-Generation Young Adults

Rubén G. Rumbaut, Roberto G. Gonzales, Golnaz Komaie, Charlie V. Morgan, and Rosaura Tafoya-Estrada

Nghi Van Nguyen is a twenty-five-year-old Vietnamese man. He works full time at Pizza Hut and lives with his girlfriend and her four-year-old son in San Diego. Without a high school diploma, Nghi is confined to a minimum-wage job with no benefits. He works six days a week and is trying to get his life back on track. Nghi was recently released from prison after serving three years of a six-year sentence for attempted burglary. With a prison record and an eleventh-grade education Nghi faces major obstacles. His life until now has been one of hardship and bad choices. After fleeing Vietnam in a boat crammed with refugees, Nghi's family was resettled in San Diego upon arrival in the United States. During those early years, times were tough for the family, which depended on public assistance through state-sponsored refugee programs. After a few years, Nghi's father landed a job at a large industrial company, making parts for airplanes; he also found companionship and remarried. Although doing better materially, the family still did not act as a cohesive unit, and parent-child bonds frayed. Nghi blames his early troubles on his dad's bad temper and his stepmom's chronic nagging.

Nghi found solace in a peer group of Vietnamese youths who were just as troubled. Together they got caught up in drugs, stealing, robberies, and shootings. He left home at sixteen to escape home life and gain freedom from parental authority. This move, however, signaled a turn for the worse. Less than a year later, Nghi was expelled from school. Out of school and on the streets, Nghi steadily increased his involvement in delinquent activity. At nineteen, he picked up his first criminal charge for petty theft, for which he paid $500 and was put on probation. Two months later he was pulled over by police for possession of a shotgun. After making up a story, he was let go by the police without being charged. But he was not so lucky on his third encounter with the police. Four years after leaving home, at the age of twenty, he was charged with commercial burglary. He confessed to the crime and was given the maximum sentence, of which he served half.

Like Nghi, many of today's children of immigrants—both the first (foreign-born) and second (U.S.-born) generations—confront a complex set of circumstances that shape their trajectories of incorporation into the American society and economy. Born or raised in the United States, they inherit their immigrant parents' customs and circumstances but come of age with a distinctively American outlook and frame of reference and face the often-daunting task of fitting into the American mainstream while meeting their parents' expectations, learning the new language, doing well in school, and finding decent jobs. Along the way, they face many obstacles. Their parents' legal status, human and social capital, cultural constraints, and economic circumstances condition their transitions to adulthood. Further, community violence, intergroup conflict, inadequate public educational systems, and an unyielding job market loom as structural barriers to social mobility. For a smaller but significant segment of this population there is a strong pull from the streets, where violence and gangs make up a large part of the realities of central cities. By the time these children of immigrants reach adulthood, the impediments and opportunities they faced as adolescents solidify. For those with troubled pasts, like Nghi, the transition to adulthood can be an especially rough process. Those without adequate education and job skills and without family safety nets are hard put to find steady work and a stable source of income. Moreover, for some, a pattern of delinquency during adolescence signals deeper future involvements in the adult criminal justice system.

Mass Immigration and Mass Imprisonment in the United States

Nghi's story, to be sure, needs to be located and understood in a larger societal and historical context. He is but one of millions of newcomers —professionals, entrepreneurs, laborers, refugees—who have made the United States once more a nation of immigrants. A new era of mass migration, accelerating since the 1970s and coming chiefly from Asia, Latin America, and the Caribbean, has transformed the ethnic and racial composition of the U.S. population and the communities where immigrants settle. The magnitude of this transformation is extraordinary. By 2000, over sixty million persons were of foreign birth or parentage—about 22 percent of all Americans, including 75 percent of all "Hispanics" and 90 percent of all "Asians."[1] They are heavily concentrated in metropolitan areas, are predominantly nonwhite, speak languages other than English, reflect a wide range of class, religious, and cultural backgrounds, and arrive with a mix of legal statuses.[2] Their process of assimilation presents a different set of complications than it did for the Europeans who came in the last era of mass migration a century ago. Their incorporation has coincided with a period of economic restructuring and rising inequality, during which the returns to education have sharply increased. As the post–World War II era of sustained economic growth, low unemployment, and rising real wages ended for most workers by the early 1970s, men with only a high school degree or less were hardest hit.[3] In this changing context, social timetables that were widely observed a half-century ago by young people for accomplishing adult transitions have become less predictable and more prolonged, diverse, and disordered.[4]

The new era of mass immigration has also coincided with an era of mass imprisonment in the United States, which has further transformed paths to adulthood among young men with low levels of education.[5] The number of adults incarcerated in federal or state prisons or local jails in the United States skyrocketed during this period, quadrupling from just over 500,000 in 1980 to 2.1 million in 2003.[6] (Indeed, the U.S. incarceration rate is the highest of any country in the world.) Two-thirds of those incarcerated are in federal or state prisons and one-third in local jails; the vast majority are young men between eighteen and thirty-nine. Those figures do not include the much larger number of those on probation (convicted offenders not incarcerated) or parole (under community supervision after a period of incarceration); when they are added to the incarceration totals, over 6.9 million adults were under correctional supervision in the United States in 2003, or 3.2 percent of all adults in the country.[7] Although the official statistics are not kept by nativity or generation, they show that imprisonment rates vary widely by gender (93 percent of inmates in federal and state prisons are men); by racial/pan-ethnic groups (there were 4,834 black male prisoners per 100,000 black males in the United States, compared to 1,778 Hispanic males per 100,000 and 681 white males per 100,000, although since 1985 Hispanics have been the group being imprisoned at the most rapidly increasing rate); and by level of education (those incarcerated are overwhelmingly high school dropouts).

This is most salient among racial minorities, for whom becoming a prisoner has become a modal life event in early adulthood: astoundingly, as Pettit and Western[8] have noted, a black male high school dropout born in the late 1960s had a nearly 60 percent chance of serving time in prison by the end of the 1990s, and recent birth cohorts of black men are more likely to have prison records than military records or bachelor's degrees. In a cycle of cumulative disadvantage, young men with low levels of education are significantly more likely to become a prisoner than same-age peers with higher levels of education. Having a prison record, in turn, is linked not only to unemployment, lower wages, marital and family instability, and severe restrictions on social and voting rights (including lifetime disenfranchisement in many states) but also to a stigmatized identity and pathways to criminal recidivism.[9]

In the wake of both phenomena—the rise of immigration and the rise of incarceration, which have occurred rapidly and in tandem—the research literatures on both immigration and incarceration have bourgeoned, but independently of each other. Surprisingly, with few exceptions,[10] scant scholarly effort has been made to connect the respective literatures. Immigration scholars, focused on the incorporation of the latest waves of newcomers, have all but ignored the areas of crime and imprisonment—although those would seem indispensable to tests of theories of segmented assimilation. And as Bursik notes in chapter 2 of this volume, criminologists have not paid much attention to the surge in immigration in recent decades. Contemporary criminology has focused largely on the stratifications of race (still largely framed in black and white terms), place, class, age, and gender, leaving out ethnicity, nativity, and generation (in part because no official criminal justice statistics are collected by national origin, immigration, or generational status). This void is similar to that seen in studies of race and pan-ethnicity, where the complexities of meaning and measurement introduced by millions of newcomers from scores of different national and often mixed ethnic origins have, until recently, also escaped scholarly scrutiny. But the sheer size, growth, diversity, and ramifications of contemporary immigration, and of the large and evolving second generation that it has spawned, now affect and will continue to affect virtually every facet of American life. The fields of criminology and immigration studies cannot continue to ignore each other.

Indeed, by default, in the absence of rigorous empirical research, myths and stereotypes about immigrants and crime often provide the underpinnings for public policies and practices and shape public opinion and political behavior.[11] Periods of increased immigration have historically been accompanied by nativist alarms, particularly during economic downturns and when the immigrants have differed substantially from the natives on such cultural markers as religion, language, phenotype, and region of origin.[12] The present period is no exception. In 2000, the General Social Survey interviewed a nationally representative sample of adults with a newly developed module to measure attitudes and perceptions toward immigration in a "multi-ethnic United States." Asked whether "more immigrants cause higher crime rates," 25 percent said this was "very likely" and another 48 percent that this was "somewhat likely"—that is, about three-fourths (73 percent) believed that immigration was causally related to more crime.[13] That was a much higher proportion than the 60 percent who believed that "more immigrants were [somewhat or very] likely to cause Americans to lose jobs" or the 56 percent who thought that "more immigrants were [somewhat or very] likely to make it harder to keep the country united."

In this chapter we aim to examine empirically the role of ethnicity, nativity, and generation in relation to crime and imprisonment. Our analysis will be elaborated at two levels. First, at the national level, we will focus on the incarceration rates of young men aged eighteen to thirty-nine, comparing differences between the foreign born and the U.S. born by national origin and by education and, among the foreign born, by length of residence in the United States. Second, at the local level, we will be relying on in-depth data collected by the Children of Immigrants Longitudinal Study (CILS) in San Diego. The decade-long study followed a large sample of first- and second-generation children of immigrants from Mexico, the Philippines, Vietnam, Laos, Cambodia, and other countries from Asia and Latin America. Unlike cross-sectional studies, which cannot establish cause-and-effect temporal sequences, the CILS data set permits the identification of factors measured in early adolescence that predict arrest and incarceration outcomes in early adulthood. As Laub and Sampson point out, whereas most studies on crime and violence use cross-sectional data, understanding patterns of criminal offense over the life course requires panel data on childhood, adolescence, and adulthood experiences.[14]

The First and Second Generations: Who Are They?

We begin, however, by sketching a broad-brush portrait of the size and ethnic diversity of the first and second generations of the population of the United States—i.e., the foreign born and the U.S. born with at least one foreign-born parent; those are the groups that will concern us principally in this chapter. As here defined, the first generation of the U.S. population numbered 34.5 million in the year 2000 (including 1.4 million island-born Puerto Ricans residing on the mainland); of them, 40 percent (almost 14 million) arrived as children under eighteen. The second generation added 29.2 million more (including 1.5 million mainland-born Puerto Ricans with island-born parents), producing a total estimate of 63.7 million persons of foreign birth or parentage in the United States in 2000.[15]

The Mexican-origin population clearly dwarfs all others in both the first and second generations. The first generation of Mexican immigrants totaled 9.3 million persons—almost 8 million more than the next sizable immigrant groups (the Filipinos, Chinese, Indians, and Vietnamese, with more than 1 million each, followed by Cubans, Koreans, Salvadorans and Dominicans, with less than 1 million each). Indeed, the Mexican total was larger than that for all other immigrants from Latin America and the Caribbean combined, and for all Asia combined. With a median age of thirty-one years, the Mexicans were one of the youngest immigrant populations as well, many of them arriving in the United States as children under eighteen. The Mexican American second generation, with a median age of only twelve years, added another 8 million persons—larger by far than any other second-generation groups. Both through sustained immigration and natural increase, the Mexican-origin first and second generations of the United States are growing rapidly; at 17.3 million they already account for 27 percent of the country's total immigrant-stock population. Except for the remnants of the "old second generation" of Europeans and Canadians, U.S.-born children of immigrants are still very young—in fact, they mostly consist *of* children, with median ages ranging from nine to thirteen years for almost all the Latin American and Asian-origin groups —a telling marker of the recency of the immigration of their parents.

What do we know in these respects about young adult children of immigrants who have been coming of age in this transformed national context and of their patterns of mobility and prospects for incarceration? At first glance, there would appear to be cause for concern. For example, despite the sizable presence of highly educated professionals among contemporary immigrant flows, who can be expected to transfer to their children their ambitions and resources, data from the 2000 census show that the foreign-born population as a whole is more likely than the U.S.-born population to be living in poverty (20 to 15 percent) and to be concentrated in central cities of metropolitan areas (42 to 24 percent); foreign-born adults are much more likely to have attained less than a high school education (37 to 17 percent) and to be working in the bottom-rung sectors of the labor force (45 to 30 percent). Those figures are much higher for the largest immigrant group: nearly 70 percent of Mexican immigrants 25 and older lack high school degrees and labored in low-wage jobs.[16]

Foreign-Born versus Native-Born Men: Who Are More Likely to Be Incarcerated?

Inasmuch as conventional theories of crime and incarceration predict higher rates for young adult males from ethnic minority groups with lower educational attainment—characteristics that describe a much greater proportion of the foreign-born population than of the native born—it follows that immigrants would be expected to have higher incarceration rates than natives. And immigrant Mexican men—who compose fully a third of all immigrant men between eighteen and thirty-nine—would be expected to have the highest rates. That hypothesis is examined empirically in tables 4.1 and 4.2, but the results turn those expectations on their head. Data from the 5 percent Public Use Microdata Sample (PUMS) of the 2000 census are used to measure the institutionalization rates of immigrants and natives, focusing on males eighteen to thirty-nine, among whom the vast majority of the institutionalized are in correctional facilities.[17]

As table 4.1 shows, 3 percent of the 45.2 million males aged eighteen to thirty-nine were in federal or state prisons or local jails at the time of the 2000 census (a total of over 1.3 million, coinciding with official prison statistics). However, *the incarceration rate of the U.S. born (3.51 percent) was four times that of the foreign born (0.86 percent)*. The latter was half the 1.71 percent rate for non-Hispanic white natives and thirteen times less than

TABLE 4.1
Percent of Males 18 to 39 Years Old Incarcerated in the United States, 2000,
by Nativity and Level of Education, in Rank Order by Ethnicity

| | Males, Ages 18–39 | | % Incarcerated, by Nativity and by Education | | | |
| | | | Nativity | | High School Graduate? | |
Ethnicity (Self-Reported)	Total in U.S. (N)	% Incarcerated	Foreign Born	U.S. Born	No	Yes
Total	45,200,417	3.04	0.86	3.51	6.91	2.00
Latin American Ethnicities						
Salvadoran, Guatemalan	433,828	0.68	0.52	3.01	0.71	0.62
Colombian, Ecuadorian, Peruvian	283,599	1.07	0.80	2.37	2.12	0.74
Mexican	5,017,431	2.71	0.70	5.90	2.84	2.55
Dominican	182,303	2.76	2.51	3.71	4.62	1.39
Cuban	213,302	3.01	2.22	4.20	5.22	2.29
Puerto Rican[a]	642,106	5.06	4.55	5.37	10.48	2.41
Asian Ethnicities						
Indian	393,621	0.22	0.11	0.99	1.20	0.14
Chinese, Taiwanese	439,086	0.28	0.18	0.65	1.35	0.14
Korean	184,238	0.38	0.26	0.93	0.93	0.34
Filipino	297,011	0.64	0.38	1.22	2.71	0.41
Vietnamese	229,735	0.89	0.46	5.60	1.88	0.55
Laotian, Cambodian	89,864	1.65	0.92	7.26	2.80	1.04
Other						
White, non-Hispanic	29,014,261	1.66	0.57	1.71	4.64	1.20
Black, non-Hispanic	5,453,546	10.87	2.47	11.61	21.33	7.09
Two or more race groups, other	1,272,742	3.09	0.72	3.85	6.24	2.24

SOURCE: 2000 U.S. Census, 5% PUMS. Data are estimates for adult males, ages 18 to 39, in correctional institutions at the time of the census.

[a] Island-born Puerto Ricans, who are U.S. citizens by birth and not immigrants, are classified as "foreign born" for purposes of this table; mainland-born Puerto Ricans are here classified under "U.S. born."

the 11.6 percent incarceration rate for native black men. The advantage for immigrants vis-à-vis natives applies to every ethnic group without exception. Almost all of the Asian immigrant groups have lower incarceration rates than the Latin American groups (the exception involves foreign-born Laotians and Cambodians, whose rate of 0.92 percent is still well below that for non-Hispanic white natives). Tellingly, among the foreign born the highest incarceration rate by far (4.5 percent) was observed among island-born Puerto Ricans—who are not immigrants as such, since they are U.S. citizens by birth and can travel to the mainland as natives.

Of particular interest is the finding that the lowest incarceration rates among Latin American immigrants are seen for the least educated groups: the Salvadorans and Guatemalans (0.52 percent) and the Mexicans (0.70 percent). However, those rates increase significantly for their U.S.-born co-ethnics. That is most notable for the Mexicans, whose incarceration rate increases to 5.9 percent among the U.S. born; for the Vietnamese, whose incarceration rate increases from 0.46 among the foreign born to 5.6 percent among the U.S. born; and for the Laotians and Cambodians, whose rate moves up to 7.26 percent, the highest of any group except for native blacks. (Almost all of the U.S. born among those of Latin American and Asian origin can be assumed to consist of second-generation persons —with the exceptions of the Mexicans and Puerto Ricans, who may include a sizable but unknown number of third-generation persons.) Thus, *while incarceration rates are found to be extraordinarily low among the immigrants, they are also seen to rise rapidly by the second generation:* except for the Chinese, Taiwanese, Koreans, Indians, and Filipinos, the rates of all U.S.-born Latin American and Asian groups exceed that of the referent group of non-Hispanic white natives.

For all ethnic groups, as expected, the risk of imprisonment is highest for men who are high school dropouts (6.91 percent) compared to those who are high school graduates (2.0 percent). However, as table 4.2 elaborates, *the differentials in the risk of incarceration by education are observed principally among native-born men, not among immigrants.* Among the U.S. born, 9.76 percent of all male dropouts aged eighteen to thirty-nine were in jail or prison in 2000, compared to 2.23 percent of those who had graduated from high school. But among the foreign born the incarceration gap by education was much narrower: only 1.31 percent of immigrant men who were high school dropouts were incarcerated, compared to 0.57 percent of those with at least a high school diploma. The advantage for immigrants held when broken down by education for every ethnic group. Indeed, *nativity emerges in these data as a stronger predictor of incarceration than education:* as noted, native-born high school graduates have a higher rate of incarceration than foreign-born non–high school graduates (2.2 percent vs. 1.3 percent).

Among U.S.-born men who had not finished high school, the highest incarceration rate by far was seen among non-Hispanic blacks, 22.25 percent of whom were imprisoned at the time of the census; that rate was triple the 7.08 percent among foreign-born black dropouts. Other high rates among U.S.-born high school dropouts were observed among the Vietnamese (over 16 percent), followed by Cubans and Puerto Ricans (over 11 percent), Mexicans (10 percent), and Laotians and Cambodians (over 9 percent). Almost of all these can be assumed to consist of second-generation persons—with the exceptions of the Mexicans and Puerto Ri-

TABLE 4.2

*Percent of U.S-Born and Foreign-Born Males 18 to 39 Years Old Incarcerated in the
United States, 2000, by Completion of a High School Education,
in Rank Order by Ethnicity*

| | Males, Ages 18–39 | | % Incarcerated, by Education and by Nativity | | | |
| | | | If Foreign Born High School Graduate? | | If U.S. Born High School Graduate? | |
Ethnicity (Self-Reported)	Total in U.S. (*N*)	% Incarcerated	No	Yes	No	Yes
Total	45,200,417	3.04	1.31	0.57	9.76	2.23
Latin American Ethnicities						
Salvadoran, Guatemalan	433,828	0.68	0.58	0.43	4.70	2.16
Colombian, Ecuadorian, Peruvian	283,599	1.07	1.54	0.54	7.01	1.58
Mexican	5,017,431	2.71	0.70	0.70	10.12	3.95
Dominican	182,303	2.76	3.99	1.24	8.67	1.82
Cuban	213,302	3.01	3.18	1.78	11.32	2.90
Puerto Rican[a]	642,106	5.06	9.01	1.96	11.54	2.66
Asian Ethnicities						
Indian	393,621	0.22	0.29	0.09	6.69	0.48
Chinese, Taiwanese	439,086	0.28	0.91	0.07	4.71	0.36
Korean	184,238	0.38	0.58	0.24	2.05	0.82
Filipino	297,011	0.64	1.73	0.23	4.73	0.81
Vietnamese	229,735	0.89	0.85	0.32	16.18	2.85
Laotian, Cambodian	89,864	1.65	1.72	0.52	9.11	5.80
Other						
White, non-Hispanic	29,014,261	1.66	1.63	0.43	4.76	1.23
Black, non-Hispanic	5,453,546	10.87	7.08	1.32	22.25	7.64
Two or more race groups, other	1,272,742	3.09	2.08	0.39	7.44	2.85

SOURCE: 2000 U.S. Census, 5% PUMS. Data are estimates for adult males, ages 18 to 39, in correctional institutions at the time of the census.

[a] Island-born Puerto Ricans are U.S. citizens by birth and not immigrants but are classified as "foreign born" for purposes of this table; mainland-born Puerto Ricans are classified under "U.S. born."

cans, who may include a sizable but unknown number of third-generation persons.

The finding that incarceration rates are much lower among immigrant men than the national norm, despite their lower levels of education and minority status, but increase significantly among their co-ethnics by the second generation, suggests that the process of "Americanization" leads to downward mobility and greater risks of involvement with the criminal justice system among a significant segment of this population. To explore this question further, we examined what happens to immigrant men over time in the United States. The results are presented in table 4.3. For every group without exception, *the longer immigrants have resided in the United States, the higher their incarceration rates are.* Here again,

TABLE 4.3
*Percent of Foreign-Born Males 18 to 39 Years Old Incarcerated in the United States, 2000,
by Length of U.S. Residence, in Rank Order by Ethnicity*

Ethnicity (Self-Reported)	Total Foreign-Born Males 18–39		Year in the United States		
	N	% Incarcerated	0–5	6–15	16+
Total	8,079,819	0.86	0.50	0.77	1.39
Latin American Ethnicities					
Salvadoran, Guatemalan	407,147	0.52	0.37	0.46	0.88
Mexican	3,082,660	0.70	0.46	0.66	1.12
Colombian, Peruvian, Ecuadorian	234,834	0.80	0.55	1.30	1.98
Cuban	127,399	2.22	1.28	1.99	3.07
Dominican	144,387	2.51	1.48	2.49	3.40
Puerto Rican[a]	240,713	4.55	2.57	4.01	6.06
Asian Ethnicities					
Indian	343,834	0.11	0.05	0.11	0.27
Chinese	347,029	0.18	0.07	0.22	0.27
Korean	152,785	0.26	0.10	0.15	0.50
Filipino	205,167	0.38	0.31	0.35	0.45
Vietnamese	210,331	0.46	0.46	0.41	0.51
Laotian, Cambodian	79,489	0.92	—[b]	0.33	1.19
Other					
White, non-Hispanic	1,266,100	0.57	0.36	0.41	0.88
Black, non-Hispanic	441,263	2.47	1.64	2.10	3.80

SOURCE: 2000 U.S. Census, 5% PUMS. Data are estimates for all foreign-born males, ages 18 to 39, in correctional institutions at the time of the census, regardless of age at arrival in the United States.

[a] Island-born Puerto Ricans are classified as "foreign born" for purposes of this table.

[b] There are too few cases for an accurate estimate.

the rates of incarceration for island-born Puerto Ricans are significantly higher—regardless of how long they have lived in the U.S. mainland—than the rates for all the immigrant groups listed in table 4.3, underscoring the unique status of the former. In contrast, foreign-born Mexican men aged eighteen to thirty-nine, by far the largest group (at over three million), have a lower incarceration rate than many other ethnic and racial groups—even after they have lived in the United States for over fifteen years. The Mexican incarceration story in particular can be very misleading when the data conflate the foreign born and the native born (as official statistics on "Latinos" or "Hispanics" routinely do). Rather than a story of upward mobility often mentioned in the straight-line assimilation literature, the data in tables 4.1 through 4.3 suggest instead a story of segmented assimilation to the criminal propensities of the native born.

Although they are not shown in this national profile, we also examined the same census data for California, the state with both the greatest number of immigrants (over a quarter of the national total, including the largest concentrations by far of Mexicans, Salvadorans, Guatemalans, Vietnamese, Filipinos, and many other immigrant groups) and the greatest number of persons in prisons and jail (in fact, California has the second highest inmate population in the world, behind China)—as well as one of the toughest mandatory-sentencing "three strikes" laws in the country.[18] Overall, native-born men aged eighteen to thirty-nine in California have *higher* incarceration rates than in the rest of the United States, while the foreign born have *lower* rates in California than in the United States. The total incarceration rate for the U.S. born is more than 1 percentage point higher in California than in the rest of the United States (4.5 to 3.4). In contrast, the incarceration rate for the foreign born in California was less than half the foreign-born rate in the rest of the country (0.4 to 1.0). We now shift our focus to a consideration of a longitudinal study of children of immigrants carried out in California's second largest city: San Diego.

The CILS Study: Ethnicity, Family,
Socioeconomic Status, and Education

To explore patterns of crime and incarceration among these populations in more depth, we draw on data from the Children of Immigrants Longitudinal Study (CILS), a decade-long panel study whose last phase of data collection ended in 2003. The CILS study has followed the progress of a large sample of youths representing seventy-seven different nationalities in two main areas of immigrant settlement in the United States: southern California (San Diego) and south Florida. The principal nationalities represented in the San Diego sample—which is our focus in this chapter —were Mexicans, Filipinos, Vietnamese, Laotians, Cambodians, Chinese, and smaller groups of other children of immigrants from Asia, Latin America, and the Caribbean. The initial survey, conducted in spring 1992, interviewed students enrolled in the eighth and ninth grades, when most were fourteen or fifteen years old.[19] They were reinterviewed three years later, in 1995, when they were in their final year of senior high school (or had dropped out of school); by then most were seventeen to eighteen years old.[20] Results from those first two waves of surveys have been reported in a series of articles and in two companion books.[21] In the third and last wave of surveys, carried out in 2001–3, the respondents were in their mid-twenties (the mean age was 24.2, ranging from 23 to 27), and although the majority had remained in the city and the region, we located the rest in twenty-seven different states plus the District of Columbia and a few military bases overseas. The survey, which included questions about ever having been arrested or incarcerated, was supplemented with a complete check of federal prison, California State Department of Corrections, and local county jail records against all of the original respondents in the baseline sample.

The San Diego sample was divided evenly by gender. By nativity, 56 percent were foreign born ("1.5" generation) and 44 percent were U.S. born ("second generation"); in 15 percent of the cases the U.S.-born respondent also had one U.S.-born parent ("2.5" generation). The modest family origins of many of these children, the highly educated backgrounds of the parents of others, and their varying patterns of homeownership and poverty are all reflected in the CILS sample. Between two-thirds and four-fifths of the foreign-born children from Mexico, Vietnam, Laos, and Cambodia had fathers and mothers who never completed secondary-level schooling; but 38 percent of Filipino mothers had college degrees, as did a third of Chinese fathers and mothers—well above U.S. norms. The proportion of homeowners ranged from 15 percent among Laotians and Cambodians to over 75 percent of the Chinese and Filipinos. And neighborhood poverty rates were wider still: the proportion of children growing up in inner-city neighborhoods of concentrated poverty (where more than 50 percent of all residents were below the poverty line) ranged from over three-fifths (62 percent) of the Cambodian and Laotian children, about half (48 percent) of the Mexican children, and 28 percent of the Vietnamese children to only 4 percent of the Chinese and 2 percent of the Filipinos.

These differences in socioeconomic status (SES) between the poorest groups (the Mexicans, Cambodians, and Laotians) and the better off (the Chinese, Filipinos, and "other Asians") are partly reflected in their school experiences and attainment from the end of junior high to the end of high school and the level of education they completed by age twenty-four—as summarized in table 4.4 and briefly highlighted below. Those variables— hypothesized as predictors of future involvement with the criminal justice system—include the number of suspensions and of days suspended from school (from 1991 to 1995), the percent who were involved in the drug scene or physically threatened while in high school, the percent classified by the school system as "inactive" annually from 1993 to 1995, national percentiles in math and reading achievement test scores in 1991–92, final high

TABLE 4.4

School Suspensions, Experiences with Drugs and Violent Threats, and Educational Achievement of Children of Immigrants in San Diego Secondary Schools (1991–95), and Education Attained by Age 24 (2001–3), by National Origin and Gender (CILS San Diego Sample)

Characteristics (in % unless noted)	Year	Mexico	Philippines	Vietnam	Cambodia, Laos	China, Taiwan	Other Asia	Other Latin America	Total
Suspended from school[a]	1991–95								
Female		17.6	8.6	5.2	6.9	0.0	9.8	12.0	10.6
Male		36.3	18.1	33.0	24.6	7.7	22.0	41.0	27.4
Total		27.1	13.4	19.6	15.3	3.9	15.9	24.7	19.0
If Yes, how many times?		1.9	1.7	2.0	1.3	2.0	2.1	1.6	1.8
If Yes, total days suspended		4.5	3.8	5.1	3.9	5.0	4.3	4.5	4.3
Was offered drugs for sale in high school more than twice	1995								
Female		6.6	4.4	2.0	1.3	0.0	5.4	7.0	4.3
Male		21.9	19.1	11.8	6.6	7.7	11.4	27.6	16.9
Total		14.3	11.8	7.1	3.8	4.0	8.3	15.3	10.6
Was physically threatened in high school more than twice	1995								
Female		1.0	1.9	2.7	0.7	0.0	0.0	4.7	1.6
Male		0.2	5.7	8.1	5.1	3.8	5.7	6.9	6.7
Total		4.6	3.8	5.5	2.8	2.0	2.8	5.6	4.1
National percentile in achievement tests in 8th or 9th grade[b]	1991								
Math		30.7	58.9	60.1	37.5	81.0	62.7	46.4	48.2
Reading		25.7	51.1	37.2	18.0	63.7	61.2	50.4	38.3
Classified as Inactive[c]	1993–95								
By fall 1993		12.7	7.9	7.7	6.3	2.0	15.9	18.0	9.6
By fall 1994		21.6	14.5	14.1	12.6	3.9	18.3	24.7	16.6
By fall 1995		26.7	17.6	18.2	17.6	3.9	23.2	31.5	20.8
GPA by end of high school[d]	1995								
Female		2.40	3.10	3.31	2.93	3.70	3.16	2.98	2.91
Male		2.09	2.63	2.76	2.49	3.70	3.15	2.44	2.50
Total		2.24	2.86	3.02	2.72	3.70	3.16	2.74	2.71
Education completed (by age 24)	2001–3								
High school graduate or less:									
Female		35.6	11.9	4.2	43.1	6.3	12.5	22.6	21.9
Male		40.9	19.4	21.3	49.4	5.3	5.0	31.3	28.4
Total		38.0	15.6	12.6	45.9	5.7	9.1	25.5	24.9
College graduate or more:									
Female		6.4	34.5	54.2	17.6	43.8	45.8	32.3	27.4
Male		10.5	18.0	28.7	8.4	47.4	45.0	31.3	18.2
Total		8.3	26.6	41.6	13.5	45.7	45.5	31.9	23.1

SOURCE: Children of Immigrants Longitudinal Study (CILS), Waves I (1992), II (1995), and III (2001–3); Rumbaut (2000).

[a] School suspensions for any reason between fall 1991 and spring 1995, collected from the school system for the full baseline sample. Suspending a student from school for one day is, except for expulsion, the most severe official reaction to student disciplinary infractions. Nearly 80 percent of the suspensions in the district are meted out for physical injury (fights, threats, attempts) and disruption/defiance; others include drugs, property damage, and weapons infractions.

[b] Standardized Stanford Achievement Test scores collected by the San Diego school system in fall 1991, when the students were in the eighth or ninth grades, for the full baseline sample. The figures given are national percentiles.

[c] "Inactive" status is a school district classification for students who have transferred out of the district for whatever reason; most involve moves to other school districts, but the status also includes students leaving school and official dropouts. "Active" students are those currently enrolled.

[d] Academic grade point averages (GPAs) collected annually from the school system for the full sample; GPA shown is by the end of high school in 1995 (or latest).

school GPA, and highest education completed by the time of the last survey in 2001–3. In a subsequent section we will examine the relationship of these antecedent variables to their arrests and incarceration outcomes by 2001–3.

Suspending a student from school for one or more days is, except for expulsion, the most severe official reaction to student disciplinary infractions. Nearly 80 percent of the suspensions in the San Diego Unified School District were meted out for physical injury (fights, threats, attempts) and disruption/defiance; others included drugs, property damage, and weapons infractions. As table 4.4 shows, nearly a fifth (19 percent) of the students were suspended at least once throughout their junior and senior high school years—*below* the suspension rate for the school district as a whole—including 27 percent of the males compared to only 11 percent of the females. There were also very significant differences between ethnic groups, ranging from the Chinese (with the lowest proportion suspended, 3.9 percent) to the Mexican youth (27 percent of whom had been suspended at least once). Similarly, males were much more likely than females to have been involved with drugs and to have been physically threatened during the high school years, with the Mexicans and other Latin Americans being much more likely to report these experiences, and the Chinese the least—although among the Asian groups the Filipinos had a much higher proportion of involvement with drugs, while Vietnamese males were most likely to have been involved in situations involving threats of violence and fights.

"Inactive" status (shown yearly from fall 1993 to 1995) is a school classification for students who have transferred out of the district for whatever reason prior to graduation and are no longer currently enrolled; many instances of this classification involve moves to other school districts, but the category includes transiency and students leaving school due to a variety of problems as well as official dropouts. Frequent moves across school districts have been associated with academic underachievement. Again stark differences were noticeable between the Chinese (by far the most stable, with only 3.9 percent classified as inactive by 1995 and *none* who were officially recorded as having dropped out of school by the end of high school) and the Mexicans and other Latin Americans (with the highest inactivity and dropout rates).

Already by eighth grade there were large ethnic differences observed in standardized math and reading achievement test scores. The Chinese collectively scored at the 81st percentile nationally on math, compared to the

60th percentile for the Vietnamese and Filipinos and the 31st percentile for the Mexican-origin students. The Cambodians and Laotians (who were also the most recent arrivals) scored lowest on reading achievement (at the 18th percentile collectively). On opposite sides of the spectrum in academic GPAs were the Chinese (averaging 3.70) and the Mexican-origin students (2.24). Except for the Chinese and "other Asians" (for whom GPA rates were virtually identical for males and females), there were significant differences in high school GPA by gender, with females outperforming males by wide margins (2.91 to 2.50 overall)—gender differentials of nearly half a grade point were observed for most ethnic groups. These differences in turn were generally reproduced in the level of education they had completed six to seven years later, by their mid-twenties, as shown in the bottom panel of table 4.4. We turn now to an analysis of the relationship of these characteristics and experiences with arrest and incarceration outcomes.

Patterns and Predictors of Arrests and Incarceration

Table 4.5 presents a set of correlates of arrests and incarceration in early adulthood among children of immigrants, broken down by nationality, sex, generation, family structure, and various educational outcomes. Being arrested and incarcerated for criminal behaviors is an overwhelmingly male experience. Overall, 17 percent of the males in the CILS sample but less than 3 percent of the women had ever been arrested by the police, and 12 percent of the men but less than 2 percent of the women had been imprisoned (which in most cases involved being convicted and sentenced for the commission of a crime, although our survey instrument did not ask respondents to specify the nature of the violation or the circumstances).

Note that the Mexicans were about *twice* as likely to report having been *arrested and incarcerated* as all of the other groups (as well as reporting that family members had been arrested and incarcerated). Given the huge size of the Mexican-origin second generation compared to all other groups in the United States, this is a finding fraught with implications for the future—not only for the downward mobility prospects of the individuals who are caught in a cycle of arrest and imprisonment, all the more given high rates of recidivism after release, but also for the effects on their communities when the prisoners return home.[22] Specifically, 29 percent of

TABLE 4.5
Correlates (Measured in 1991–95) of Arrests and Incarceration (Measured in 2001–3) in Early
Adulthood among Children of Immigrants, by Gender (CILS San Diego Longitudinal Sample)

Correlates	Year	Males		Female	
		% Arrested	% Incarcerated	% Arrested	% Incarcerated
Total		16.6	11.9	3.2	1.6
National origin		***	NS	***	NS
Mexican		29.3	20.2	5.5	2.7
Filipino		10.7	6.8	3.0	1.6
Vietnamese		16.7	14.6	2.1	1.0
Cambodian, Laotian		9.5	9.5	1.0	0.0
Chinese		5.3	0.0	0.0	0.0
Asian, other		19.0	9.5	4.2	4.2
Latin, other		18.8	18.8	0.0	0.0
Immigrant generation[a]		*	*	NS	NS
"1.5"		10.6	8.2	1.6	1.1
"1.75"		15.6	11.8	2.5	1.5
"2.0"		19.6	14.0	3.9	2.1
"2.5" (one U.S-born parent)		21.4	14.3	4.8	3.2
Family structure	1992	NS	*	***	**
Intact family		15.2	10.3	2.2	1.2
Step family		18.6	15.3	11.1	6.3
Single-parent family		22.3	17.9	3.8	1.5
Academic GPA (8th–9th grade)	1991–92	***	***	**	*
Under 2.0		30.5	24.7	8.6	6.2
2.0–2.5		20.0	14.1	3.6	1.3
2.5–3.0		11.7	7.6	3.2	1.6
3.0–3.5		11.3	6.5	2.8	1.2
Above 3.5		6.9	5.4	1.4	0.7
School suspensions (8th–12th grade)	1991–95	***	***	***	***
None		11.1	8.0	2.3	1.1
One		28.1	18.8	6.1	2.0
Two		36.4	24.2	18.2	9.1
Three or more		50.0	41.7	42.9	42.9
Inactive status	1993–95	***	***	*	*
No		13.8	8.7	2.6	1.1
Yes		37.2	34.9	7.4	5.3
Physically threatened in high school	1993–95	***	***	**	***
Never, or once or twice		13.6	8.9	2.9	1.4
More than twice		57.1	53.1	18.2	18.2
Was offered drugs to buy in high school	1993–95	***	***	***	***
Never, or once or twice		12.9	8.4	2.1	0.9
More than twice		34.4	28.7	24.3	16.2
Education completed	2001–3	***	***	***	***
Some high school		29.5	18.2	7.7	7.7
High school graduate		20.8	17.5	4.1	3.4
Some college		13.5	9.3	3.8	1.5
College graduate		7.1	1.6	0.9	0.0

SOURCE: Children of Immigrants Longitudinal Study (CILS), Waves I (1992), II (1995), and III (2001–3). Data on arrests and incarceration were collected in 2001–3; data on high school experiences with drugs and physical threats were collected in 1995; data on GPA, inactive status, and school suspensions were obtained from the San Diego City Schools, 1991–92 and 1993–95.

[a] Generational cohorts: "1.5" = foreign born, 6–12 years old at U.S. arrival; "1.75" = foreign born, age 0–5 at U.S. arrival; "2.0" = U.S. born, both parents born in foreign country; "2.5" = U.S. born, on parent foreign born, one parent U.S. born.

*** $p < .001$; ** $p < .01$; * $p < .05$; NS = not significant.

Mexican-origin men in our sample reported having been arrested, and 20 percent reported having been incarcerated, since 1995—that is, between the ages of eighteen and twenty-four—a much higher proportion than the Vietnamese men, who came next at 17 percent arrested and 15 percent incarcerated, as well as the smaller samples of other Asians and other Latin Americans, with rates of arrest and incarceration approximating the latter. Even the reported degree of arrest and incarceration among the Laotians and Cambodians (just under 10 percent) was substantial. Moreover, *among males who were arrested and incarcerated, the U.S. born were significantly more likely to have become involved with the criminal justice system than the foreign born, reflecting the national-level data presented earlier on adult men between the ages of eighteen and thirty-nine.*

As table 4.5 clearly shows, family structure, academic GPA, school suspensions, inactive status, education attained, and being physically threatened and offered drugs in high school all show strong linear relationships with arrest and incarceration, especially among males. That is, respondents from single-parent families, with low GPAs and a history of multiple school suspensions and inactive status, who were physically threatened or offered illegal drugs more than twice in high school, and who have no high school diploma are much more likely to be arrested and incarcerated. In some instances the magnitude of these associations is dramatic—as is evident from the data on suspensions, being physical threatened, and involvement with the drug subculture.[23] In turn, arrests and incarceration (especially for the men) emerge as turning points likely to derail post–high school trajectories for a substantial segment of these young adults.

To determine the independent effects of these predictor variables on the odds of being incarcerated, we ran a series of logistic regression models, entering sets of predictors into the equation in sequence. All the predictor variables were measured either in 1991–92 or between 1991 and 1995 —preceding the outcome variables by as long as ten years and thus clearly establishing the temporal order of effects. The set of predictors included age and gender, national origin, immigrant generation, parental SES, family structure in adolescence (intact two-parent family or not), and all of the school-related variables listed in table 4.5. The main findings from the multivariate analysis can be briefly summarized as follows. (The results of these models are available upon request.)

With all the predictor variables controlled, only a handful retained significant independent effects. The strongest, as expected, is gender—incarceration is an overwhelmingly male phenomenon. That is followed in predictive strength by a set of critical school events and experiences, of which the most significant are (1) having been physically threatened more than twice in high school (much more prevalent in lower-SES inner-city schools with significant gang activity); (2) the number of days suspended from school between eighth and twelfth grades (suspensions emerge here as a strong indicator of likely future problems in early adulthood); (3) "inactive" school status (indicative of additional transience or instability); (4) lower GPAs in school; and (5) involvement with illegal drugs in high school (more prevalent in higher-SES suburban public schools, where the students who reported involvement with buying or selling drugs came from more affluent homes and were more likely to have the money to spend on drugs).

Our measure of immigrant generation retained a weaker but nonetheless significant positive effect on the likelihood of being jailed for a criminal offense: that is, the U.S. born (2.0 and 2.5 generational cohorts) were more likely to get involved in the correctional system than the foreign born (1.5 and 1.75 generational cohorts), further supporting the national and local-level data presented earlier. As different sets of predictors were entered into the logistic regression, family structure (an intact family in the teen years) initially exerted a significant negative effect on the odds of being jailed, until school suspensions, inactive status, and GPA were entered into the equation, whereupon the effect of family structure washed out—suggesting that its buffering effect is mediated through those latter variables (respondents in intact families had significantly higher GPAs and fewer suspensions and were least likely to have transferred out of the district or dropped out of school). Similarly, parental SES and neighborhood poverty retained no significant effect on incarceration in the final model.

More important, only one of our dummy variables for ethnicity (Vietnamese) exhibited a significant association with the dependent variable— even though Mexicans had by far the highest rates of arrest and incarceration. Something about Vietnamese ethnicity in this sample, as illustrated by the story of Nghi at the outset of this chapter, remains significantly associated with the likelihood of being jailed that is not explained by the predictor variables included in our model.[24] More consequential still, given the importance for public policy of the Mexican case, the effect of Mexican ethnicity in our models, which is initially strongly associated with incarceration when the demographic and socioeconomic measures are entered into the logistic regression, washes out when the measures of school status are subsequently entered (especially suspensions, inactivity, lower GPA), suggesting that the latter variables (and not ethnicity as such) "explain" the Mexican association.

These results, based on longitudinal survey data collected over a decade from a representative sample of children of immigrants in southern California, are enlightening up to a point, but while they alert us quantitatively to significant patterns and predictors of criminal justice outcomes, they are nonetheless constrained qualitatively in depicting the complex mechanisms and contexts through which those outcomes are produced. Our in-depth, open-ended qualitative interviews, in combination with the survey data, provide a clearer and fuller sense of the paths and processes of "downward assimilation" involved in the dynamics of arrest and incarceration, as illustrated by the opening vignette of Nghi and by this concluding case history of a Mexican American CILS respondent:

José, twenty-six years old, was born and raised in San Diego County by parents of Mexican descent. Like his parents, José did not finish high school. He left school after tenth grade due to his heavy involvement with drugs and gangs. José's parents did not have high educational expectations for him; they only told him to work hard. At the age of sixteen, when his parents divorced, he moved in with his father while his younger brother moved in with his mother. At nineteen he moved out of his father's house and in with his girlfriend.

Early on José began having negative encounters with the law. When he was fifteen years old he got into a domestic dispute with his girlfriend, for which he was detained but released a few hours later. Later that year he was caught with stolen property and arrested for robbery. He tried to get his life back on track but in 1995 was arrested for possession of drugs. After this, his life took a turn for the worse. His addiction to drugs led to his being arrested three more times for the same offense, in 1996, 1998, and 2000. The mother of his baby left him shortly after his first incarceration. His second arrest forced him to leave his first jobs as a gardener and street cleaner during high school. Finally, his third stint in jail, at the age of seventeen, disrupted his full-time employment at Target. The subsequent arrests made it difficult for him to hold a steady job.

At twenty-six, José is now employed as a newspaper delivery boy. Although he regrets the time spent in jail, he does not blame anyone. He is satisfied with his job but acknowledges that he needs to be making better money. He knows that he could do better and is still hopeful for a positive future. His aspirations, however, are modest. He wants to get his GED by the age of thirty and hopes for a good job in computers and a car. He is still with his longtime girlfriend and wants to have children with her. José currently has an eleven-year-old daughter from a previous relationship with an African American woman. He has not seen his daughter in three years but speaks with her by phone on a weekly basis.

Conclusions and Implications

We noted earlier that, in the absence of rigorous empirical research, myths and stereotypes about immigrants and crime often provide the underpinnings for public policies and practices and shape public opinion and political behavior. Such myths and stereotypes tend to thrive in periods of increased immigration such as the present, which have historically been accompanied by nativist alarms, particularly during economic downturns and when the immigrants have differed substantially from dominant native groups in race, language, religion, and region of origin. We also pointed out that a new era of mass immigration—which by 2000 had produced a rapidly growing population of foreign birth or parentage already then exceeding sixty million persons—has coincided with an era of mass imprisonment in the United States, transforming paths to adulthood among young men with little education. Because many immigrants, especially labor migrants from Mexico and Central America and refugees from Southeast Asia, are young men who arrive with very low levels of education, conventional wisdom—in the form of both nativist stereotype and standard criminological theory—tends to associate them with high rates of crime and incarceration.

But correlation is not causation, and such presumptions and assumptions are misbegotten. Both the national and local-level findings presented in this chapter turn conventional wisdom on its head and present a challenge to criminological theory. For every ethnic group without exception, the census data show an *increase* in rates of incarceration among young men from the foreign-born to the U.S.-born generations, and over time in the United States among the foreign born—exactly the opposite of what is typically assumed. Paradoxically, incarceration rates are lowest among immigrant young men, even among the least educated, but they increase sharply by the second generation, especially among the least educated— evidence of downward assimilation that parallels the patterns observed for native minorities. The proportions involved are not trivial but comprise millions of individuals—nationally in 2000, about 15 percent of all young men twenty-five to thirty-nine had failed to graduate from high school (including 31 percent of the foreign born who came as children under eighteen), and among them about 2 percent of the foreign born and 10 percent of the U.S. born were in prison. Still, nativity emerges in this analysis as a stronger predictor of incarceration than education; when immigration and generational status are taken into account, the association between (lower) education and (higher) crime and incarceration rates is complicated in ways not anticipated by canonical perspectives. It is in the context of the study of immigrant groups and generational cohorts that such paradoxes are revealed,[25] further underscoring the importance of connecting the research literatures on immigration and on crime and imprisonment, which have largely ignored each other—to the impoverishment of both and the enrichment of popular prejudice.

Contemporary criminology has focused largely on the stratifications of race (still largely framed in black and white terms) and place, class, age, and gender, leaving ethnicity, nativity, and generation out of the analysis —in part because official criminal justice statistics are not collected on national origin, immigration, or generational status (as measured by age at arrival and parental nativity). This is compounded by the national bad habit of lumping individuals into a handful of one-size-fits-all racialized categories (black, white, Latino, Asian) that obliterate different migration and generational histories, cultures, frames of reference, and contexts of reception and incorporation—omitting from scholarly scrutiny the complexities introduced by millions of newcomers from scores of different national and ethnic origins. It may not be too much of an exaggeration to suggest that much current research resembles the classic story of the drunk who loses his keys in a dark alley at night but continues to search for them under a streetlight a block away, where there is more light to "see." Similarly, empirical investigations into the correlates and causes of imprisonment may be looking under the "streetlight" of currently available data—but the locus of their search may be mistaken, particularly when they are dealing with immigrant populations.

Given the limitations of both criminal justice statistics and cross-sectional national data, we turned to the longitudinal CILS data set to probe the determinants and dynamics of arrest and incarceration outcomes in a panel of young adult children of immigrants observed across the span of a decade, from ages fourteen to twenty-four on average. The results are clearly patterned, interrelated, and cumulative and suggest that much of the determination of arrest and incarceration outcomes in early adulthood can be traced to specifiable factors, events, and contexts observable and measurable in early to mid-adolescence. In the process, although the findings presented here must be considered preliminary, they underscore the value of comparative longitudinal studies and of mixed-methods research, combining quantitative and qualitative approaches across a significant span of the life course, from early adolescence to early adulthood. They also indicate the importance of bringing criminological research into the study of the incorporation of immigrants and of the segmented assimilation of their children born or raised in the United States. Serious efforts along these lines would add significantly to our store of empirical knowledge and help to develop both better social science and more informed public opinion about two highly consequential and highly charged areas of American national life.

NOTES

An earlier version of this chapter was presented to the National Consortium on Violence Research conference, "Beyond Racial Dichotomies of Violence: Immigrants, Race and Ethnicity," University of California, Los Angeles, November 6–8, 2003. The support provided by research grants from the Russell Sage Foundation and the Andrew W. Mellon, Spencer, and National Science Foundations to the Children of Immigrants Longitudinal Study (CILS), 1991–2005, is gratefully acknowledged.

1. Rumbaut (2004).

2. Alba and Nee (2003); Bean and Stevens (2003); Portes and Rumbaut (1996, 2001); Waldinger and Lee (2001).

3. Danziger (2004).

4. Settersten, Furstenberg, and Rumbaut (2004).

5. Pettit and Western (2004).

6. U.S. Department of Justice (2004).

7. U.S. Department of Justice (2004).

8. Pettit and Western (2004).

9. Sampson and Laub (1993); Western, Kling, and Weiman (2001); Western (2002); Pager (2003); Visher and Travis (2003).

10. Butcher and Piehl (1997); Hagan and Palloni (1999); Martinez (2002); Lee, Martinez, and Rosenfeld (2001); Lee (2003); Martinez, Lee, and Nielsen (2004).

11. Chávez (2001); Hagan and Palloni (1999); Lee (2003).

12. Fry (2001); Warner and Srole (1945).

13. Rumbaut and Alba (2003).

14. Laub and Sampson (2003).

15. For a breakdown by national origin, see Rumbaut (2004).

16. Rumbaut (2004).

17. Butcher and Piehl (1997); Rumbaut (1997).

18. Domanick (2004, 2005).

19. The sample was drawn in the junior high grades, a level at which dropout rates are still relatively rare, to avoid the potential bias of differential dropout rates between ethnic groups at the senior high school level. Students were eligible to enter the sample if they were U.S. born but had at least one foreign-born parent, or if they themselves were foreign born and had come to the United States at an early age (all before age twelve).

20. We obtained from the school systems complete academic histories for them, including data on achievement test scores, GPAs, suspensions, transfers outside the school district ("inactive" status), and official dropout status.

21. Portes and Rumbaut (2001); Rumbaut and Portes (2001).

22. Petersilia (2003).

23. Of the more than 2 million men and women now behind bars in the United States, an estimated 1.6 million offenders (80 percent) either violated drug or alcohol laws, were high at the time they committed their crimes, stole property to buy drugs, or had a history of drug and alcohol abuse and addiction—or some combination of those characteristics. Moreover, criminal recidivism is strongly associated with a history of drug and alcohol abuse. See National Center on Addiction and Substance Abuse (1998).

24. Rumbaut and Ima (1988); Kibria (1993); Zhou and Bankston (1998).

25. Rumbaut (1997); Harris (1999).

REFERENCES

Alba, Richard D., and Victor Nee. 2003. *Remaking the American Mainstream: Assimilation and Contemporary Immigration.* Cambridge, MA: Harvard University Press.

Bean, Frank D., and Gillian Stevens. 2003. *America's Newcomers: Immigrant Incorporation and the Dynamics of Diversity.* New York: Russell Sage Foundation.

Butcher, Kristin F., and Anne Morrison Piehl. 1997. "Recent Immigrants: Unexpected Implications for Crime and Incarceration." NBER Working Paper 6067, National Bureau of Economic Research, Cambridge, MA.

Chávez, Leo R. 2001. *Covering Immigration: Popular Images and the Politics of the Nation.* Berkeley: University of California Press.

Danziger, Sheldon. 2004. "Poverty and Low-Wage Work 40 Years after the Declaration of War on Poverty." Working paper, National Poverty Research Center, University of Michigan, Ann Arbor.

Domanick, Joe. 2004. *Cruel Justice: Three Strikes and the Politics of Crime in America's Golden State.* Berkeley: University of California Press.

———. 2005. "Stop L.A.'s Crime Engine." *Los Angeles Times,* January 23.

Fry, Brian N. 2001. *Responding to Immigration: Perceptions of Promise and Threat.* New York: LFB Scholarly Publishing.

Hagan, John, and Alberto Palloni. 1999. "Sociological Criminology and the Mythology of Hispanic Immigration and Crime." *Social Problems* 46:617–32.

Harris, Kathleen M. 1999. "The Health Status and Risk Behavior of Adolescents in Immigrant Families." In *Children of Immigrants: Health, Adjustment, and Public Assistance,* edited by D. J. Hernández, 286–347. Washington, DC: National Academy of Sciences Press.

Kibria, Nazli. 1993. *Family Tightrope: The Changing Lives of Vietnamese Americans.* Princeton: Princeton University Press.

Laub, John H., and Robert J. Sampson. 2003. *Shared Beginnings, Divergent Lives: Delinquent Boys to Age 70.* Cambridge, MA: Harvard University Press.

Lee, Matthew T. 2003. *Crime on the Border: Immigration and Homicide in Urban Communities.* New York: LFB Scholarly Publishing.

Lee, Matthew T., Ramiro Martinez Jr., and Richard B. Rosenfeld. 2001. "Does Immigration Increase Homicide? Negative Evidence from Three Border Cities." *Sociological Quarterly* 42:559–80.

Martinez, Ramiro, Jr. 2002. *Latino Homicide: Immigration, Violence and Community.* New York: Routledge.

Martinez, Ramiro, Jr., Matthew T. Lee, and Amie L. Nielsen. 2004. "Segmented Assimilation, Local Context and Determinants of Drug Violence in Miami and San Diego: Does Ethnicity and Immigration Matter?" *International Migration Review* 38:131–57.

National Center on Addiction and Substance Abuse. 1998. *Behind Bars: Substance Abuse and America's Prison Population.* New York: Columbia University Press.

Pager, Devah. 2003. "The Mark of a Criminal Record." *American Journal of Sociology* 108:937–75.

Petersilia, Joan. 2003. *When Prisoners Come Home: Parole and Prisoner Reentry.* New York: Oxford University Press.

Pettit, Becky, and Bruce Western. 2004. "Mass Imprisonment and the Life Course." *American Sociological Review* 69:151–69.

Portes, Alejandro, and Rubén G. Rumbaut. 1996. *Immigrant America: A Portrait.* Berkeley: University of California Press.

———. 2001. *Legacies: The Story of the Immigrant Second Generation.* Berkeley: University of California Press.

Rumbaut, Rubén G. 1997. "Assimilation and Its Discontents: Between Rhetoric and Reality." *International Migration Review* 31:923–60.

———. 2004. "Ages, Life Stages, and Generational Cohorts: Decomposing the

Immigrant First and Second Generations in the United States." *International Migration Review* 38:1160–1205.

Rumbaut, Rubén G., and Richard D. Alba. 2003. "A Distorted Nation: Perceptions of Racial/Ethnic Group Sizes and Attitudes towards Immigrants and Other Minorities." Paper presented at the annual meetings of the American Sociological Association, Atlanta.

Rumbaut, Rubén G., and Kenji Ima. 1988. *The Adaptation of Southeast Asian Refugee Youth: A Comparative Study.* Washington, DC: U.S. Office of Refugee Resettlement.

Rumbaut, Rubén G., and Alejandro Portes, eds. 2001. *Ethnicities: Children of Immigrants in America.* Berkeley: University of California Press.

Sampson, Robert J., and John H. Laub. 1993. *Crime in the Making: Pathways and Turning Points through Life.* Cambridge, MA: Harvard University Press.

Settersten, Richard A., Jr., Frank F. Furstenberg Jr., and Rubén G. Rumbaut, eds. 2004. *On the Frontier of Adulthood: Theory, Research, and Public Policy.* Chicago: University of Chicago Press.

U.S. Department of Justice. Bureau of Justice Statistics. 2004. "Adult Correctional Populations in the United States, 1980–2003." Retrieved October 25, 2005, from www.ojp.usdoj.gov/bjs/glance/tables/corr2tab.htm.

Visher, Christy A., and Jeremy Travis. 2003. "Transitions from Prison to Community: Understanding Individual Pathways." *Annual Review of Sociology* 29:89–113.

Waldinger, Roger, and Jennifer Lee. 2001. "New Immigrants in Urban America." In *Strangers at the Gates: New Immigrants in Urban America,* edited by Roger Waldinger, 30–79. Berkeley: University of California Press.

Warner, W. Lloyd, and Leo Srole. 1945. *The Social Systems of American Ethnic Groups.* New Haven: Yale University Press.

Western, Bruce. 2002. "The Impact of Incarceration on Wage Mobility and Inequality." *American Sociological Review* 67:1–21.

Western, Bruce, Jeffrey R. Kling, and David F. Weiman. 2001. "The Labor Market Consequences of Incarceration." *Crime and Delinquency* 47:410–27.

Zhou, Min, and Carl L. Bankston III. 1998. *Growing Up American: How Vietnamese Children Adapt to Life in the United States.* New York: Russell Sage Foundation.

Chapter 5

Immigration and Asian Homicide Patterns in Urban and Suburban San Diego

Matthew T. Lee and Ramiro Martinez Jr.

A well-established body of research has identified what Rubén Rumbaut refers to as an "immigration paradox"—unexpectedly favorable social and health outcomes for immigrant groups despite community conditions that sociologists traditionally associate with "social disorganization."[1] For example, in the last few decades low-income immigrants (largely from Mexico and Asia) have had better outcomes than native-born Americans, often including non-Latino whites, in studies on such diverse outcomes as infant health, risky adolescent behavior, and educational attainment.[2] An emerging research agenda has expanded the notion of an immigration paradox to include crime. Initial studies have found that immigration generally does not increase crime rates in areas in which immigrants settle and that immigrants tend to be less involved in crime than natives.[3] Although these early findings are intriguing, much work remains to be done before we will have definitive answers on the immigration-crime relationship. In this spirit, this chapter is the first to extend the investigation of the immigration paradox to community-level patterns in contemporary Asian homicide. To do this, we compare and contrast Asian homicide in the three largest Asian communities in San Diego, using data from the San Diego Police Department and the U.S. Census Bureau. We concentrate on the late 1980s and early 1990s because this period exhibited the highest rate of immigration in the contemporary era, both nationally and in San Diego. Findings are discussed in the context of refining criminological theories that relate to immigration.

Immigration and Violence

Few studies consider the impact of recent immigration on violence. But although the empirical data are sparse, there are good theoretical reasons to suspect that immigrants may be more likely to engage in violence than similarly situated native groups.[4] The social disorganization perspective is perhaps the most prominent sociological theory to posit a positive relationship between immigration and crime.[5] This theory suggests that levels of crime will increase due to the negative impact on community social control wrought by the increases in poverty and population turnover that are associated with an influx of immigrants. The notion that compositional heterogeneity disrupts a community's regulatory capacity has since been elaborated and widely disseminated by contemporary social disorganization scholars.[6] Warner has concisely summarized current thinking: "Heterogeneity also diminishes community ties, as racial and ethnic differences among people may impose barriers to friendships and broad-based organizational ties, thereby limiting the breadth of neighborhood networks and the consequential potential for informal control."[7] Indeed, as Bursik notes in chapter 2 of this volume, immigrants are in a "doubly weak position," being unable to maintain social bonds to primary group members in their homeland and also prevented from forming strong ties to members of the population of the host country. Crime rates are likely to be much higher under these conditions. San Diego provides us with an opportunity to examine this claim using data on an immigrant population that has largely escaped the attention of criminologists—Asians—thus answering Bursik's call to examine "rich racial and ethnic distinctions" beyond the traditional black/white dichotomy that has characterized much contemporary criminological scholarship.[8]

Although the theoretical propositions of social disorganization theory are compelling, research on the "immigration paradox" for crime has provided support for a counterclaim that immigration stabilizes impoverished communities, increases community social control, and suppresses violent crime.[9] For example, in a comparison of two adjacent communities in the northern part of Miami, Lee and Martinez found that the heavily immigrant Little Haiti neighborhood had much lower rates of black homicide than Liberty City, an African American neighborhood with similar levels of poverty.[10] Similarly, Lee, Martinez, and Rosenfeld present findings based on a multivariate analysis that directly challenge stereotypes of the "criminal immigrant" as well as notion that immigration, as a social process, disorganizes communities and increases crime.[11] This study of Miami, El Paso, and San Diego neighborhoods shows that, controlling for other influences, immigration generally does not increase levels of homicide among Latinos and African Americans. The authors argue that immigrants' strong ties to the labor market and family may offset the potential crime-producing consequences of disadvantage and community instability and thereby suppress levels of crime in immigrant communities.

This research is consistent with numerous other studies, such as one conducted by Portes and Stepick that found that, rather than disorganizing communities, immigrants stabilized and revitalized Miami's economic and cultural institutions.[12] The implication is that community social control has been strengthened by immigration. In fact, sociologists have long argued against the "myth" that residents of impoverished urban areas are poor (or victimized by criminals) because they are "disorganized" in the sense that they lack common values or strong ties to each other.[13] The question addressed by the current study is whether this characterization holds for Asians in San Diego. Given the educational achievement of children, as well as the professional or entrepreneurial backgrounds of parents, of many recent arrivals from Asian countries, it is likely that an exploration of Asian homicide patterns may provide further support for the immigration paradox.[14]

Little contemporary research has been conducted on Asian crime in the United States, and most research on the topic focuses on Asian gangs[15] or delinquency.[16] The research that does exist has revealed important within-group differences over time and across social space, which suggests that such differences must be understood in their local social contexts. Scholarship on Asian crime in the United States dates at least to the 1931 Wickersham Commission, which reported that Chinese immigrants had the highest arrest rate of any group in San Francisco, while research from the same era in Vancouver found that Asians (Chinese and Japanese) had much lower rates of delinquency than non-Asians, a result attributed to "unusually strong family ties" among Asians in that city.[17] From the earliest studies, and continuing today, scholarship has produced contradictory images of Asians as both a "model minority" and unusually crime prone, especially with regard to gang activity, depending on the specific ethnic group (e.g., Vietnamese, Chinese, Laotian) and time period. There are even wide variations in criminal involvement within a specific type of Asian group. For example, rates of commitment to the California Youth

Authority among Laotian refugees in the 1990s were highest for Mien and lowest for Hmong, with ethnic Lao falling in between.[18] Although there was some variation over time, these patterns persisted throughout the 1990s.

The relationship between immigration (Asian or otherwise) and gangs has been the subject of ongoing debate. It is clear that immigration does affect gang composition, in that the hostile reception of immigrants by the host country can encourage the formation of gangs and in that the ethnic groups that initially form gangs may be replaced by newer arrivals. For example, new waves of Asian immigrant groups changed the ethnic composition of gangs in San Francisco across different decades, from early domination by recent Chinese immigrants in the 1960s, to the inclusion of Chinese refugees from Vietnam in the 1970s and, more recently, Cambodians.[19] The initial formation of Asian gangs in San Francisco was shaped by federal immigration policies and the unique problems faced by new Chinese immigrants in that city upon their arrival (e.g., exclusion from job opportunities, ethnic violence perpetrated by Italians and established Chinese), suggesting that Asians facing discrimination and ethnic conflict respond like other ethnic minorities in forming gangs.[20] But much of the assumed distinctiveness of Asian gangs has not been supported by research. Whereas the popular imagination conceives Asian gangs as particularly vicious and well organized, a review essay on the Asian gang literature disputes such images and finds instead that Asians represent "only a small percentage" of the gang problem in the United States, that most Asian gang members join gangs that are not exclusively, or even largely, Asian in composition, and that Asian gang members are affected by the same social factors that drive gang membership for other ethnic groups.[21]

Because of the inordinate focus on gangs and delinquency, research on other Asian crime patterns, such as homicide, is scarce. One exception is a study of homicide based on death certificates in California from 1970 to 1992.[22] This study, which focused on the most homicide-prone age group (fifteen to thirty-four years old), points out that there are many reasons to suspect overinvolvement of immigrant groups, including Asians, in homicide because such groups "contain a high proportion of young men of color, the very group at highest risk of homicide."[23] Indeed, the data revealed that, overall, immigrants were more likely than native-born Californians to become homicide victims. But there were important differences over time and by ethnicity within this broad trend. For example, although foreign-born Asians had higher homicide victimization rates than native-born Asians from 1970 to 1974, these two groups exhibited virtually identical rates from 1975 to 1992. More importantly for the current study, from 1975 to 1992 Asian immigrants had homicide rates comparable to those of native-born whites, which were much lower than those of both foreign- and native-born blacks and Latinos, as well as those of foreign-born whites. There were some limitations in this study, which the current research seeks to overcome, including an inability to disaggregate Asians and Native Americans and a lack of data on social conditions, but the results make the important point that Asian homicide patterns differ from those of other social groups. The question is why. This question cannot be answered without first considering the history of immigration in the United States and especially in San Diego, as this social process has had a profound effect on contemporary life in Asian communities.

Immigration in National Context

Before we turn to a discussion of San Diego's immigration context, it is important to highlight ways in which the arrival of newcomers from abroad has substantially transformed many cities in recent decades. While previous waves of immigrants "provided the cheap labor force essential to industrialization and expansion in America," the most recent wave (largely Latino and Asian) has encountered "an increasingly post-industrial, service-oriented society."[24] This has important implications because sociological theories of immigrant crime were developed using data on earlier waves of European immigrants to Northeast and Midwest cities with industrial economies. The context is quite different in Sunbelt cities, in terms of both population characteristics and the nature of the labor market. Scholars have demonstrated that immigrants do not simply seek out existing jobs; in many cases they "fill occupational niches that would not exist in their absence."[25] The "enclave economy" created by Cuban immigrants, which transformed the city of Miami, is a classic example.[26]

Immigration in the 1980s surpassed any previous decade in U.S. history, and legal admission records were set in both 1990 and 1991.[27] By 1990, over 80 percent of immigrants originated in Latin America and Asia.[28] Looking at Asian immigration specifically, the 1980 census reported that among the foreign born 87.4 percent of Asians entered the United States between 1960 and 1980.[29] This group has had a significant impact on a number of large American cities, including San Diego, where they constituted 11.3 percent

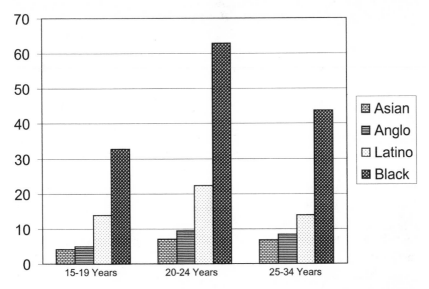

Fig. 5.1. National Homicide Victimization Rates per 100,000 by Race, Ethnicity, and Age, 2001

of the population, according to the 1990 census. Asian immigration and settlement patterns continue to affect this country's structural characteristics, despite the lack of attention to them by criminology scholars.

At present, no original research on Asian homicide patterns has been conducted at the city or neighborhood level. To provide national context for the current study, we compare and contrast Asian homicide victimization rates in the United States for 2001—the latest time period available— with other racial/ethnic groups, as reported in data based on death certificates collected by the Centers for Disease Control.[30] As figure 5.1 shows, Asian homicide victim rates in the crime-prone years (i.e., ages fifteen to nineteen, twenty to twenty-four, and twenty-five to thirty-four) are lower than the rates for whites, blacks, and Latinos.[31] This is powerful evidence that an examination of Asian homicide patterns has great potential for criminological theory, especially social disorganization. Asians appear to be underinvolved as homicide victims, at least on the national level, and given these figures it is likely that the influx of Asians into the United States since 1965 has not contributed to a disproportionate rise in homicide. The question for the current study is, What impact, if any, have Asians had on homicide in San Diego?

Immigration Patterns in San Diego

According to 1990 census figures, San Diego, home to the busiest border crossing in the country, is one of the top ten largest cities in the United States. In terms of race/ethnicity, it is 59 percent white, 9 percent black, 20 percent Latino, and 11 percent Asian, making it one of most racially and ethnically diverse (and underexamined) cities in the country. So although native-born whites remain the most populous group in San Diego, Mexicans have maintained a strong presence throughout the city's history, with some neighborhoods approaching 80 percent by the time of the 1990 census.[32] As with California more generally, San Diego's Mexican population increased drastically because of the Bracero program—a World War II policy designed to import cheap immigrant labor to deal with the domestic labor shortage caused by the war, particularly in the agricultural sector.[33]

In addition to a steady stream of arrivals from Mexico, San Diego has experienced substantial immigration from Asia, especially since the 1965 Immigration Act allowed Asians to enter the United States under family reunification provisions and occupational preferences. The 1965 legislation encouraged immigration among highly educated and well-trained Asian professionals. For example, in 1964 only 14 percent of immigrant scientists and engineers came to the United States from Asia. By 1970, the number had climbed to 62 percent.[34] San Diego certainly has its share of Asian professionals. But Asians in this city are a diverse lot, including a relatively recent wave of less educated and impoverished arrivals from Vietnam, a large middle-class contingent of Filipinos employed by the U.S. Navy, and refugees from Laos and Cambodia.[35] Census figures report almost ninety-six thousand Filipinos in San Diego County, and although "increasing geographical dispersion of the community is an obstacle to its cohesion," there are still a large number of newly arrived professionals settling in affluent areas of the city.[36] While we may expect that the presence of such immigrants should suppress homicide,[37] the impact of other impoverished Asian immigrant groups remains an empirical question.

Recent research in the San Diego area documents the relationship between ethnicity, poverty, and immigration. Alejandro Portes and Rubén Rumbaut, in a survey of 2,842 high school students, found that "Southeast Asian" refugees and undocumented Mexican immigrants were clustered in a handful of highly impoverished San Diego neighborhoods and routinely exposed to crime, drugs, fights, and family conflict.[38] Still, a connection to the "old country" in the community, family, church, or temple or through quick trips "back home" helped preserve parental authority and stem the deleterious effects of acculturation in the new urban environment.[39] Thus San Diego represents an ideal site to investigate the relationship between Asians, immigration, and violence.

Analytical Method

Our analytical strategy is to compare and contrast Asian homicide and immigration patterns in three San Diego neighborhoods.[40] The term *Asian* incorporates a broad range of heterogeneous "Eastern-origin" groups of people, which in San Diego includes Filipinos, Vietnamese, and Chinese, among others. Ideally, the homicide patterns of these subgroups would be compared and contrasted, but these ethnic distinctions were not consistently coded in the San Diego police files that we collected for this study. Nevertheless, much can be learned by focusing attention on homicide patterns of Asians as a group, something that has not yet been done in criminological research, as Eastern-origin group members have a very different social and intellectual history than Westerners, a category that includes whites, blacks, and Latinos.[41] This difference may have substantial effects on homicide involvement and may require a modification of traditional criminological theories, such as social disorganization, that were developed to explain the criminal involvement of Westerners, especially European immigrants.[42] Our analysis therefore uses a unique population (Asians) to test a key proposition of the social disorganization perspective, which predicts a positive relationship between immigration, ethnic heterogeneity, and homicide, relative to the competing claim, which suggests that recent immigration revitalizes urban communities and suppresses crime. Because we are testing a theory (social disorganization) with a clearly specified set of propositions along with circumstances under which the propositions are assumed to be true, we are conducting a version of the single case study method known as the *critical case*.[43]

Consistent with previous research,[44] we argue that neighborhoods may have a distinctive character, often unmeasured by variables commonly included in statistical models, that influences the relationship between structural conditions and crime. Crutchfield, Glusker, and Bridges found such an effect at the city level, particularly with regard to a city's historically situated niche in a changing economy, in their study of homicide in three cities.[45] They found strong effects for education in a "high-tech city" (Seattle), both education and the presence of an underclass in an "old rust belt city" (Cleveland), and a more straightforward underclass effect in a "service sector" city (Washington, D.C.). These researchers have identified a "milieu effect" at the city level, an issue that has often concerned ethnographers at the neighborhood level.

We argue that research in the social disorganization tradition would profit from a methodological approach that attempts to determine elusive qualities of "character" with regard to crime and violence at the neighborhood level—and that the presence of Asian groups can be used as a proxy for the existence of a different (i.e., non-Western) cultural outlook that may moderate the impact of commonly used structural covariates of lethal violence, such as poverty. Lind provides an example of the value of such an approach in his early research on within-city variations in crime.[46] His examination of two neighborhoods with similar poverty characteristics revealed widely differing rates of crime. He used maps and other methods to investigate the differences of ethnically homogeneous but poor "ghettos" compared to heterogeneous, disorganized, and poor "slums." According to Lind's view, crime might flourish in slums but not in ghettos, even though both were characterized by economic deprivation and other deleterious social conditions, because ghetto residents exerted a degree of control over neighbors that was missing in disorganized slums. Lind argued that the "social atmosphere" was markedly different in ghettos and slums: "One [the ghetto] breathes of warmth, intimacy, color; the other of anonymity, chilling distances, drabness. In the one life is on the plane of close, compelling, family and neighborhood disciplines and in the other of impersonal relationships and private convenience."[47] As an example, Lind discussed patterns of Japanese delinquency in two neighborhoods in Honolulu, Hawaii. One, an exclusively Japanese community, exhibited a "complete absence of juvenile delinquency."[48] The other, an ethnically heterogeneous area, was characterized by a high level of delinquency for all groups living there, including the Japanese.

Our strategy is to use maps and descriptive statistics, as Lind does, in a critical case study of social disorganization and Asian homicide in San Diego.[49] Multivariate statistical methods are not particularly helpful in this study because of the spatial segregation of the Asian population in a relatively small number of census tracts and the low overall number of Asian homicides. As figure 5.2 shows, San Diego's Asian population is diverse, including a large number of Filipinos (the dominant Asian group in

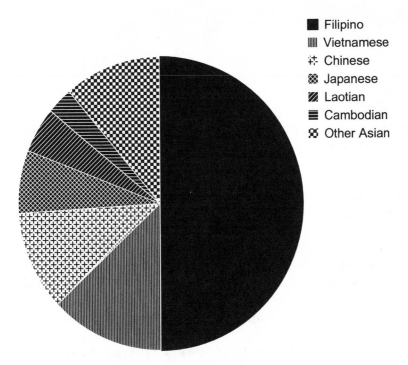

Fig. 5.2. Percentage of Total Asian Population, San Diego (1990)

the city), as well as Vietnamese, Chinese, Japanese, Laotian, Cambodian, and other Asian groups. Previous research has shown that these groups vary in their levels of crime and deviance and in the social factors that affect such variations.[50] Therefore, it is important to disaggregate the Asian population in the three communities under study in order to better understand within-group variations in homicide and associated structural characteristics.

Data Collection

To compare and contrast the macro-level conditions influencing Asian homicide events in the three San Diego communities, we collected original data on all homicides that occurred in these areas during 1985–95 directly from the homicide investigations unit of the San Diego police department. The eleven-year time period was chosen to generate sufficient

numbers of the rare event of Asian homicide ($N = 90$). Access to the detailed internal files allowed us to distinguish Asians from other ethnic
groups, a process not fully possible with the FBI's Uniform Crime Reports.
Most widely available data sets are useless for the purposes of this study
because crime surveys do not capture homicides, while race-specific homicide data sets that include groups like Asians are rare. Equally important
for the present analysis, the police files contain the street address of each
homicide incident, information that enabled the mapping of the spatial
distribution of homicide events and allowed each case to be linked to data
from the 1990 decennial census. Citywide, over 98 percent of all homicide incident addresses were successfully geocoded with Arcview GIS 3.2a
software.[51] The remaining addresses were not captured in Arcview's map
database.

Coding for variables discussed below, other than obvious ones (vacant
buildings and percent Asian, Black, Latino, and Anglo), is as follows: (1)
Asian homicide rate is annualized and expressed per 100,000, using a
count of Asian homicide victims from internal police files (1985–95) in the
numerator and a count of Asians from the 1990 census in the denomina-
tor; (2) the "recent immigrant" variable captures the proportion of the
population that entered the United States between 1980 and 1990; and (3)
Asian poverty, male joblessness, and female-headed family variables are all
expressed as a proportion of the Asian population.

Results

The extent of ethnic diversity that epitomizes San Diego stands in sharp
contrast to its level of violent crime like homicide and its levels of ethnic-
specific crime. San Diego has one of the lowest levels of homicide for cities
over one million in population size. Yet that rate varies dramatically for
the city's four largest racial groups. As figure 5.3 shows, from 1980 to 1995
African Americans had a much higher homicide rate than Latinos, and
both of those rates were strikingly high when compared to that of Asians,
a group with a rate that is in line with that of Anglos (whites). In fact, the
Asian rate was lower than the Anglo (non-Latino white) rate throughout
the 1980s and, after a slight increase in the early 1990s, matched the Anglo
rate in 1995. The Asian and Anglo rates never exceeded 10 per 100,000
throughout this period, while the African American rate ranged from
about 25 to 40 per 100,000, depending on the year, and the Latino rate

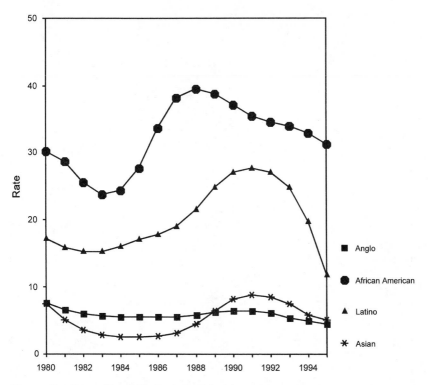

Fig. 5.3. San Diego Homicide Rates by Ethnicity, 1980–95

ranged from about 15 to 25. These findings are largely consistent with the national figures reported above in figure 5.1 and suggest that a more detailed study of Asian homicide patterns in San Diego could increase our understanding of how immigrant groups maintain low levels of violent crime despite significant structural disadvantages.[52]

Mapping all Asian homicides in San Diego reveals that this violent crime is concentrated in a few areas of the city. These areas, not coincidentally, also contain the highest concentration of Asian residents and are contained within twenty-one census tracts. The tracts form three distinct clusters, or what we may consider natural areas or communities (see figure 5.4). Two of the communities are "inner city" in location, although one is "urban" and the other "suburban" in terms of its population demographics and housing characteristics. The third is well outside the city center and comprises a much larger land mass, with much lower population density than the other two.

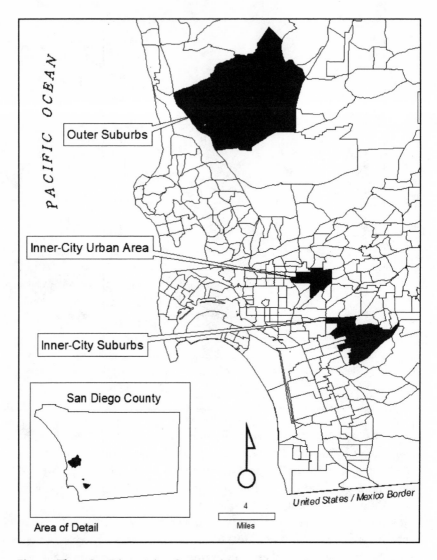

Fig. 5.4. Three San Diego Asian Communities

A map showing population change between the 1980 and 1990 censuses indicates that these three heavily Asian areas became increasing foreign born over time, relative to other areas of the city (not shown here but available from the authors). Another map indicates that the concentration of Asians also increased in these three areas between 1980 and 1990.[53] This suggests that these three Asian communities are well suited as critical cases for testing the social disorganization proposition that immigration should weaken community social control and increase violent crime levels. To assess this claim, we compare and contrast patterns of Asian homicide and structural characteristics in the three areas.

Turning first to table 5.1, we see that the inner-city urban area has by far the highest Asian homicide rate of the three communities (18.46 per 100,000), compared to 3.93 for the inner-city suburbs and 3.24 for the outer suburbs. The urban area is well above the citywide tract average Asian homicide rate of 10.23, while the other two are well below this figure. This suggests that there is indeed substantial variation across space in Asian homicide rates, but the question is to what degree this variation is related to immigration and other structural covariates of homicide.

To begin to answer this question, table 5.1 provides data on recent immigration, vacant buildings, Asian poverty, Asian male joblessness, Asian female-headed families, the dominant Asian group, and the ethnic makeup of each of the three communities. As expected, Asian poverty is quite high in the urban area (42.49 percent) and is well above the mean, as well as the figures for the other two communities. A similar relationship is apparent for the percentage of vacant buildings, a factor long thought to contribute to the social disorganization of a community. The figure for the inner-city urban area is more than double the percentage for either of the other two communities. But the relationship with recent immigration is

TABLE 5.1
Demographic Characteristics by Area, San Diego (1990)

	Inner-City Urban	Inner-City Suburban	Outer Suburban	Tract Mean (Citywide)
Asian homicide rate[a]	18.46	3.93	3.24	10.23
% Asian poverty	42.49	2.79	5.86	16.49
% vacant buildings	7.59	3.10	3.54	5.51
% new immigrants	27.88	21.51	11.87	9.62
% Asian male joblessness	39.54	30.25	17.19	32.01
% Asian female-headed families	14.97	13.63	6.06	14.87
% dominant Asian group	41.52	87.76	52.94	50.00[b]
	(Viet/Cambo)	(Filipino)	(Filipino)	(Filipino)
% Asian	20.02	37.90	25.66	11.31[c]
% Black	20.93	17.29	3.54	9.01[c]
% Latino	31.05	18.16	8.27	20.14[c]
% Anglo	26.94	25.91	62.04	58.83[c]

[a] Per 100,000, 1985–95.
[b] Percentage of all Asians at the city level.
[c] Group-specific percentage at the city level.

less clear. The high-homicide, high-poverty urban area does have the highest concentration of new immigrants (27.88 percent), yet the inner-city suburbs are also heavily immigrant (21.51 percent) without the poverty or homicide levels of the urban community. Even the outer suburban area is above the mean for recent immigration, so two of three areas received large numbers of immigrants but exhibited relatively low levels of poverty and homicide. This finding highlights the diversity of immigration patterns in San Diego and suggests a qualification of the social disorganization thesis regarding the effects of immigration on crime, in that poverty and vacancy may be more influential in Asian communities than the disorganization that is presumed to accompany immigration.

Turning to the other variables in table 5.1, we see that the inner-city urban and suburban areas are quite similar with regard to Asian male joblessness and female-headed families, despite their differences concerning homicide and poverty. We find mixed support for the social disorganization thesis on ethnic heterogeneity and crime in that the high-homicide inner-city area has no clearly dominant Asian group (41.52 percent of the Asian residents are Vietnamese or Cambodian) and thus has potentially weaker community social control, while the low-homicide inner-city urban area does have a dominant Asian group (87.76 percent of Asians are Filipino). The outer suburban area has only a slim Filipino majority (52.94 percent), and Asians account for only 25.7 percent of the total population, but this community exhibits a low Asian homicide level. The percentage of Asians in the outer suburban area is more similar to that of the inner-city urban area than that of the inner-city suburban area. In fact, the former is composed mostly of Anglos (62 percent), with Asians a distant second and only a handful of blacks and Latinos. Asians are the dominant group in the inner-city suburban area, constituting 37.9 percent of the residents, which may partly account for the ability of this community's residents to control behavior and inhibit crime (in addition to the poverty findings discussed above).

Interestingly, there is no clear ethnic majority in the inner-city urban neighborhood, which is consistent with Lind's findings about ghettos versus slums discussed above.[54] In other words, the inner-city urban area is best described as a high–Asian homicide, high-poverty, high-immigrant, ethnically homogeneous slum; the inner-city suburban area is a low-homicide, low-poverty, but high-immigrant, community that is dominated by Asians; and the outer suburban neighborhood is characterized by low homicide, low poverty, slightly above average recent immigration, and Anglo dominance.

Table 5.1 reveals important variations from the social disorganization model of urban crime, in that predictions about the impact of immigration and ethnic heterogeneity on homicide levels seem to hold in one community, but not in two others. Basic social conditions, such as poverty and physical incivilities (i.e., vacant buildings), seem to be more influential. But the story is more complicated than that, as an examination of within-community variations reveals even more differences (see figures 5.5–5.7). These maps present bar graphs with tract-level data for each of the three communities on the annualized Asian homicide rate per 100,000 (hom), percent Asian poverty (pov), percent recent immigration (imm), percent Asian male joblessness (job), and percent Asian female-headed families (fem).

Looking first at the inner-city urban area in figure 5.5, we see that in most tracts high levels of recent immigration and Asian poverty are indeed associated with high levels of homicide (tracts 2200, 2300, 2701, and 2600). Yet in others this is not the case, as tracts 2400 and 2704 have Asian homicide rates substantially lower than the other tracts and lower than the citywide tract mean, despite having poverty rates that are above the mean. It is also important to note that only one tract (2200) in this community had a clearly dominant Asian group. In this case, 70 percent of the Asians in this tract were Vietnamese (Asians constituted roughly 18 percent of the tract population). This subethnic group was also the largest Asian group in tracts 2400 and 2704, but in both cases the Vietnamese accounted for only 37 percent of the Asian residents. Cambodians constituted the largest Asian group in the other tracts in this figure, with a range of 28 percent to 44 percent of the tracts' Asian populations.

Figure 5.6 reveals more interesting within-community variations, this time for the inner-city suburban area. Note that Asian homicide is concentrated in three tracts in this community (tracts 3109, 3110, and 3209) and is totally absent in the others. This provides support for research on units of analysis smaller than the city or neighborhood, possibly directing our attention to "hot spots" at the block group level, a subject to be taken up in future research. Notice also that one of the most heavily immigrant tracts (3102) in this community has no Asian homicides at all. In addition, common structural covariates of homicide (e.g., poverty, joblessness, female-headed families) do not seem to be associated with Asian homicide

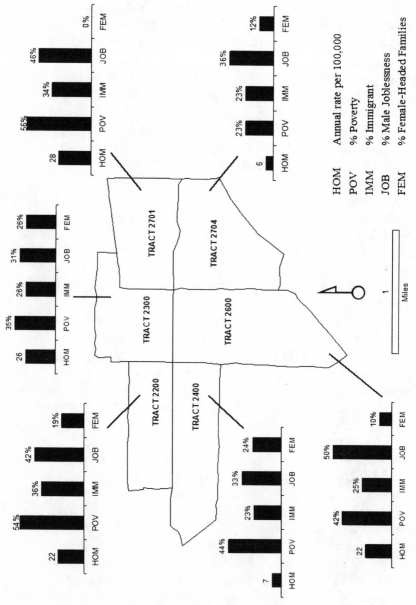

Fig. 5.5. Asian Homicide and Structural Characteristics in an Inner-City Urban Area (City Heights East/Oak Park)

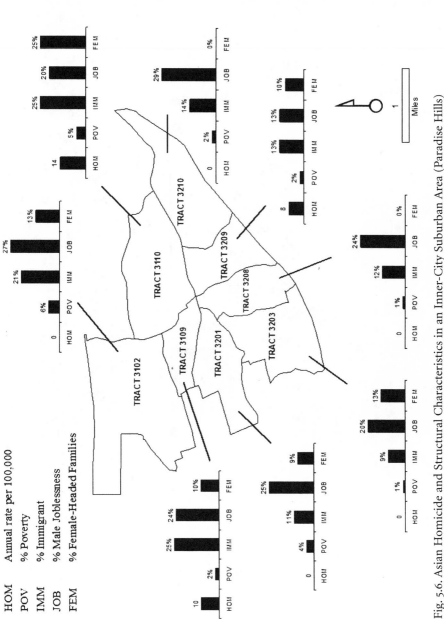

HOM   Annual rate per 100,000
POV   % Poverty
IMM   % Immigrant
JOB   % Male Joblessness
FEM   % Female-Headed Families

Fig. 5.6. Asian Homicide and Structural Characteristics in an Inner-City Suburban Area (Paradise Hills)

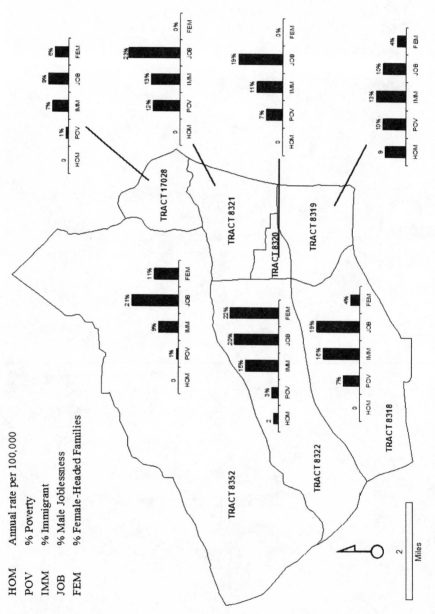

HOM — Annual rate per 100,000
POV — % Poverty
IMM — % Immigrant
JOB — % Male Joblessness
FEM — % Female-Headed Families

Fig. 5.7. Asian Homicide and Structural Characteristics in an Outer Suburban Area (Mira Mesa/Sorrento Valley)

in this part of San Diego, suggesting that widely accepted structural theories of crime etiology may not adequately predict levels of violent crime for this group at the tract level. Filipinos constitute the vast majority, between 78 percent and 96 percent, of all Asian residents in the tracts in this neighborhood. Figure 5.7 paints a similar picture for the outer suburbs: Asian homicide is concentrated in only two tracts (8322 and 8319), again directing our attention to within-community variations. As in the inner-city suburban area, Filipinos are the dominant Asian group. But in the outer suburban area their share of the Asian population is much lower, ranging from a low of 37 percent to a high of only 61 percent.

Conclusion

This study attempted to uncover community-level patterns in Asian homicide, recent immigration, and other community characteristics in order to test the social disorganization proposition that immigration weakens social control and contributes to high levels of crime. Using maps and descriptive statistics in an analytical method similar to that employed by Lind,[55] we uncovered important community and within-community variations in homicide, immigration, and structural characteristics suggesting that neighborhoods do have a distinctive character (or social milieu) that might be obscured in statistical studies based on larger units of analysis (e.g., cities or counties). These variations suggest that fundamental tenets of the social disorganization perspective must be modified when examining groups such as Asians in San Diego.[56] Although in some census tracts immigration appeared to be associated with higher levels of Asian homicide, abundant data from this study also supported the "immigration paradox" that recent immigration does not have the deleterious consequences expected by sociological theories.[57]

Previous research has demonstrated the value of the theory of segmented assimilation for explaining within-group variations in Asian delinquency and drug use.[58] The descriptive findings of the current study, especially as reported in table 5.1, which revealed vastly different Asian homicide rates across the three communities, suggest that the social disorganization approach to understanding violent crime in urban areas could also benefit from attention to issues raised by segmented assimilation theory. The low rates of Asian homicide in suburban Filipino neighborhoods contrast sharply with the high Asian homicide level in the impoverished inner-city urban community—where "downward assimilation" to norms and values of the underclass may be disproportionately affecting Vietnamese and Cambodian residents. Thus the presumed disorganizing effects of recent immigration on communities are not universal, or even typical, but are rather mediated by processes of segmented assimilation.

Explicit attention to this issue in future research using multivariate methods is imperative, but because of the small number of Asian homicides in San Diego and their concentration in a handful of tracts where Asians reside, we were prevented from conducting multivariate analyses that would disentangle the relative importance of the structural factors that we examined. However, it did seem clear that basic social conditions, such as poverty and vacant buildings, were more directly related to Asian homicide than recent immigration, although within-community variations somewhat complicated this picture. The findings for ethnic heterogeneity were mixed, with high homicide levels associated with high ethnic heterogeneity in one neighborhood (inner-city urban) but not the other two. In the inner-city suburban area, Asians were the dominant ethnic group; many of them were Vietnamese and Cambodians, and Filipinos constituted the overwhelming majority. In the outer suburban area, Anglos were by far the dominant group, but a quarter of the residents were Asian, and the majority of these were also Filipino. This underscores the need to take into consideration within-group differences in future research on Asian homicide, as Filipinos have a very different social and economic history in San Diego than Vietnamese and Cambodians.

Although within-group differences are important, all Asian groups are likely to have a great deal in common with each other in terms of social and intellectual heritage, regardless of their particular country of origin.[59] Abundant research highlighting the different social psychologies of "Easterners" and "Westerners" has important implications for the impact of social disorganization processes and other structural covariates on crime. Despite the interesting variations across Asian areas in San Diego uncovered in this study, it is important to remember that Asians as a group are less involved in homicide than other ethnic groups, including Anglos, both in San Diego (recall figure 5.3) and nationwide (figure 5.1).[60] Research reported by Nisbett demonstrates that Westerners, who trace their intellectual heritage to the Greeks, and Easterners, who trace theirs to Confucian China, continue to have very different worldviews even today.[61] Westerners tend to emphasize personal agency, individual rights, and competitive success through adversarial confrontation; Easterners are more likely to emphasize harmony, interconnectedness, and community and family obligations. These different outlooks affect processes of causal attribution and responses to social circumstances and situations. The implications for crime are suggestive—Asian populations may contribute to a milieu effect that suppresses violent confrontations as a result of their cultural emphasis on harmony and "seeking the Middle Way" (as opposed to the Western obligation to assert that one is "right" and win competitions).

This cultural imperative provides a strong ideological foundation for the development of mutual aid organizations among Asian immigrants, which to some extent ameliorates the deleterious effects of adverse social conditions in impoverished urban centers.[62] Asian culture, as institutionalized through mutual aid organizations and informal social practices organized around notions of harmony, therefore provides clues to explaining why Asians fare so much better on a variety of outcomes, including crime, than native-born citizens living in the same or surrounding neighborhoods. Integration into social organizations based on notions of ethnic identity and honor helped Asian immigrants resist the disorganizing and atomizing effects of urban life.[63] "Caste subordination" beginning with slavery deprived blacks of similar institutions, and, as a result, "blacks were free to act as individuals quite apart from group approval . . . [and] rampant individualism contributed to the disorganization of social life in the slums."[64] The disparity in homicide rates between African Americans and Asians in San Diego, many of whom live in the same areas, is one indicator of the legacy of caste subordination that continues to afflict African American inner-city communities but has been mitigated by Asian culture and institutions. It is important to point out that although there is a long history of discrimination against Asian groups in this country, Asian institutions were not obliterated by the practice of involuntary servitude and the associated devaluation of ethnic identity that has shaped African American social conditions.

In sum, it is clear that structural covariates of violence, such as poverty, can shape Asian homicide patterns in important ways, but much can also be learned from a research agenda that examines how Asian history and culture might modify the impact of these structural covariates on lethal violence, in a context of segmented assimilation across Asian immigrant groups. It is entirely plausible that Asians operate under a very different "code of the street"[65] than Westerners, such that they are less likely to operationalize into violence the frustrations associated with deleterious social conditions—and that these frustrations are lessened in the first place by mutual aid groups and a strong ethnic identity. The patterns in Asian homicide uncovered in this initial study suggest that this possibility is worthy of serious consideration.

NOTES

We wish to thank Bob Bursik, Bob Crutchfield, and Al Blumstein for helpful comments on an earlier version of this chapter.

1. Rumbaut (1999); see also Pedraza (1996); Portes (2000).
2. Rumbaut (1999).
3. Butcher and Piehl (1997); Hagan and Palloni (1999); Lee (2003); Lee and Martinez (2002); Lee, Martinez, and Rosenfeld (2001); Martinez (2002).
4. Lee (2003).
5. Cf. Shaw and McKay (1931).
6. Cf. Bursik (1999).
7. Warner (1999: 101).
8. Martinez (2002).
9. Cf. Lee (2003); Lee and Martinez (2002).
10. Lee and Martinez (2002).
11. Lee, Martinez, and Rosenfeld (2001).
12. Portes and Stepick (1993); see also Muller (1993) on the revitalizing effects of recent immigration on "gateway" cities.
13. Portes (2000: 5).
14. Muller (1993).
15. Knox and McCurrie (1997); Toy (1992).
16. Nagasawa, Qian, and Wong (2001); Waters (1999).
17. Waters (1999: 30).
18. Waters (1999).
19. Toy (1992).
20. Toy (1992); Knox and McCurrie (1997).
21. Knox and McCurrie (1997: 303).
22. Sorenson and Shen (1996).
23. Sorenson and Shen (1996: 97).
24. Pedraza (1996: 2).
25. Linton (2002: 58).
26. Portes and Stepick (1993).
27. Rumbaut (1996).
28. Rumbaut (1996).
29. Rumbaut (1992).
30. R. Anderson and Smith (2003); see also Sorenson and Shen (1996) for the California context.

31. Similar results were found in 2000 and 1999; see R. Anderson (2001, 2002).
32. Martinez (2002).
33. Rumbaut (1992).
34. Ong and Liu (1994).
35. Carino (1996); Ong and Liu (1994).
36. Espiritu (1995: 24).
37. Waters (1999: 58).
38. Portes and Rumbaut (2001: 194).
39. Portes and Rumbaut (2001: 232).
40. For a similar method, see Valdez (1993).
41. Nisbett (2003).
42. Cf. table 2.2 in Bursik, ch. 2 of this volume.
43. Yin (1994).
44. Cf. Lee and Martinez (2002).
45. Crutchfield, Glusker, and Bridges (1999).
46. Lind (1930a, 1930b).
47. Lind (1930a: 208).
48. Lind (1930a: 209).
49. See also Lee and Martinez (2002).
50. Nagasawa, Qian, and Wong (2001); Waters (1999).
51. This is available from the Environmental Systems Research Institute at www.esri.com.
52. Cf. Lee, Martinez, and Rosenfeld (2001); Lee and Martinez (2002).
53. Available from the authors.
54. Lind (1930a).
55. Lind (1930a, 1930b).
56. See also Lee and Martinez (2002) for the case of Haitians in Miami.
57. Rumbaut (1999).
58. Nagasaw, Qian, and Wong (2001); Portes and Zhou (1993).
59. Nisbett (2003).
60. See also Sorenson and Shen (1996).
61. Nisbett (2003).
62. Muller (1993); Light (1972).
63. Light (1972).
64. Light (1972: 189–90).
65. E. Anderson (1999).

REFERENCES

Anderson, Elijah. 1999. *Code of the Street: Decency, Violence, and the Moral Life of the Inner City.* New York W. W. Norton.

Anderson, Robert N. 2001. *Deaths: Leading Causes for 1999.* National Vital Statistics Reports 49:11. Washington, DC: Centers for Disease Control.

———. 2002. *Deaths: Leading Causes for 2000.* National Vital Statistics Reports 50:16. Washington, DC: Centers for Disease Control.

Anderson, Robert N., and Betty L. Smith. 2003. *Deaths: Leading Causes for 2001.* National Vital Statistics Reports 52:9. Washington, DC: Centers for Disease Control.

Bursik, Robert J., Jr. 1999. "The Informal Control of Crime through Neighborhood Networks." *Sociological Focus* 32:85–97.

Butcher, Kristin F., and Anne Morrison Piehl. 1997. "Recent Immigrants: Unexpected Implications for Crime and Incarceration." NBER Working Paper 6067, National Bureau of Economic Research, Cambridge, MA.

Carino, Benjamin V. 1996. "Filipino Americans: Many and Varied." In *Origins and Destinies: Immigration, Race, and Ethnicity in America,* edited by Silvia Pedraza and R. G. Rumbaut, 293–301. Belmont, CA: Wadsworth.

Crutchfield, Robert D., Ann Glusker, and George S. Bridges. 1999. "A Tale of Three Cities: Labor Markets and Homicide." *Sociological Focus* 32:65–83.

Espiritu, Len Le. 1995. *Filipino American Lives.* Philadelphia: Temple University Press.

Hagan, John, and Alberto Palloni. 1999. "Sociological Criminology and the Mythology of Hispanic Immigration and Crime." *Social Problems* 46:617–32.

Knox, George W., and Thomas F. McCurrie. 1997. "Asian Gangs: Recent Research Findings." *Journal of Contemporary Criminal Justice* 13:301–8.

Lee, Matthew T. 2003. *Crime on the Border: Immigration and Homicide in Urban Communities.* New York: LFB Scholarly Publishing.

Lee, Matthew T., and Ramiro Martinez Jr. 2002. "Social Disorganization Revisited: Mapping the Recent Immigration and Black Homicide Relationship in Northern Miami." *Sociological Focus* 35:363–80.

Lee, Matthew T., Ramiro Martinez Jr., and Richard B. Rosenfeld. 2001. "Does Immigration Increase Homicide? Negative Evidence from Three Border Cities." *Sociological Quarterly* 42:559–80.

Light, Ivan H. 1972. *Business and Welfare among Chinese, Japanese, and Blacks.* Berkeley: University of California Press.

Lind, Andrew W. 1930a. "The Ghetto and the Slum." *Social Forces* 9:206–15.

———. 1930b. "Some Ecological Patterns of Community Disorganization in Honolulu." *American Journal of Sociology* 36:206–20.

Linton, April. 2002. "Immigration and the Structure of Demand: Do Immigrants Alter the Labor Market Composition of U.S. Cities?" *International Migration Review* 36:58–80.

Martinez, Ramiro, Jr. 2002. *Latino Homicide: Immigration, Violence, and Community.* New York: Routledge.

Muller, Thomas. 1993. *Immigrants and the American City.* New York: New York University Press.

Nagasawa, Richard, Zhenchao Qian, and Paul Wong. 2001. "Theory of Segmented Assimilation and the Adoption of Marijuana Use and Delinquent Behavior by Asian Pacific Youth." *Sociological Quarterly* 42:351–72.

Nisbett, Richard E. 2003. *The Geography of Thought: How Asians and Westerners Think Differently . . . and Why.* New York: Free Press.

Ong, Paul, and John M. Liu. 1994. "U.S. Immigration Policies and Asian Migration." In *The New Asian Immigration in Los Angeles and Global Restructuring,* edited by Paul Ong, E. Bonacich, and L. Cheng, 45–73. Philadelphia: Temple University Press.

Pedraza, Silvia. 1996. "American Paradox." In *Origins and Destinies: Immigration, Race, and Ethnicity in America,* edited by Silvia Pedraza and R. G. Rumbaut, 479–91. Belmont, CA: Wadsworth.

Portes, Alejandro. 2000. "The Hidden Abode: Sociology as Analysis of the Unexpected." *American Sociological Review* 65:1–18.

Portes, Alejandro, and Rubén G. Rumbaut. 2001. *Legacies: The Story of the Immigrant Second Generation.* Berkeley: University of California Press.

Portes, Alejandro, and Alex Stepick. 1993. *City on the Edge: The Transformation of Miami.* Berkeley: University of California Press.

Portes, Alejandro, and Min Zhou. 1993. "The New Second Generation: Segmented Assimilation and Its Variants." *Annals* 530:74–96.

Rumbaut, Rubén G. 1992. "The Americans: Latin American and Caribbean Peoples in the United States." In *Americas: New Interpretive Essays,* edited by A. Stepan, 275–307. New York: Oxford University Press.

———. 1996. "Origins and Destinies: Immigration, Race, and Ethnicity in Contemporary America." In *Origins and Destinies: Immigration, Race, and Ethnicity in America,* edited by S. Pedraza and R. G. Rumbaut, 21–42. Belmont, CA: Wadsworth.

———. 1999. "Assimilation and Its Discontents: Ironies and Paradoxes." In *The Handbook of International Migration: The American Experience,* edited by C. Hirshman, P. Kasinitz, and J. DeWind, 172–95. New York: Russell Sage.

Shaw, Clifford R., and Henry D. McKay. 1931. *Social Factors in Juvenile Delinquency.* Washington, DC: U.S. Government Printing Office.

Sorenson, Susan B., and Haikang Shen. 1996. "Homicide Risk among Immigrants in California, 1970 though 1992." *American Journal of Public Health* 86:97–99.

Toy, Calvin. 1992. "A Short History of Asian Gangs in San Francisco." *Justice Quarterly* 9:647–65.

Valdez, Avelardo. 1993. "Persistent Poverty, Crime, and Drugs: U.S.-Mexican Border Region." In *the Barrios: Latinos and the Underclass Debate,* edited by J. Moore and R. Pinderhughes, 173–94. New York: Russell Sage.

Warner, Barbara D. 1999. "Whither Poverty? Social Disorganization Theory in an Era of Urban Transformation." *Sociological Focus* 32:99–113.

Waters, Tony. 1999. *Crime and Immigrant Youth.* Thousand Oaks, CA: Sage.

Yin, Robert K. 1994. *Case Study Research: Design and Methods.* 2nd ed. Thousand Oaks, CA: Sage.

Chapter 6

Delinquency and Acculturation in the Twenty-first Century

*A Decade's Change in a
Vietnamese American Community*

Min Zhou and Carl L. Bankston III

"It used to be that the Vietnamese students were always the best in my classes. Any time I saw a Vietnamese name on my roster, I knew that person was going to be a star. Now, it isn't like that. I still get some good students who are Vietnamese, but a lot of them seem even worse than the others. And it's weird, because these kids today were all born here and speak good English." These observations, made by an instructor at a local college in California to one of the authors, seemed to echo opinions we have heard from many professionals in education, law enforcement, and social services. It is possible that anecdotes like this simply reflect the clash between stereotypes and realities. It is also possible that a few Vietnamese academic success stories in the 1980s and the early 1990s led to the idealization of Vietnamese youth. As people come to face the fact that Vietnamese adolescents and young adults are as complex, diverse, and troubled as any other young Americans, this harsh reality may have provoked an excessive reaction.

Our own interest in investigating an apparent increase in problem behavior among Vietnamese young people stems from our research on the "valedictorian-delinquent" phenomenon in the early and mid-1990s. In our book *Growing Up American: How Vietnamese Children Adapt to Life in the United States* and in a series of published articles, we argued that popular, and seemingly contradictory, views of Vietnamese young people as "valedictorians" and "delinquents" were rooted in actual social tendencies.[1] Although this research was primarily based on a case study of a

Vietnamese enclave in New Orleans, it shed lights on the understanding of this new ethnic group in the United States.

Findings in the Mid-1990s

Vietnamese emerged on the American scene in significant numbers only after the fall of Saigon in the mid-1970s, and most arrived in the United States as refugees. By the early 1990s, many had been in the United States for about a decade and a half. This meant that the adolescents we studied in *Growing Up American* and other works were the first cohort who either had been born in the United States (the second generation) or had been born abroad but had spent much of their lives here (the "1.5" genera-tion) and that the parent generation was a war-traumatized, ill-prepared, and economically deprived refugee group. Although Vietnamese refugees had no preexisting ethnic communities in the United States to shelter them and their resettlement here was almost entirely determined by gov-ernment agencies or nongovernment organizations, the outcomes of their adaptation were uneven. On the one hand, many children were adapting to the American environment, particularly the academic environment, surprisingly well on the basis of media accounts and a number of case studies.[2] On the other hand, however, there were numerous reports of gang activities and other forms of serious delinquent activities among Vietnamese youth.[3] Local police reports also showed a rising concern with the growth of violent criminal activity among Vietnamese juveniles.[4]

Vietnamese parents were aware of and extremely concerned about the two major possibilities—scholarship and delinquency—facing their chil-dren. For example, in a survey of Vietnamese living in the Los Angeles metropolitan area administered by the *Los Angeles Times* in 1994, respon-dents with children under eighteen years of age were asked to identify the most important problem facing their children. Their answers were reveal-ing: while 30 percent said that their children had no problems, 27 percent identified studying and doing well in school as the most important prob-lem for their children, and 20 percent identified staying away from gangs as the most important problem. No other potential problem came close to these two—academic excellence and gang involvement—in the eyes of the parents.[5]

The findings from the *Los Angeles Times* survey of the Vietnamese in Los Angeles were quite consistent with evidence from the survey data, face-to-face interviews, and field observations that we gathered in the Vietnamese enclave in New Orleans in 1993 and 1994. In *Growing Up American*, we argued that the apparently contradictory stereotypes of Vietnamese youth and the polarized concerns of Vietnamese parents both derived from the fact that Vietnamese American young people were indeed moving in two contrary directions in their adaptation to American society. The bifurcation, as we called it, resulted from their being subject to two opposing sets of contextual influences. On the one hand, the ethnic community was tightly knit and encouraged behaviors such as respect for elders, diligence in work, and striving for upward social mobility into mainstream American society. The local American community, on the other hand, was socially marginalized and economically impoverished, and young people in it reacted to structural disadvantages by erecting oppositional subcultures to reject normative means to social mobility.

Drawing on the segmented assimilation theory, which predicts the assimilation among children of immigrants into different segments of the American society rather than into a single mainstream middle-class America, we conceptualize these contextual influences on bifurcated outcomes of Vietnamese youth in a model of multilevel social integration.[6] Individual young people, we argue, are embedded in families, and these families are also embedded in multiple sets of social contexts and social relations. Ethnic social networks and ethnic institutions constituting an ethnic community are the primary set of social relations. Moreover, the individuals and their families are located in particular neighborhoods and surrounded by local social environments where social relations are largely secondary and beyond ethnic boundaries. Whether or not contextual influences contribute to positive adaptation to the larger society depends on how consistent the ethnic and local social environments are with the goals and means of the larger society. When the local social environment is not consistent with the goals and means of the larger society but the ethnic social environment is, young people may benefit from integration into families that connect them to the ethnic community and from intense involvement in social relations in ethnic networks and institutions that connect them to that community.

Our case study of a New Orleans Vietnamese enclave provided empirical evidence in support of this model.[7] We found that although Vietnamese young people lived in a socially marginal local environment they were shielded from the negative influences of that environment by being tightly bound up in a system of ethnic social relations providing both control and direction. The adults in this ethnic enclave were relatively new arrivals in the country. They placed great emphasis on striving for opportunities in the new land and expected young people to obtain these opportunities through the American educational system. They also enforced in their young people the cultural values, such as respect for elders, obedience and hard work, that they brought with them from Vietnam, believing that these values were beneficial in achieving their goal of communal upward mobility. As a result, adolescents who were closely connected to their communities through families and peer groups were directed in ways likely to pay off through school success.

We also found that some Vietnamese young people living in the same neighborhood were rejected by other Vietnamese as "outsiders," or at-risk youth. Some of these youth were simply disoriented drifters and school dropouts, while others were lawless gangsters. Many of these alienated youth had families characterized by absent parents, poor relations among family members, weak connections to other Vietnamese families, or a lack of involvement in the Vietnamese community. We called these families "absent or partially absent family systems" and considered them problematic because they were isolated from the ethnic community. These families' own social isolation led their children astray, so that they drifted into peer groups or street gangs that stood out as being "too Americanized." In fact, being labeled as "Americanized" by other Vietnamese in that enclave did not mean that these youth had become part of mainstream American society; it simply meant that they had become like local American youth living in the same neighborhood, whose attitudes and forms of behavior were disapproved of by both the Vietnamese community and mainstream American society.

Social contexts, therefore, gave rise to a tendency among Vietnamese American youth to diverge into two distinct categories: a larger group that was closely tied to an ethnic identity and ethnic social relations and a smaller but visible group that was at the margins of the ethnic community with stronger behavioral and attitudinal ties to the local American youth subculture. Has bifurcation continued to perpetuate itself among the children of Vietnamese? In this chapter, we examine current behavioral and attitudinal trends among Vietnamese youth, using recently gathered data from the same Vietnamese neighborhood in New Orleans that we studied almost a decade ago. We aim to reevaluate and update our earlier findings by looking at whether Vietnamese American young people still fall into these two categories and, if they do, whether the categories continue to be

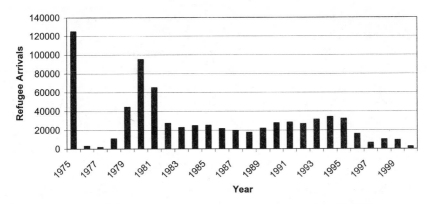

Fig. 6.1. Refugee Arrivals from Vietnam in the United States, 1975–2000

as distinct as they were nearly ten years ago. Then we attempt to address any changes, using our model of ethnic social relations to discuss how these changes may be the consequences of changing social contexts.

A New Cohort Coming of Age at a New Time

Over the past decade, a new cohort of Vietnamese American adolescents has reached high school age. The young people that we studied in 1993 and 1994 are now in their mid- to late twenties. Intensifying the cohort effect, the large-scale movement of Vietnamese refugees to the United States that began in 1975 essentially ended by the beginning of the twenty-first century. As figure 6.1 shows, the greatest waves of refugees from Vietnam arrived in the United States occurred in the late 1970s and early 1980s. From the early to mid-1980s until about 1995, just after we concluded most of our data collection for *Growing Up American,* refugee arrivals continued at a substantial rate, totaling around twenty thousand to thirty thousand annually. In addition to the first wave in 1975 and the second wave around 1980, there was a smaller third wave around 1990. This probably reflected programs, such as the Humanitarian Operation Program (HO), completed between the United States and Vietnam in 1989 to allow former political prisoners and their families to settle in this country. The HOs and other new arrivals were still being settled during the research period of our earlier work. After 1995, the influx of people classified as refugees slowed to a trickle, partly because so many people had already arrived in the United States and partly because of normalized relations between Vietnam and the United States.

The trends of Vietnamese refugee and immigrant influx have important implications for contextual differences between the adolescent cohort of 1993–94 and that of 2003. The decline in the refugee influx means that the parents of this recent cohort are much less likely than the parents of the earlier cohort to have fled Vietnam as refugees and that, among those born abroad, the recent cohort is less likely than the earlier cohort to be child refugees. Perhaps even more important, the young people of the early twenty-first century experienced drastically different family processes shaped by immigrant settlement as opposed to refugee resettlement. Members of the recent cohort are much less likely than those in the earlier cohort to be in absent or partially absent family systems as a consequence of the disruptions of flight. They are also more distant from the immediate sufferings and nerve-racking ordeals of war and flight that traumatized so many families and individuals in the earlier years, since the whole resettlement experience was something that largely took place before their personal memories. The Vietnam War had been over and Vietnamese refugee resettlement in the United States had already taken place by the time a fifteen-year-old in 2003 was in early childhood. One logical contextual consequence of this cohort effect would be an intensification of generation gaps between parents, who still had fairly clear memories of the original homeland, and their children, for whom Vietnam was an obscure and faraway place in Asia.

Apart from generation gaps within families, the changing nature of Vietnamese migration to the United States also suggests that the ethnic population has become increasingly diverse and that ethnic social relations between adolescents and their elders have arguably weakened, partly because of the lack of a shared experience, which was the trauma of war and flight for the refugees, and partly because of acculturation. For example, in our studies in the mid-1990s we found that the local Vietnamese Catholic church was the single most authoritative ethnic institution and the unequivocal center of social relations in the enclave. When we spoke with a pastor at this same church in May 2001, he remarked that it had become necessary to hold masses in English as well as Vietnamese because increasingly large numbers of young people did not have a sufficient command of the Vietnamese language. Young people and their elders today are literally speaking different languages. Moreover, as the group is settled in one location for a long time, its members inevitably increase the frequency and intensity of contacts with non-co-ethnic members in the neighbor-hood and in workplaces. In the case of Vietnamese Americans, the stabi-lization of the ethnic population can mean that direct cultural influences from Vietnam are largely thinning out, giving way to influences from the larger society or from the people around them.

Delinquency in a Vietnamese American Community: A Decade's Change

To contrast the situation of Vietnamese youth a decade ago with the situa-tion today, we use data from two periods. For the first period, we revisited the quantitative and qualitative analyses in *Growing Up American,* based primarily on an in-school survey of 402 Vietnamese students and on field-work conducted in the Vietnamese enclave in New Orleans in 1993 and 1994. To contrast the early 1990s with the early 2000s, we administered another survey to 214 Vietnamese young people who lived and attended school in the same neighborhood in small groups and in various locations outside the school during the spring and summer of 2003. The use of these two survey data sets may raise some questions of comparability, since the initial survey not only included a greater number of respondents but was conducted in schools. It is entirely possible that young people would respond to the same survey questions differently in school and out of school. However, we think the fact that the surveys at both points in time were anonymous does give them comparability. We also use informal interviews, conducted in the same manner and in the same neighborhood as the set from the first period, to obtain some qualitative information.

Overall, the 2003 cohort was in a better situation than the 1994 cohort in several ways. The current cohort was more likely to be U.S. born and less likely to be recent arrivals. Their parents were generally better edu-cated. With fewer disruptions associated with refugee flight, they were more likely to live in two-parent homes. However, contradictory outcomes emerged despite such favorable contextual factors.

We highlight the delinquency trend using the three measures that we found most central from our research in *Growing Up American:* drug use, alcohol use to the point of drunkenness, and confrontation with the police. We caution that, because our 1994 survey was a school-based sur-vey and the current one is a neighborhood-based survey, responses of the two surveys may not be entirely consistent with each other. Thus our

TABLE 6.1
*Frequency of Drug Use, Alcohol Use, and Confrontations with the Police among
Vietnamese Youth, 1994 and 2003*

	1994		2003	
	%	N	%	N
Drug Use				
Never	89.3	359	37.9	81
1 to 5 times	2.0	8	47.1	101
More than 5 times	8.7	35	15.0	32
Alcohol Use				
Never	77.4	311	31.8	68
1 to 5 times	7.9	32	45.3	97
More than 5 times	14.7	59	22.9	49
Times Stopped by Police				
Never	77.9	313	37.4	80
1 to 5 times	14.9	60	57.9	124
More than 5 times	7.2	29	4.7	10
N	100	402	100	214

interpretation of the data focuses more on highlighting the trends and patterns among Vietnamese youth in the neighborhood than on generalizing them to the entire group in the United States.

Disturbingly, all three forms of delinquency seem to have become more common from one cohort to another, as shown in table 6.1. Almost all (90 percent) of those we surveyed reported that they had never used illegal drugs in 1994, but by 2003 this percentage had gone down to only 38 percent. The percentage of those who had used drugs more than five times had increased from under 9 percent to 15 percent.

Alcohol use to the point of drunkenness had also increased. Most (77 percent) of the respondents surveyed in 1994 said in the earlier survey that they had never been drunk, but around one-third (32 percent) reported so in the current survey. Nearly a quarter in the current survey said that they had been drunk more than five times, compared to just 15 percent in 1994.

Confrontation with the police had become more frequent too. The majority of the respondents (nearly 80 percent) surveyed in 1994 reported that they had never been stopped by the police, but only 37 percent reported so in the current survey. The percentage of those who said they had been stopped by the police more than five times was slightly smaller in 2003 than in 1994. Still, the general trend was much more contact with law enforcement at the later date.

While the number of Vietnamese youth who had never been involved in any form of delinquent behavior dropped substantially, by more than 100 percent, it was no longer as easy as it had been a decade ago to place young people into two distinct categories, "delinquents" and "nondelinquents," as we did in our research for *Growing Up American*.[8] Table 6.2 illustrates the trend in more detail. Using cluster analysis of the 1994 survey, shown in the first two columns, we found that the Vietnamese youth fell fairly distinctly into two separate groups on the three measures of delinquency. Moreover, the delinquents were a relatively small portion of all the adolescents in this neighborhood (less than 1 percent). Further, the U-shape distribution was easily discernible: 94 percent of those in the delinquent cluster reported using drugs more than five times, while 98 percent of the nondelinquents reported that they had never used drugs; nearly 92 percent of those in the delinquent cluster had used alcohol to the point of drunkenness, while 85 percent of those in the nondelinquent cluster reported that they had never been drunk; and 47 percent of those in the delinquent cluster reported that they had been stopped by the police for more than five times, while 84 percent of those in the nondelinquent cluster reported that they had never been stopped by the police. The 1994 data suggest that the delinquents and the nondelinquents were distinctly "bad" and "good" kids. In fact, both adults and youth in the Vietnamese enclave that we studied could easily tell the "good kids" from the

TABLE 6.2

Drug Use, Alcohol Use, and Confrontations with the Police among Vietnamese Youth by Delinquency Clustering, 1994 and 2003

	1994		2003	
	Delinquent Cluster	Nondelinquent Clluster	Delinquent Cluster	Nondelinquent Cluster
Drug Use				
Never	0	98.1	0	100.0
1 to 5 times	0	1.9	75.9	0
More than 5 times	94.4	0	24.1	0
Alcohol Use				
Never	0	85.0	2.3	80.2
Once	8.3	7.9	59.9	19.8
More than 5 times	91.7	7.1	36.8	0
Times Stopped by Police				
Never	19.4	83.6	12.8	77.8
Once	33.3	13.1	79.7	22.2
More than 5 times	47.3	3.3	7.5	0
N	100	402	100	214

"bad kids." And this general observation reflected an actual split in the young people.

Nearly a decade later, our cluster analysis of the 2003 survey showed that nearly two-thirds of Vietnamese youth fell into the "delinquent" cluster (133 in the delinquent cluster as opposed to 81 in the nondelinquent cluster), which alarmingly contrasts with less than 1 percent in the earlier survey. However, the clustering itself appeared less distinct and more problematic. We no longer see a U-shaped distribution as revealed in our earlier survey, with respondents reporting either a great deal of undesirable behavior or none at all. In 2003, for example, fewer of those in the delinquent cluster reported using drugs, getting drunk, or being stopped by the police more than five times, but more reported engaging in these kinds of behavior one to five times. Even among those in the nondelinquent cluster in 2003, the percentages of those who had been drunk once or had been stopped by the police once were much higher than in the earlier survey.

The seemingly more advantageous contextual factors—more likely to be born in the United States, to have college-educated parents, and to live in two-parent families—did not seem to significantly reduce the overall tendency of the current cohort to engage in delinquent behavior. In our 1994 survey, 67 percent of the respondents were U.S. born, while 33 percent were foreign born (including those arriving at very young ages). By contrast, 84 percent of the respondents in our 2003 survey were U.S. born. Nativity was associated with delinquency clustering differently at two time points. In 1994, 91 percent of those in the delinquent cluster were U.S. born. But by 2003, the association became even more pronounced: almost all (99 percent) of those in the delinquent cluster were U.S. born.

Parental education seemed to be closely associated with delinquency clustering at two time points. For example, those in the delinquent cluster were more likely than those in the nondelinquent cluster to have fathers and mothers with less than high school educations and less likely to have parents with at least some college education. However, such associations became less discernible in the current cohort. For example, none of those in the 1994 delinquent cluster had college-educated fathers or mothers, but more than a third of those in the 2003 delinquent cluster had college-educated fathers, and 9 percent had college-educated mothers.

Family structure continued to suggest a positive association with delinquency clustering, given that family disruption was usually found to be related to problematic behavior among juveniles. Those from two-parent families were less likely to fall into the delinquent cluster than into the nondelinquent cluster in 1994. However, this association had nearly disappeared by 2003: those from two-parent families were as likely to fall into the delinquent cluster as into the nondelinquent cluster.

To address these obvious contradictory outcomes, we turn now to our earlier conclusions about acculturation and maladaptation in the Vietnamese community and attempt to understand changes in the light of these conclusions.

Acculturation

In our research for *Growing Up American*, we found that Vietnamese parents, other adults, and young people had specific stereotyped ideas about "bad" kids. They usually gave concrete descriptions of the attitudes and behaviors of those they considered "bad" kids: spending too much of their time "hanging out" on streets or public places, rather than staying at home; while at home, not getting along or cooperating with parents or other family members and not contributing to family chores; dressing and acting like other American youth in their schools and in the neighborhood; acquiring the tastes and interests of other American youth, such as playing loud American music; showing little interest in Vietnamese culture and Vietnamese ways of doing things. In short, the "bad" kids in the eyes of many Vietnamese adults were those who had been acculturated into American youth subcultures.

The descriptions of problem youth given by Vietnamese parents and other adults prompted us to include in our 1994 survey a number of items regarding tastes and interests. We asked respondents how much they liked or disliked Vietnamese music, helping around the house, reading, participating in school clubs, watching television, hanging out on streets or in public places, having one's nose pierced, and listening to rap music. For the purpose of brevity, we report in table 6.3 only the percentages that gave "likes or likes very much" answers.

Our earlier survey showed clearly that the delinquent and nondelinquent clusters were divided in their interests and activities along lines suggested by the Vietnamese. Those in the delinquent cluster were less likely than those in the nondelinquent cluster to report that they liked listening to traditional Vietnamese music, helping around the house, reading, and participating in school clubs but were more likely to report that they liked

TABLE 6.3
*Tastes or Interests (Rated "Likes" or "Likes Very Much") by Delinquency
Clustering among Vietnamese Youth, 1994 and 2003*

| | 1994 | | 2003 | |
	Delinquent Cluster	Nondelinquent Cluster	Delinquent Cluster	Nondelinquent Cluster
Traditional Vietnamese music	9.5	67.7	1.5	32.1
Helping around the house	19.1	58.8	0	22.2
Reading	7.1	49.8	3.8	43.2
Participating in school clubs	14.2	52.9	9.0	45.7
Watching TV	95.2	82.3	78.9	80.2
Hanging out	95.2	82.3	93.2	76.5
Pierced noses	21.5	2.7	20.3	43.2
Rap music	83.4	33.5	92.5	76.5
N	36	366	133	81

watching television, hanging out, having their nose pierced, and listening to rap music. That is, the delinquents were more detached from things Vietnamese or things approved by the Vietnamese and more attracted to things viewed by Vietnamese adults as "too American," while the non-delinquents leaned more toward tastes and interests approved of by the adult Vietnamese community.

In 2003, there was a tendency toward a greater detachment from things Vietnamese or things approved by the Vietnamese community for both the delinquent and nondelinquent groups. The putative delinquents who enjoyed traditional Vietnamese music went down from less than 10 percent to barely 2 percent, while the putative nondelinquents who liked it decreased by half, from 68 percent to 32 percent. Both groups also declined in their interest in doing housework over time. While 19 percent of those in the delinquent cluster and nearly 60 percent of those in the nondelinquent cluster reported that they liked helping around the house in 1994, none of the delinquents and only 22 percent of the nondelinquents expressed such interest in 2003. Moreover, the taste for reading decreased substantially for both groups over the period between the two surveys. The interest in participating in school clubs also decreased, although this retained somewhat greater popularity than reading. While those in the nondelinquent cluster were more likely than those in the delinquent cluster to be interested in reading and school social activities, these nonproblematic young people seemed to become more like the problematic ones in their interests in things that used to be considered desirable by the Vietnamese community.

It is odd, but interesting, that watching television became less popular with both groups. However, perhaps we should not make too much of this, considering that the overwhelming majority of young people in both groups and at both points in time liked watching television. Perhaps the slight decrease was due to an increase in the availability of other sorts of entertainment, such as computer games, but this is purely speculation.

"Hanging out" was often taken as a key characteristic of delinquent youth in the Vietnamese enclave under study. As a police document on Vietnamese gangs that we quoted in *Growing Up American* observed, "Being a gang member involves a lot of 'hanging out.'" Gangbangers hang out in pool halls, in coffee shops, in game rooms, and on the street.[9] Still, there is hanging out on streets or in public places, and there is hanging out in private homes. Meeting one's friends at the mall or at home may qualify as "hanging out" just as well as standing on the street corner smoking cigarettes. We should be mindful that this item may reflect a wide range of behavior. The majority of young people in both groups and at both points in time actually liked hanging out. Still, the delinquents were notably more likely to say that they liked it or liked it very much. There was a light decrease in this activity over time for both groups. It may be that there was very little real change in this behavior because it was so popular among adolescents to begin with.

Having one's nose pierced was another characteristic associated by the ethnic community with delinquency in the mid-1990s. Even though it was not as popular as hanging out, delinquents were seven times as likely as nondelinquents to express an interest in having it done, as revealed in our 1994 survey (22 percent vs. 3 percent). Strangely enough, those in the delinquent cluster were only half as likely as those in the nondelinquent cluster to report that they liked or liked very much this type of ornamentation in 2003 (20 percent vs. 43 percent).

Finally, rap music picked up in popularity. This reflected general trends in the larger popular culture. In the 1990s, rap and associated forms of music were beginning to enter the mainstream, and they have spread more widely since then. Our 2003 survey showed that most Vietnamese youth in both groups liked listening to rap music, although it was still somewhat more popular in the delinquent cluster than in the nondelinquent cluster.

Some of the differences between the two surveys, as shown in table 6.3, may simply be due to changes in fashions. Nevertheless, we can identify two important trends: First, the nondelinquents became more like the delinquents in their tastes and interests. Second, not only did the number

of young people classified as nondelinquents shrink, but the kinds of activities and interests associated by people in the community with the
"good kids" became less favored by most of the young people. If we com-
bine these results with those shown in tables 6.1 and 6.2, there would
appear to be a definite shift toward less desirable behavior and toward the
kinds of self-presentation and self-expression associated with less desirable behavior.

In the mid-1990s, we argued that looking at the tastes and interests of
Vietnamese adolescents could provide some insight into what their elders
meant by describing the problematic young people as being too "Americanized." In the elders' eyes, "Americanized" youth included those who
were highly acculturated into the local youth subculture and those who
were sharply distinguished in tastes and interests from those who remained strongly attached to the Vietnamese community. Today, a general
trend has become clear: more and more adolescents are moving closer to
the subculture of their American peers and away from their Vietnamese
community. However, those in the nondelinquent cluster tended to report
having more white friends than those in the delinquent cluster.

Peer Group Association

Acculturation, as we pointed out in Growing Up American, is a matter of
social contact, or peer group association, as well as of cultural expression.
Since so many young people liked to "hang out," we might want to ask:
Who are they hanging out with? Table 6.4 shows the racial composition
of friendship groups. In 1994, we found that about one-third of the Vietnamese youth in either group had no white friends and that no one in the
delinquent group had mostly white friends. By 2003, there was a significant increase in contact with whites for both groups, although such contact still remained limited.

Similarly, contact with blacks was not very frequent, even though the
Vietnamese lived in a black-dominant neighborhood and attended black-
majority schools, but such contact had increased over time. In 1994, the
modal category for both groups was having "some" black friends. In 2003,
a clear majority of those in the delinquent cluster and nearly half of those
in the nondelinquent cluster reported that at least half of their friends
were black. It also seems that social contact with African American young
people was more common among those in the delinquent cluster than

TABLE 6.4

Distribution of Vietnamese, Black, and White Friends by Delinquency
Clustering among Vietnamese Youth, 1994 and 2003

	1994		2003	
	Delinquent Cluster	Nondelinquent Cluster	Delinquent Cluster	Nondelinquent Cluster
White Friends				
None	36.1	32.0	44.4	37.0
Some	63.9	63.4	26.3	27.2
At least half	0	4.6	29.3	35.8
Black Friends				
None	2.8	20.2	9.0	32.1
Some	63.9	70.2	12.0	21.0
At least half	33.3	9.6	79.0	46.9
Vietnamese Friends				
None	8.3	0.5	1.5	0.0
Some	8.4	8.8	12.8	3.7
About half	16.7	.3	22.6	17.3
Most or almost all	66.6	81.4	63.1	79.0
N	36	366	133	81

among those in the nondelinquent cluster at both points in time. At this point, some caveats may be in order. First, it would be incorrect and unfair to infer, on the basis of this association, that there is anything intrinsically "delinquent" about having black friends. In fact, the data showed that quite a few nondelinquents reported having many black friends, and this reporting told us nothing about who those friends were, other than their race. Second, we were not sure whether someone who said that at least half of his or her friends were black or white actually had a friendship group that was composed of mostly non-co-ethnic members.

On the first caveat, those familiar with our earlier work may recall that this Vietnamese enclave is located in a low-income, minority neighborhood in which blacks make up nearly all the non-Vietnamese residents and that most of the Vietnamese children attended black-majority public schools. It makes sense, then, that our respondents in both surveys would report more contact with black peers than with white peers. It is also clear that the Vietnamese young people who had friendship ties with non-Vietnamese in the neighborhood would be associating with African American young people. On the second caveat, it should be kept in mind that these items are fairly rough ordinal indicators of the extent of social contacts with different peer groups. We do not believe that our respondents actually calculated the proportions of white, black, and Vietnamese friends at either point in time.

With regard to contacts with Vietnamese friends, it is fairly clear that the peer groups of these young people in both clusters and at both points in time were primarily Vietnamese. The nondelinquents were slightly more likely to report primarily Vietnamese social circles than the delinquents, and this remained constant over time. While those in the delinquent cluster tended to have more ties to outsiders than those in the nondelinquent cluster, a large majority in both clusters reported that "most or almost all" of their friends were Vietnamese in 1994 as well as in 2003.

Given that most of these young people liked hanging out and that they were apparently hanging out mostly with other Vietnamese adolescents, the question arises: Who were these Vietnamese friends? Would the Vietnamese friends of the delinquents be more "Americanized" than those of the nondelinquents? To explore this possibility, we looked at the language use of our respondents. Table 6.5 shows reported frequencies of speaking Vietnamese with friends in 1994 and in 2003.

Vietnamese youth who said that they never spoke Vietnamese with their friends were definitely in the minority at both points in time, but the percentages who said so did increase significantly for both groups, from 17 percent to 31 percent for the delinquent group and from 3 percent to 10 percent for the nondelinquent group. It is interesting to note that the percentages of those who said that they always spoke Vietnamese with their friends also increased over time but increased most markedly in the nondelinquent group, from 17 percent to 31 percent. Overall, those in the delinquent group remained much less likely to speak Vietnamese with their friends than those in the nondelinquent group.

TABLE 6.5

Frequency of Speaking Vietnamese with Friends by Delinquency Clustering among Vietnamese Youth, 1994 and 2003

	1994		2003	
	Delinquent Cluster	Nondelinquent Cluster	Delinquent Cluster	Nondelinquent Cluster
Never	16.7	2.5	30.8	9.9
Seldom	22.2	9.0	35.3	13.6
Sometimes	27.8	31.7	18.8	28.4
Usually	30.6	39.9	11.3	17.2
Always	2.7	16.9	3.8	30.9
N	36	366	133	81

What are we to make of these changes over time? In *Growing Up American,* we quoted a social worker active among troubled Vietnamese youth who told us that the youth he worked with wanted "to be American." But he went on to explain: "[W]hat they know about America is usually the worst part of it. They listen to rap songs about shooting policemen and watch movies with everybody killing each other. A lot of the American kids they know are kids who skip school, or quit school, and get in a lot of trouble. So, I think the problem is they're becoming part of the wrong part of America."[10] We argued that the so-called "bad" kids had not just failed to find a place in their own ethnic community. Instead, they had their own established social networks, their own systems of support and control, and their own accepted values and attitudes. They had formed something of an ethnic oppositional culture, existing both at the margins of their own community and at the margins of mainstream American society. But why should the characteristics of this oppositional culture have spread, so that the number of those showing signs of problem behavior increased? Why would even those who were apparently not problematic at all have taken on so many of the traits of the problematic group? To answer these questions, we return to the idea of contexts and look more closely at how the social contexts of Vietnamese American youth may have changed over time.

Multiple Contexts of Alienation and Integration

Our research in the mid-1990s led us to conclude that the apparent bifurcation of Vietnamese American youth was related to their acculturation to American society. In our fieldwork and survey data, we found that problematic behavior seemed more common among those who had spent almost all their lives in the United States and had become highly acculturated. Increasing problematic behavior would be consistent with the fact that most Vietnamese American youth now spend all their lives in the United States and have generally become more acculturated than their uncles, aunts, and much older siblings. Still, to understand why the trend toward problematic behavior may have occurred and may have affected more young people over time, it will be helpful to turn to a revised and updated version of the model of multilevel social integration that we developed in *Growing Up American.*[11]

We have proposed an approach to social integration that takes into account the effects of alienation or integration of Vietnamese youth at four

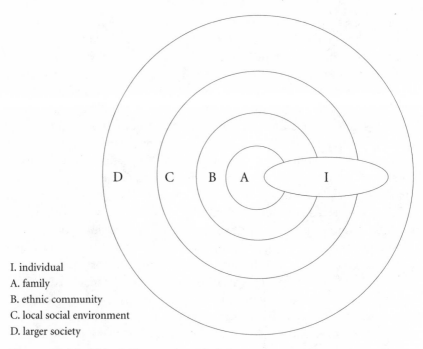

I. individual
A. family
B. ethnic community
C. local social environment
D. larger society

Fig. 6.2. Multilevel Social Integration, Ideal Case

contextual levels: the family, the ethnic community, the local environment, and the larger society. Following Uri Bronfenbrenner, we conceive of a set of relations among family members as an ecosystem, in which ongoing processes promote adaptation to a larger environment.[12] However, the immediate social environment may also be seen as an ecosystem, a pattern of interdependence among families and other social units, which makes possible adaptation to a still larger environment. Thus interactions among individual family members enable them to function in a community setting, and interactions among families and other primary groups determine how the community will act as a mechanism for adapting to broader social and economic exigencies.

The circles in figure 6.2 offer an approximate illustration of how a family system may integrate an individual into larger systems. Note that the oval representing the individual overlaps all of the systems, since individuals do participate in their own families, in their ethnic communities, in the local social environment, and in the larger society. In this ideal representation, however, the family is at the very center of the systems in which the

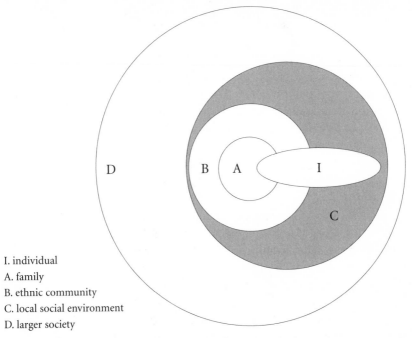

I. individual
A. family
B. ethnic community
C. local social environment
D. larger society

Fig. 6.3. Multilevel Social Integration, in the Marginal Social Environment

individual participates, and each larger circle symmetrically contains each smaller circle. In the ideal case, the family is well integrated into the ethnic community, the ethnic community is well integrated into the local social environment, and the local social environment is well integrated into the larger society.

In this concentric model, problems in adaptation may occur because an individual is insufficiently integrated into an effective family system, because the family is insufficiently integrated into an immediate social system (such as an ethnic community), or because of problems in the integration of the immediate system into the larger surrounding social patterns. When the local social environment is a marginal one (i.e., a relatively low-income area with high rates of crime and juvenile delinquency), integration into the family and community systems is especially important because family and community must direct young people away from the local social environment to prepare those young people for society at large. Figure 6.3, representing the situation of family and community in a marginal local social environment, captures this possibility.

Under the conditions signified by figure 6.3, successful integration into the larger society depends on the fit between familial and ethnic social systems on the one hand and on the fit between the ethnic social systems and the larger society on the other. The local social environment, including both American and Americanized peer groups, pulls young people toward normative orientations that are at variance with those of the larger society. The more that families function to pull young people into the ethnic community and the more the ethnic community guides them toward normative orientations consistent with those of the larger society, the less those young people are drawn toward the alternative social circles of local youth.

In our earlier work, we argued that individual young people had moved toward the local social environment of the oppositional youth subculture because their families were marginal to the ethnic community, and therefore insufficient to connect them to the ties of that community, or because absent or inadequately functioning families were unable to counter the attractions of the local environment. However, as shown above, today's Vietnamese American young people are more likely than those of the 1990s to come from intact families and have more educated parents. We believe that what has happened is that both the families and the community have become more porous, more open to outside influences over time. We illustrate this phenomenon in figure 6.4.

Systems of ethnic social ties still exist, and families still take part in them. But those systems pose less of a barrier to the outside than they did previously. As one resident of the Vietnamese neighborhood remarked to one of the authors recently, "It's so hard to keep up our culture and traditions when you've been in this country so long. Our children think that Vietnam is very far away, and sometimes we just can't pass things on to them." Even with intact families and with an existing Vietnamese community, it is increasingly difficult for families or communities to function as sealed subsystems. English-speaking children in Vietnamese families are bringing a world different from that of their parents and other elders into their homes and neighborhoods.

Conclusion

Despite the glowing media praise for Vietnamese overachievers in past decades, Vietnamese Americans are facing serious challenges in the twenty-first century. In this chapter, we have examined behavioral and attitudinal

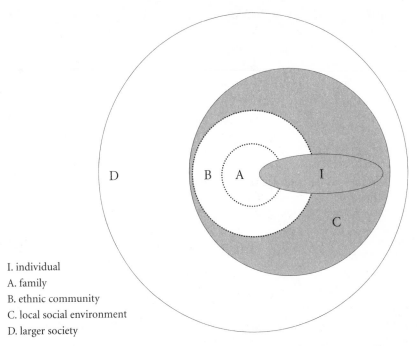

I. individual
A. family
B. ethnic community
C. local social environment
D. larger society

Fig. 6.4. Multilevel Social Integration, in the Marginal Social Environment, Porous Families and Communities

trends among Vietnamese youth, contrasting recently gathered data with data collected in the mid-1990s from the same Vietnamese enclave in New Orleans that we studied nearly ten years ago. This recent cohort of Vietnamese adolescents is mostly U.S. born and is growing up in an ethnic context quite different from that of the older cohort of the mid-1990s. We find that bifurcation is continuing but that the ranks of the "valedictorians" or "achievers" are getting smaller, while those of the "delinquents" are growing. Moreover, generation gaps within Vietnamese families are becoming greater, and the families are less able than previously to channel their children through systems of ethnic social relations.

Our examination leads us to conclude that delinquency is likely to become a more serious problem among Vietnamese adolescents in the foreseeable future. While the "Vietnamese valedictorians" celebrated in the media in earlier years will not disappear, it does seem that they will become less common, and it does look as if the parents of today's Vietnamese youth are likely to face more of the kinds of problems that affect other minority communities in the United States. For immigrant groups in general, these results suggest that we should see acculturation and assimilation into American society as neither purely positive nor purely negative. However, our findings suggest that the acculturation of new immigrant groups is likely to be attended by some serious difficulties as new generations grow up in this country.

NOTES

1. Zhou and Bankston (1994, 1998); Bankston and Zhou (1995a, 1995b, 1996, 1997); Banskton, Caldas, and Zhou (1997).
2. Ashton (1985); Arias (1987); Caplan, Whitmore, and Choy (1989); Caplan, Choy, and Whitmore (1991).
3. Bergman (1991); Butterfield (1992); Davidian (1992).
4. Willoughby (1993).
5. *Los Angeles Times* (1994).
6. Portes and Zhou (1993); Zhou and Bankston (1998).
7. Zhou and Bankston (1998).
8. Zhou and Bankston (1998: ch. 8).
9. Willoughby (1993: 2).
10. Zhou and Bankston (1998: 201).
11. Zhou and Bankston (1998: ch. 8).
12. Bronfenbrenner (1979).

REFERENCES

Arias, Roberto. 1987. "Twelve Years out of Vietnam Air Force Cadet Hoang Nhu Tran Discovers the Sky's the Limit." *People's Weekly,* 27 (June 15): 45–46.

Ashton, Gail. 1985. "Vietnamese Make Grade in Classroom." *Times-Picayune,* April 23, A1+.

Bankston, Carl L., III, Stephen J. Caldas, and Min Zhou. 1997. "The Academic Achievement of Vietnamese American Students: Ethnicity as Social Capital." *Sociological Focus* 30:1–16.

Bankston, Carl L., III, and Min Zhou. 1995a. "The Effects of Minority Language Literacy on the Academic Achievement of Vietnamese Youth in New Orleans." *Sociology of Education* 68:1–17.

———. 1995b. "Religious Participation, Ethnic Identification, and Social Adjustment among Vietnamese American Adolescents." *Sociological Quarterly* 36: 523–34.

————. 1996. "The Ethnic Church, Ethnic Identification, and the Social Adjustment of Vietnamese Adolescents." *Review of Religious Research* 38:18–37.

————. 1997. "The Social Adjustment of Vietnamese American Adolescents: Evidence for a Segmented Assimilation Approach." *Social Science Quarterly* 78: 508–23.

Bergman, Bryan. 1991. "Terror in the Streets: Ruthless Asian Gangs Bring a New Wave of Violence to Canadian Cities." *Maclean's*, March 25, 18+.

Bronfenbrenner, Yuri. 1979. *The Ecology of Human Development.* Cambridge: Cambridge University Press.

Butterfield, Fox. 1992. "Gangs Terrorize Asians near Boston." *New York Times*, February 7, A17.

Caplan, Nathan, Marcella H. Choy, and John K. Whitmore. 1991. *Children of the Boat People: A Study of Educational Success.* Ann Arbor: University of Michigan Press.

Caplan, Nathan, John K. Whitmore, and Marcella H. Choy. 1989. *The Boat People and Achievement in America: A Study of Family Life, Hard Work, and Cultural Values.* Ann Arbor: University of Michigan Press.

Davidian, Geoff. 1992. "Dread in Port Arthur: Viet Community Fears Retribution after Arrests in Slayings." *Houston Chronicle*, September 18, A1.

Los Angeles Times. 1994. *Los Angeles Times Poll: Vietnamese in Southern California.* Storrs, CT: Roper Center for Public Opinion Research.

Portes, Alejandro, and Min Zhou. 1993. "The New Second Generation: Segmented Assimilation and Its Variants." *Annals of the American Academy of Political and Social Science* 530 (November): 74–96.

Southeast Asia Resource Action Center. 2003. "Americans from Cambodia, Laos, and Vietnam: Statistics." January 27. Retrieved November 8, 2005, from www.searac.org.

Willoughby, Jack. 1993. "Vietnamese Gangs and Other Criminals." Training aid for novice police officers. New Orleans Police Department, New Orleans, LA.

Zhou, Min, and Carl L. Bankston III. 1994. "Social Capital and the Adaptation of the Second Generation: The Case of Vietnamese Youth in New Orleans." *International Migration Review* 28:821–45.

————. 1998. *Growing Up American: How Vietnamese Children Adapt to Life in the United States.* New York: Russell Sage Foundation.

Chapter 7

Beyond Conflict and Controversy
Blacks, Koreans, and Jews in Urban America

Jennifer Lee

Racial violence in the United States may be as old as the nation itself, but in no single period of the twentieth century was there anything that approached the chain reaction of race riots that began on July 18, 1964, in Harlem. The Harlem riot of 1964 began the prolonged urban black protest that raced through seven major cities before ending in Philadelphia on the last day of August. During the riots, people of all ages dashed through the commercial thoroughfares, broke windows, and looted merchandise from neighborhood businesses. They worked over small and large businesses alike, taking groceries, liquor, furniture, appliances, clothing, drugs, and items held in pawnshops. Rioters generally looted stores whose merchandise they could drink, wear, or readily sell, and what they could not carry they threw in the streets. Credit records in pawnshops, furniture stores, and grocery markets were consistently destroyed, providing evidence that there was some method involved in the frenzy and fury of the riots.[1]

Black storeowners were spared as long as they made it to their shops in time to place identifying insignia outside their store. Signs such as "Blood Brother," "Colored," and "Poor Working Negro" were placed in their windows in the hopes that rioters would bypass their own. Even the owners of a Chinese restaurant displayed a sign that read, "We are colored too," sparing them from the rioters.[2] Black business owners who lived further away and were unable to make it to their stores in time were not as fortunate; their stores, too, were ransacked. Service-oriented businesses such as beauty salons and barbershops—typical black retail niches—received the least amount of damage during the riots, partly because they were black owned and partly because looters had nothing to take. When the riots finally died down on August 31, 1964, the toll count amounted to 112 damaged stores in Harlem and 726 damaged stores and offices in Philadelphia.[3] Jewish storeowners, who predominated in black neighborhoods at the time, were particularly hard hit.

Following the wave of riots in the 1960s, the overall mood was one of desperation and fear, and most Jewish merchants expressed panic at the possibility of being looted, robbed, or personally harmed. Their fears were not unwarranted, prompting many of them to carry weapons, reduce their inventory, close up shop early, and place barricades on all windows and doors.[4] Jewish merchants in black neighborhoods faced a quandary— Should they stay or leave? Some Jewish intellectuals argued that it was time for Jews to move out of neighborhoods like Harlem and Watts. For instance, conveying his opinion in the *National Review*, Max Geltman maintained that "Jewish storekeepers who remain today in Harlem or in Watts, encamped as it were in enemy territory, can expect future forays into their business establishments when the next riot breaks out. For them a process of disengagement should suggest itself, away from Harlem and away from Watts and away from other such volatile neighborhoods in other cities."[5]

Convinced that they had not seen the last of the violence and certain that police protection was inadequate, more than half of the Jewish business owners in the inner city wished to sell their businesses and relocate.[6] The decision to leave was complicated because following the riots there were few prospective buyers, and to simply close up shop would have resulted in financial ruin. However, faced with rising crime, cancellation of insurance policies, and decreasing profitability, and surrounded by residents who questioned their legitimacy in neighborhoods in which they did not reside, some Jewish merchants simply boarded up stores if they could not find interested buyers.

By the early 1970s, the future of small business in the United States seemed bleak. The consequences of the riots were disastrous for retail businesses and affected both the objective and the subjective situation of inner-city retailers.[7] While Jewish merchants phased out of the inner city, a new group of immigrants were positioned to enter the inner-city retail niche. What nobody predicted in the early 1970s was that this retail niche would soon become a vibrant and profitable economy with the entrance of America's newcomers. Although Jews still retained a strong hold on some of the largest and most lucrative retail niches such as appliances and furniture, ethnic succession has altered the face of inner-city retailing from Jewish to Korean ownership.

Like Jewish merchants who once dominated the inner-city retail niche, Korean immigrant merchants experienced their share of violence and urban riots, especially during the final decade of the twentieth century, which rivaled the 1960s as one of the most tumultuous periods in black communities across the United States. The decade opened with an eighteen-month boycott of a Korean-owned fruit and vegetable market in the Flatbush section of Brooklyn, New York. The relationship between black customers and Korean immigrant merchants was quickly popularized and exploited by the media with splashy newspaper headings that read "Will Black Merchants Drive Koreans from Harlem?" "Blacks, Koreans Struggle to Grasp Thread of Unity," "Cultural Conflict," and "Scapegoating New York's Koreans."[8]

Racial tensions climaxed in South Central on April 29, 1992, after an all-white, Simi Valley jury acquitted four white police officers of beating twenty-five-year-old African American motorist Rodney King. The "not guilty" verdict sparked the Los Angeles riot—the first multiethnic riot in U.S. history. The nation remained transfixed as it witnessed buildings in South Central and Koreatown set aflame while inner-city residents looted neighborhood stores, taking everything from televisions and VCRs to food and diapers. The L.A. riot proved to be the worst domestic uprising in the twentieth century, ending with 16,291 arrested, 2,383 injured, 500 fires, and 52 dead. Korean merchants suffered almost half of the property damage, amounting to more than $400 million and affecting more than 2,300 Korean-owned businesses in Los Angeles.

However, racial violence was not limited to Korean immigrant merchants. Several years later on December 8, 1995, an African American man named Roland Smith walked into Freddy's, a Jewish-owned clothing store on Harlem's 125th Street, with a .38 caliber gun and a can of paint thinner. Four men—three white and one Guyanese Indian—dashed for the door, and Smith shot each of them, critically wounding two. Moments later the police arrived, but it was too late. Smith had set Freddy's clothing store ablaze and then made his way to the back of the store, where he shot himself. Unable to escape, the seven nonblack employees of Freddy's were trapped in the store and died in the flames. The firebombing of Freddy's made the front page of the New York Times, with headlines that read, "In Nightmare of Anger, Store Becomes Flaming Madhouse" and "Death on 125th Street: A Scene of Carnage."[9]

I purposely begin this chapter with images of urban riots, picket lines, and firebombings because these powerful images have seared into the public's consciousness that racial warfare is a fact of life in black communities, with immigrant merchants pitted against black customers. And because few people living outside black communities have firsthand experience of the commercial life in these neighborhoods, journalistic accounts often become a major means of defining reality.

However, I argue that media accounts have been biased toward conflict and controversy and do not reflect the full range of commercial life and merchant-customer relations in black communities. Conflict may be raw material for newspaper headlines, television leads, and even scholarly research, but there is a wide gap between the nature of merchant-customer relations in black communities and the public image of these relations. In this chapter, I provide a more nuanced portrait of the commercial relations between immigrant merchants and black customers in black communities and demonstrate that the prevailing image of racial conflict is at odds with most merchant-customer interactions. This reassessment of ethnic conflict contributes to a number of literatures, including the scholarly work on the immigration-violence nexus, which has thus far tended to concentrate on completed acts of violence (e.g., homicide) while ignoring the many ways in which immigrants seek to prevent violent outcomes. In this chapter, immigrants attempt to ameliorate conflict in a way that is at odds with popular stereotypes of immigrants as crime prone.

I contend that an important, untold story is the ordinariness, civility, and routine that immigrant business owners and their employees work to maintain each day. Using an ethnomethodological lens, I examine the ways in which social order, routine, and civility are negotiated and maintained through hundreds of daily interactions between merchants and customers. I demonstrate that while merchant-customer relations are in no way uniform the majority are civil because merchants actively work to manage tensions and smooth out incidents before they escalate into racially charged anger. I dispel the myth of the ubiquity of conflict and argue that civility, routine, and business as usual—rather than conflict—is the norm. Moreover, I argue that the everyday interactions between merchants and customers are *not* the cause of collective protest and conflict. However, because these interactions occur in a context of group subordination, merchant-customer conflict can ignite protest motivations and spur collective action.

Previous Research

Research on merchant-customer relations in poor, urban neighborhoods focuses on points of contention, stressing that disagreements between merchants and customers frequently arise over faulty merchandise, high prices, and exchange policies.[10] Past research has often emphasized Jewish and Korean merchants' role as middlemen who provoke resentment because they are caught between the elites who manufacture products and the poor consumers who buy them.[11] Moreover, customers often believe that middlemen minorities compete with native-born groups and take away opportunities from them. The middleman minority framework is based on the presumption that the merchant-customer relationship is inherently conflictual, and it in turn serves as the basis for the emergence of ethnic conflict. Other researchers underscore the media's role in constructing and reifying interracial conflict among minority groups.[12] And yet another line of research emphasizes the structural context in which Jewish and Korean merchants come into contact with black customers, highlighting that nonblack merchants often serve black customers in urban neighborhoods where poverty, unemployment, and inequality are extreme. Structural conditions such as these create ripe conditions for the emergence of racial conflict in the form of boycotts, firebombings, and urban riots.[13]

However, what these bodies of research have failed to reconcile is that boycotts, firebombings, and riots are anomalous events in inner cities while structural conditions such as poverty, unemployment, and inequality are ever present. Hence, by focusing only on structural conditions or the role of middleman minorities, past researchers have allowed few options beyond conflict and in essence have overpredicted the level of conflict between merchants and customers in urban neighborhoods. In short, these studies may help to explain why conflict emerges, but they cannot account for what happens the rest of the time.

In contrast, I adopt a different approach to the study of merchant-customer relations—an ethnomethodological one—meaning that I focus on the everyday and the local rather than on the larger events like riots, firebombings, or boycotts that erupt only rarely. Ethnomethodology's main theoretical proposal is that there is a self-generating order in concrete activities, and its principal task is to identify the mechanisms by which the social order is locally produced. I argue that this approach is particularly fruitful because, apart from dramatic and contentious events such as boycotts and firebombings, we know little about the nature of merchant-customer relations in black communities.

Using an ethnomethodological lens, I argue that what previous research has overlooked is how nonblack merchants make investments to foster civility, abate tensions, and socially embed their businesses in black communities in order to thwart conflict. However, Jewish and Korean merchants recognize that their efforts to create civility exist within a context of group subordination, where inequality is extreme, and within a framework in which race can inflect interactions. So while black customers may have positive relations with Jewish and Korean merchants, protest motivations emerge against nonblack merchants because of what their businesses symbolize: black economic subordination to other racial and ethnic groups.

Data and Methods

Because merchant-customer relations have been cited as a source of animosity and as a catalyst to conflict, I focus on these interactions as the site of interracial contact and tension. The data are based on seventy-five semistructured, in-depth interviews of African American, Jewish, and Korean merchants, seventy-five semistructured, in-depth interviews with black customers, and participant observation. I chose to interview Jewish and Korean merchants because both of these groups have experienced mobility through self-employment and both have prospered by serving the black community.[14] Korean immigrants today are achieving rates of socioeconomic mobility that parallel the experience of the Jewish immigrants in earlier decades.[15] The media, the politicians, and the public have touted both groups as "model minorities" who have battled discrimination and achieved success through hard work and grit.[16]

However, Jewish and Korean merchants' economic success has come with social costs. Black customers have charged both groups with disrespectful treatment, prejudice, and exploitation of their communities. In addition, black nationalists have accused Jewish and Korean business owners of buying all of the stores in their neighborhoods, draining them of their resources, and failing to "give back" by hiring local residents.[17] Jewish and Korean merchants have also been the targets of boycotts, strikes, and urban riots. Clearly, there are striking parallels between the Jewish and Korean entrepreneurial experience. Therefore, I decided to compare black-Jewish and black-Korean merchant-customer relations in black communities. I then decided to interview African American merchants and compare their experiences with those of their Jewish and Korean counterparts. By adding African American merchants to the study, I am able to understand what merchant-customer relations are like when we hold race constant.

The interviews with the merchants and customers took place in five predominantly black neighborhoods in New York City and Philadelphia with some class variation. Of the five neighborhoods, three are low income and have median household incomes under $20,000 (East Harlem and West Harlem in New York and West Philadelphia), and two are middle income with median household incomes slightly over $35,000 (Jamaica, Queens and Mount Airy, Philadelphia). Table 7.1 illustrates the various characteristics of the five research sites.

Each of the neighborhoods has bustling commercial strips lined with small businesses that offer a variety of merchandise, some of which is

TABLE 7.1
Characteristics of Cities Where Interviews Were Conducted: 1990

Characteristic	New York			Pennsylvania	
	West Harlem	East Harlem	Jamaica, Queens	West Philadelphia	Mount Airy
Total population	55,142	28,448	53,127	48,672	27,675
Median household income ($)	16,767	11,348	35,224	18,394	35,152
% on public assistance	22	42	8	21	8
% below poverty line	34	46	13	27	8
Race (%)					
Black	60	54	28	93	95
White	26	18	39	5	4
Other race	14	27	33	2	1
Place of birth					
% native born	81	90	51	96	97
% foreign born	19	10	49	4	3
Sex (%)					
Male	44	46	49	44	45
Female	56	54	51	56	55
Occupational Status (%)					
Employed	48	40	61	46	67
Unemployed	7	9	6	8	7
Not in labor force	45	51	33	46	26
Education (%)					
Completed high school or more	64	42	72	58	70
Completed college or more	27	4	26	8	17

SOURCE: U.S. Bureau of the Census (1990).
NOTE: West Harlem, East Harlem, and West Philadelphia are low-income neighborhoods; Jamaica, Queens, and Mount Airy are middle-income neighborhoods.

geared specifically to a black clientele, including wigs, ethnic beauty supplies, inner-city sportswear, soul food restaurants, beauty salons, and barbershops. There are also a variety of other businesses that offer furniture, sneakers, jewelry, fruits and vegetables, fresh fish, electronics, and discount household supplies. However, on these shopping strips the large retail chains and department stores that are nearly ubiquitous in white, middle-class neighborhoods and suburban shopping malls are noticeably missing. The absence of large retail chains has left a vacant niche for small-scale entrepreneurs to set up shop in these black communities.[18] The business owners in these neighborhoods include Koreans, Jews, Asian Indians, Latinos, African Americans, and West Indians, while the customers are primarily black. I interviewed fifteen merchants from each of the five research sites, totaling seventy-five merchant interviews.

Additionally, I benefited from participant observation while I worked as a bag checker in a clothing store on 125th Street in West Harlem in July 1996 and as a cashier in a sneaker store in March 1997 on 52nd Street in West Philadelphia. These positions allowed me to be at the field site as an inconspicuous observer and witness the merchants' daily activities and their interactions with customers, providing rich data that would have been missed had I relied on the interview data alone.

To get a complete understanding of the merchant-customer relationship, I hired African American research assistants to conduct interviews of the black customers, something no study has done to date.[19] The research assistants interviewed fifteen black customers from each site, totaling seventy-five customer interviews. All of the customers were local residents who resided and shopped in these communities and were asked specifically about their shopping experiences in Jewish-, Korean-, and black-owned stores in their neighborhoods.

New York and Philadelphia provide a fascinating comparison of two eastern cities that are similar on a number of key dimensions, such as the self-employment rate, the proportion of service sector employment, the rate of unemployment, and the percentage living below the poverty line. However, the two key dimensions on which these cities differ remarkably are the rate of immigration and the number of race riots. New York City leads the country in the percentage of foreign born, with 28.4 percent of its residents born outside the United States, whereas Philadelphia lags far behind, ranking thirty-seventh among U.S. cities, having only 6.6 percent of its residents foreign born.[20] And while Korean immigrants constitute a relatively small portion of New York and Philadelphia's immigrant stream

—rarely more than 3 percent of the legal immigrants who come to these cities each year—they play an important and visible role in the cities' economies.[21]

A second point of divergence is the number of race riots that each city has experienced. Although the Northeast has been a common site of racial unrest, New York has experienced nearly four times as many black race riots as Philadelphia in the latter half of the twentieth century. From 1960 to 1993, there have been twenty-two black race riots in New York compared to only six in Philadelphia.[22] The design of the study allows me to compare merchant-customer relations between African American, Jewish, and Korean merchants on the one hand and black customers on the other in low- and middle-income neighborhoods in two strategically selected cities.

Everyday Commercial Life in Black Communities

Merchant-customer life in New York's Harlem or West Philadelphia is an odd mixture of prosaic routine and explosive tension, friendly customer relations and racial anger. Yet despite the media focus on incidents like the L.A. riot or the firebombing in Harlem, I was most struck by the sheer ordinariness of most merchant-customer relationships. The majority of the interactions between merchants and customers that we witnessed were characterized by civility, routine, and the simple philosophy of business as usual.

In fact, when we interviewed the black customers, the majority said that they routinely experienced positive interactions with the merchants in their communities, and perhaps most surprising is that there is not a great deal of variation across race lines. For example, 59 percent of the black customers we interviewed said their experiences with African American merchants were positive, 55 percent said the same of Jewish merchants, and 53 percent said the same of Korean merchants. About a third of customers said that they received mixed treatment, meaning that they said that they were treated "okay" or "all right."

These figures vary more in terms of the negative experiences, but not as much as one would expect according to the scholarly and journalistic accounts that emphasize conflict. Seven percent of the black customers we interviewed said that they routinely experienced negative treatment in African American–owned businesses, and the figures for Jewish- and

Korean-owned stores were 8 and 16 percent, respectively.[23] Contrary to public opinion, the majority of merchant-customer interactions were, in fact, not negative. The point is that there is a wide gap between the nature of merchant-customer relations in black communities and the public image of these relations. However, what I originally thought to be ordinariness and routine was something much more complex. I soon discovered that merchants, their employees, and the customers made substantial investments to create normalcy and foster civility.

Cultural Brokers

One important way in which nonblack merchants create civility is by hiring black employees and managers to act as "cultural brokers" between them and their predominantly black clientele. They realize that black employees are generally better at dealing with co-ethnics, something that black employees readily recognize. As an African American manager of a Jewish-owned clothing store explained to me, "Sometimes you have to develop a way of talking to people. You have to know who you're talking to. And with most of our trade coming here that's 95 percent black, if you don't have the right way of talking, you're in trouble."

While I was interviewing him, three black customers (one male and two females) interrupted us to purchase a T-shirt. The following conversation between the African American manager and a male customer who attempted to bargain for a discount on his friend's behalf was caught on tape:

Customer: [Begins by saying to the manager] Don't charge her tax, she's broke.
Manager: Why not?

Customer: She's broke.
Manager: No she's not. Nobody's broke. You're never broke. And besides I can see why you have so much money. I can see the all the money written all over your faces. That's the money sign you have on your faces there. It's only $9.73. We'll wait till you're broke. We'll wait till you're broke, and then we'll make a deal. We'll wait till an emergency. It's $9.73 today, and next week we'll talk about it.
Customer: Only $9.73. Next week we'll work on our bargain. Okay, see you next week.

The three young customers left the store without even a grumble. In this interaction, the manager refused to give the customers a discount, yet he handled the interaction with aplomb. In effect, he used flattery to convey to his customers that they appeared to have money and therefore should not need a discount.

This interaction stands in sharp contrast to one that I witnessed unfold between a black male customer and a Korean storeowner while I worked as a cashier in a sneaker store. The customer intended to purchase four pairs of sneakers, each ranging in price from $100 to $140. As the salesman placed the sneakers on the counter for me to ring up, the customer asked him, "How much do I get off for buying all these shoes?" The salesman turned to the Korean storeowner, who replied, "We don't do that here." The customer then fired back, "I'm buying four pairs of shoes, and you won't work with me? Who can I talk to here?" The storeowner repeated more firmly, "Nobody does that here." The customer walked to the register and slammed a wad of bills on the counter. After counting the money and bagging up the sneakers, I handed the customer the four bags and said, "Thanks. Have a nice day." Without looking in my direction, the customer grabbed the bags and walked out of the store.

Although both the Korean merchant and the African American manager denied their customers a discount, the way in which they said "no" was remarkably different. In the first case with the African American manager the customers left without any signs of dissatisfaction, whereas in the second the customer avoided eye contact and abruptly left the store after paying. Here the Korean merchant could have handled the situation very differently and conveyed to the customer that if he could afford to purchase four pairs of expensive sneakers he certainly did not need a discount. The point is that merchants and managers can say "no" to customers in many ways, but most immigrant shop owners do not have the sophisticated interpersonal skills to artfully deal with such customer requests. This may partially account for the fact that the percentage of black customers who said that they routinely experienced negative treatment by Korean-owned businesses was double the percentage of those who said they experienced such treatment by black-owned ones.

More crucially, black employees serve another function; they defuse and deracialize anger. While most merchant-customer interactions are civil, from time to time they erupt into arguments, usually over small economic disputes such as bringing back an item without a receipt or bringing something back that has been used or damaged. These seemingly trivial arguments can quickly become racialized when the merchants are Jewish, Korean, or, for that matter, any nonblack racial group. Here Robert K. Merton's concept of "in-group virtues" and "out-group vices" is useful.[24] Merton noted that the same behavior by members of the in-group and out-group can be differently perceived and defined by in-group members.

While working as a bag checker in West Harlem, I observed the defusing process in action as a Korean merchant was explaining his reliance on black employees to smooth out incidents. He said to me, "If you have black management, no problem, but if you have a Korean manager or whatever, you can get into trouble." On the heels of this logical explanation, a black customer tried to exchange the dirty pants he was wearing for a new pair. The storeowner immediately handed him off to the black manager, who told the man, "I'm not disputing that you bought the pants here, sir, but we wouldn't have sold them to you like that. Look at all our pants here, none of them look like that. That's your hand that made them like that. Here, look at my pocket. If I'm reaching in there all the time and my hand is dirty, then they're going to get dirty. That's just your hand." The Korean storeowner, visibly nervous that the man was not accepting the manager's explanation said, "Call the police." But the black manager reassured him, "We don't need to call the police, he's just drunk. When he comes around tomorrow, he'll come back and apologize." The storeowner then turned to me and said, "If that was a Korean manager, there would have been a little bit of commotion."

Korean merchants are not the only ones to have adopted the strategy of hiring black employees to deracialize tensions; Jewish merchants, too, have embraced this tactic. For instance, a white salesman in a Jewish-owned furniture store explained how easily the "racial element" could disappear if he simply handed the customer off to a black salesperson. As he explained,

> I'm white, and I deal with the black customers. Sometimes you have problems, but 99 percent of the time you never have problems because we always try to deal with the customer. We always have the philosophy that they're right. But always, you're going to have problems that we're not able to solve, but you see that if it gets to a racial point, or if the customer feels that it's racial, then you give him to somebody of his own race, and he cannot say that anymore.

From the perspective of black managers and sales associates, brokering and mediating arguments between the customers and their nonblack employers is just part of the job. They realize all too well that there would be many more racial disputes between the black customers and the nonblack storeowners if they were not present to handle customer gripes. For example, a black manager of a clothing store in Harlem admitted:

> It's an absolute fact that if I weren't the manager they would have more problems with exchanges. It's a fact because the customers always think, "Whitey's trying to get over them." They use that expression. So they will get hostile very fast. The owners would have to change their way of talking very much or either take back a lot of stuff they don't want to take back just to keep the peace because there really would be a hostile situation.

In this instance, the manager noted how customers could easily interpret the refusal to exchange merchandise within a racialized framework.

Racial and ethnic stereotypes are readily available, and when tempers flare, stereotypes can easily be evoked and quickly adopted. Although an individual may have experienced hundreds or even thousands of positive encounters with individuals from out-groups, one negative experience can easily conjure up negative stereotypes that have little to do with the situation at hand. This is especially easy to do when there exist ready-made antiwhite, anti-Semitic, anti-Asian, and anti-immigrant frameworks in which customers can situate their negative experiences with Jewish and Korean merchants. Correlatively, the ready-made negative frameworks about blacks in our society make it all too easy for nonblack merchants to situate their negative encounters with black customers within a racialized frame.

Maternal Brokers

Female merchants fill a similar role to that of black employees. Women—regardless of race or ethnicity—are more likely to perform the "emotional labor" in these stores.[25] Women are more likely to adopt work roles in which they have more contact with their customers. They are more likely to greet and talk to their customers—asking about their families, their children, and other bits of daily trivia and thereby bringing a more humanizing dimension to the commercial encounter. And because women are better able—or simply more willing—to perform the emotional labor, they are positioned at the "front end" in these businesses—usually behind the cash register or on the selling floor—while men assume inconspicuous positions in the background.

Gender also works as an "interactional resource" in fostering civility, since customers perceive women as less threatening. By illustration, while working in West Philadelphia, I witnessed a fight break out between two black male customers outside the store. The middle-aged Korean female merchant immediately ran outside to break up the fight, physically wedging herself between the two young men. They pushed her aside and began fighting again, but the female merchant persisted and managed to break it up, yelling at both of them to stop. After exchanging a few curse words, the men parted in opposite directions.

Visibly shaken by the encounter, the female merchant marched back into the store and yelled at her husband and the male employees for failing to intervene. When I asked why she decided to risk harm to herself and come between the men to break up the fight, she replied, "If they break one of my store windows, that's a big problem! If another customer gets hurt, that's another problem!" Still upset by the fight, she walked to the back room of the store to cool off. I then turned to her husband and asked why he refused to jump to her aid. Initially, he replied, "I don't know." But after a pausing for few seconds, he answered, "They could turn around and fight me, maybe. I don't know."

The Korean man refused to intervene because he feared that the two black men could turn their anger on him. He understood that race and ethnicity could become salient in a way that they did not for his wife. Because her gender made her less of a threat, the Korean female merchant's act of breaking up the fight was interpreted as maternalism rather than confrontation. In essence, cultural and maternal brokers work to ensure that the day-to-day routine runs as smoothly as possible and go to considerable lengths to preserve it.

How Customers Foster Civility

Not only do the merchants and managers actively work to foster civility, but customers also do their part in maintaining the everyday routine, largely by tolerating and not complaining about what could easily be defined as offensive security measures. For instance, some sneaker stores in

West Philadelphia and Harlem give only one sneaker at a time to customers as they try them on for size. Employees initially provide customers —especially teenagers—with only the right sneaker, and if customers wish to try on the left, they must take off the right sneaker and hand it back to the employee. Very seldom did customers complain about this one-shoe-at-a-time try-on policy; instead, most accepted the norms without raising an eyebrow.

Moreover, none of the customers complained about having to check their bags when I worked as a bag checker in a clothing store. Nor did the customers comment on the employees who perched themselves on top of high ladders and watched as they browsed through the store. And while some customers complained about being followed in some of the stores, the complaints largely came from teenagers rather than all customers.

In short, civility was maintained from day to day because merchants, their employees, and customers actively worked to manage and preserve it. Jewish and Korean merchants hired black employees, placed women at the front end of the business, and succumbed to customers' demands to keep the routine in place. And the customers certainly did their part by not voicing complaints against what many could easily interpret as offensive consumer treatment.

From Civility to Conflict and Controversy

Against the backdrop of civility, how can we explain overt incidences of conflict such as the firebombing of the Jewish-owned store or the boycotts of Korea-owned businesses throughout the nation? Herein lies the paradox: although most merchants and customers may have positive relations on an individual level, racial and ethnic conflict persists on a collective level because groups jockey for position in America's racially and ethnically stratified society. Here it is critical to differentiate between individual interactions and group-level dynamics. When tensions run high, something powerful blocks the generalization from positive feelings about individual members of out-groups to the out-group as a whole. In other words, although blacks, Jews, and Koreans may regularly engage in positive interpersonal encounters, individual interactions do not necessarily translate into positively changed views of other groups. This is because imported into interethnic relationships are beliefs and ideologies about opportunity structure and group position.[26] It is precisely when subordinate groups develop a new conception of themselves and challenge their group position in the ethnic hierarchy that everyday routine breaks down and protest motivations surface.[27]

As Jews move up and out of black neighborhoods and new immigrants such as Koreans move in, African Americans witness a succession of groups moving up and out—realizing the American dream of success. The image of immigrants coming into black communities, buying the businesses, and leaving with the profits at night is a provocative one for poor African Americans. They may not object to immigrants per se, but the African Americans we interviewed *do* object to the notion that the foreign born of all types are moving ahead of them, presumably with governmental aid and seemingly at their expense. For instance, an African American resident in West Philadelphia lamented:

> Koreans are getting loans from the banks that Jews own, and I believe that the Jews and the Koreans work together to do African Americans in. And I feel that if it's so easy to come to our country and get these loans and get these grants and get all these different types of things, then why isn't it easy for our people to do this? Because we have been discouraged and we have been stepped on, and it's just a continuous pattern. And it will never stop.

What is especially interesting here is that while black residents may complain about the commercial domination of nonblacks, they continue to patronize Jewish- and Korean-owned stores, sometimes even at the expense of African American merchants. When we asked why they preferred shopping in non-black-owned businesses, the black customers stated that black storeowners generally charged higher prices, sold substandard goods, and offered inferior service. For instance, a male customer in Mount Airy explained why he preferred shopping in Korean- and Jewish-owned stores:

> With the blacks, they get their prices and they try to get more than what it's really worth. But then when you go into the Korean store and the Jew store, they have a reasonable price for you, and not only is it reasonable, they make the price so that they can get you to come back. And that keeps their business going. But in the black store, with the prices being so high, they kind of turn you away, and the business will turn down. After a while they'll close down, and they wonder why.

Black merchants, on the other hand, charged that black customers refused to patronize their own, opting instead to buy from neighboring Jewish and Korean merchants because they had a problem dealing with co-ethnics. For example, a Harlem resident admitted, "Blacks don't buy from each other. They complain about the Koreans, the Jews, and the Arabs, but if a black opens a store in the middle, they go to the same people they complain about. They won't go to the black."

When presented with the choice between racial loyalty and getting the best deal, black customers—like all customers—choose to shop where they can get the most for their money, regardless of who is doing the selling. However, what is important to point out here is that black store-owners charge higher prices not because they want to but because their suppliers charge them higher prices, which is reflected in a higher retail markup. Yet constraints such as these are not visible to the consumer, who is simply looking for the best deal.

One of the ironic twists to this story is that despite the in-group criticism that black customers level against black merchants, the customers we interviewed said that they would like to see more black-owned businesses in their neighborhoods. Most stated that they would like at least three-fourths of the businesses in their communities to be owned by blacks. Initially, this seemed paradoxical, since the customers had just listed a host of complaints about black merchants, but I soon realized that this contradiction reflected the contention between the real and symbolic meaning behind black business ownership.

Although black customers may not patronize "their own" as frequently as immigrant-owned businesses, and may even level complaints about black merchants, the question of who owns the stores in the community is laden with symbolism, translating into far more than what these businesses generate in profit. For the black customers we interviewed, business ownership in their neighborhoods was a powerful indicator of America's racial and ethnic order. It reflected their sense of "group position," that is, where they believed they *ought* to stand vis-à-vis other groups. The dominating presence of non-black-owned businesses, then, was a visible symbol of black economic subordination to other racial and ethnic groups.

Communities such as Harlem and West Philadelphia are spaces that symbolize black culture, pride, and perhaps most importantly, black autonomy. Here blacks are the numerical majority, and black culture is pervasive and celebrated. Images of Martin Luther King Jr., Adam Clayton Powell, Malcolm X, and black autonomy grace storefronts, billboards, street signs, and bookstands. Black neighborhoods are pieces of America over which blacks feel they have—or at the very least should have—authority and control. Therefore, when blacks choose to boycott a Korean-owned fruit and vegetable market or picket a Jewish-owned clothing store, their cause transcends the individual Korean or Jewish retailer. Imported into boycotts and protest motivations are beliefs about group position and black control over black communities, something that became readily apparent in the events that surrounded the firebombing of Freddy's, the Jewish-owned clothing store in Harlem.

The Firebombing of Freddy's

When Fred Harari, the previous owner of Freddy's clothing store in West Harlem, decided to expand his business, he in effect terminated the lease of his African American subtenant, Sikhulu Shange. Shange appealed to both Harari and the African American church that owned the property, but neither would change their minds. Shange then pleaded with the local African American leaders in Harlem's community, who organized a boycott of Freddy's clothing store to protest Harari's decision. Interestingly, the African American church that owned the property supported Harari's decision to terminate Shange's lease, and the pastor actually marched his congregation across the picket line to show his support.

Initially, it was easy enough to ignore the protestors, but when they began to shout caustic remarks like "Kill the Jew bastards," Harari decided it was time to file a restraining order. By the time the order was granted, it was too late. Roland Smith, an African American resident of Harlem, entered Freddy's with a .38 caliber gun and a can of paint thinner and set the store ablaze, trapping and killing all seven of the store's nonblack employees and killing himself.

When asked about the incident at Freddy's, Harlem's merchants and customers overwhelmingly agreed that it was Harari's right to terminate the sublease with Shange, but most agreed that it was not the "morally right" thing to do. For instance, a Jewish sneaker store owner in Harlem remarked, "You just don't kick a black man out of Harlem," while an African American customer rhetorically asked, "How can you move blacks out of Harlem when that's all we have?" An East Harlem resident and former customer of Freddy's commented on why the incident had elicited such strong emotions. She explained, "I think when a black man has been in business for a long length of time, and he's in danger of losing his business, emotions are going to run high."

While incidents like the firebombing of Freddy's come few and far between, the emergence of protest motivations and collective action against the backdrop of everyday routine demonstrates the fine balance between civility and conflict. When business ownership in black communities is at stake, customers and merchants battle over far more than the intricacies of the economic exchange. Imported into boycott motivations of individual storeowners are ideologies of opportunity structure and group position. Business ownership represents group position, and the dominating presence of non-black-owned businesses in black communities symbolizes black economic subordination to other groups.

Hence the boycotting by African American leaders, local residents, and customers of an individual business becomes emblematic of the larger issue of black control over black communities. Chants such as "Whose streets? Our streets," "What time is it? Black nation time," and "Too black, too strong" ring through the community during boycotts, taking on collective proportions.

Here it is crucial to distinguish between individual merchant-customer interactions and collective group interest. While merchant-customer interactions are not the cause of group conflict, because the interactions occur in a context of group subordination they can readily inspire and ignite collective protest. Hence, in a context in which merchant-customer interactions are embedded in extreme inequality, nonblack merchants understand that while they actively work to preserve civility their efforts do not preclude the possibility of racial conflict.

Previous research on merchant-customer relations in poor, black neighborhoods underscores the context in which Jewish and Korean merchants serve black customers. These researchers argue that because merchants serve customers who reside in inner-city neighborhoods where poverty, inequality, and joblessness are extreme, merchant-customer interactions are typically conflictual and serve as a catalyst to boycotts and firebombings of Jewish- and Korean-owned stores. However, critical examination of merchant-customer interactions in black neighborhoods reveals they are not fraught with racial animosity but are instead civil and ordinary.

In this chapter, I illustrate that civil relations prevail because merchants make considerable investments to maintain civility under conditions of extreme inequality. Jewish and Korean merchants do not take the everyday routine for granted but instead actively work to preserve it. They hire black employees to act as cultural brokers who help socially embed their businesses in black neighborhoods, and they place women at the front end of the business to serve as maternal brokers. Furthermore, they succumb to customers' demands in order to thwart potential conflict. The customers also do their part by accepting certain norms that are in place to prevent shoplifting. Constructing ordinariness, merchants realize, is an important goal, especially when the failure to do so can have dramatic consequences.

While merchants work to preserve civility, Jewish and Korean storeowners realize that regardless of their efforts, their nonblack status in poor, black neighborhoods can easily make them visible targets for angry customers, residents, and political entrepreneurs. Because merchant-customer interactions are embedded in a context in which inequality is extreme, nonblack merchants recognize that their efforts to maintain civility do not preclude the emergence of protest motivations. However, it is important to keep in mind that protest motivations do not emerge because merchant-customer interactions in themselves are conflictual. Instead, motivations for protest arise because groups struggle for their position in the ethnic hierarchy, and the dominating presence of non-black-owned businesses in poor, black neighborhoods symbolizes black economic subordination to other groups.

NOTES

Paper prepared for the National Consortium on Violence Research conference, "Beyond Racial Dichotomies of Violence: Immigrants, Race, and Ethnicity," University of California, Los Angeles, November 6–8, 2003. I thank the International Migration Program of the Social Science Research Council, the Andrew W. Mellon Foundation, and the National Science Foundation (SBR-9633345) for the research support on which this chapter is based. This chapter was partially completed while I was a Fellow at the Center for Advanced Study in the Behavioral Sciences with generous financial support provided by the William and Flora Hewlett Foundation, Grant #2000-5633. For comments and suggestions I thank Richard Rosenfeld, Ramiro Martínez, Abel Valenzuela, and the other participants at the NCOVR conference.

1. Kolack and Kolack (1969: 7, 28–31).
2. Berson (1966: 41).

3. Quarantelli and Dynes (1968: 7); Berson (1966: 40).

4. Kolack and Kolack (1969: 7).

5. Geltman (1966: 623).

6. Aldrich and Reiss (1970: 187–206).

7. Aldrich and Reiss (1970: 205–6).

8. Noel (1981); Jones (1986); Njeri (1989); *New York Post* (1990).

9. *New York Times* (1995: A1).

10. For a discussion of merchant-customer disputes, see Jo (1991: 395–410); Min (1996); Yoon (1997).

11. Bonacich (1973: 583–94); Min (1996).

12. Abelmann and Lie (1995).

13. Cheng and Espiritu (1980: 521–34); Gans (1969: 3–15); Jacobs (1996: 1238–72); Kim (2000); Ong, Park, and Tong (1994); Selznick and Steinberg (1969); Weitzer (1997: 587–606); Yoon (1997).

14. Light and Bonacich (1988); Marx (1967); Selznick and Steinberg (1969).

15. One caveat about the relationship between small business ownership and group mobility is worth mentioning here. While I do not argue that entrepreneurship is essential to the collective mobility of all ethnic groups, I do argue that it has been an essential element to the mobility patterns of Jews and Koreans in the United States. Moreover, I do not argue that African Americans should emulate the patterns of Jews or Koreans. However, because business ownership in black communities causes contention in black communities, it is important to study. For further elaboration on this, please refer to Lee (2002).

16. Peterson (1966); *U.S. News and World Report* (1966); *Newsweek* (1982); Bell (1985: 24–31).

17. Lee (1999); Min (1996).

18. Lee (1999: 1398–1416).

19. As a Korean, I was not certain that the black customers would speak candidly to me about their experiences and perceptions (especially if they were negative) of the Korean, Jewish, and African American merchants in their neighborhoods. Therefore, to minimize the possibility of unreliable data, I hired African American research assistants to conduct the interviews with the black customers (see Schaeffer 1980).

20. U.S. Bureau of the Census (1990).

21. Waldinger (1995: 275–79).

22. Olzak, Shanahan, and McEneaney (1996: 590–613).

23. For more detail on the reasons behind the differential rates of positive and negative merchant-customer interactions, see Lee (2002).

24. Merton ([1948] 1968).

25. Arlie Hochschild defines emotional labor as "unpaid labor of a highly interpersonal sort" that involves nurturing, managing, adapting, and cooperating to others' needs. See Hochschild (1983: 170).

26. Bobo and Kluegel (1994: 443–64); Bobo and Hutchings (1996: 951–72); Quillian (1995: 586–611).

27. See also Sheppard (1947: 96–99).

REFERENCES

Abelmann, Nancy, and John Lie. 1995. *Blue Dreams: Korean Americans and the Los Angeles Riots.* Cambridge, MA: Harvard University Press.

Aldrich, Howard, and Albert J. Reiss Jr. 1970. "The Effect of Civil Disorders on Small Business in the Inner City." *Journal of Social Issues* 26:187–206.

Bell, David. 1985. "The Triumph of Asian Americans: America's Greatest Success Story." *New Republic,* July, 24–31.

Berson, Lenora E. 1966. *Case Study of a Riot: The Philadelphia Story.* New York: Institute of Human Relations Press.

Bobo, Lawrence, and Vincent Hutchings. 1996. "Perceptions of Racial Group Competition: Extending Blumer's Theory of Group Position to a Multiracial Social Context." *American Sociological Review* 61:951–72.

Bobo, Lawrence, and James Kluegel. 1994. "Opposition to Race Targeting: Self-Interest, Stratification Ideology, or Racial Attitudes?" *American Sociological Review* 58:443–64.

Bonacich, Edna. 1973. "A Theory of Middleman Minorities." *American Sociological Review* 38:583–94.

Cheng, Lucie, and Yen Le Espiritu. 1980. "Korean Businesses in Black and Hispanic Neighborhoods: A Study of Intergroup Relations." *Sociological Perspectives* 32: 521–34.

Gans, Herbert J. 1969. "Negro-Jewish Conflict in New York City." *Midstream* 15:3–15.

Geltman, Max. 1966. "The Negro-Jewish Confrontation." *National Review,* June 28, 623.

Hochschild, Arlie. 1983. *The Managed Heart.* Berkeley: University of California Press.

Jacobs, Ronald N. 1996. "Civil Society and Crisis." *American Journal of Sociology* 101:1238–72.

Jo, Moon H. 1991. "Korean Merchants in the Black Community: Prejudice among the Victims of Prejudice." *Ethnic and Racial Studies* 15:395–410.

Jones, Von. 1986. "Blacks, Koreans Struggle to Grasp Thread of Unity." *Los Angeles Sentinel,* May 1.

Kim, Claire J. 2000. *Bitter Fruit: The Politics of Black-Korean Conflict in New York City.* New Haven: Yale University Press.

Kolack, Sol, and Shirley Kolack. 1969. "Who Will Control Ghetto Businesses?" *National Jewish Monthly* 7 (July–August): 7, 28–31.

Lee, Jennifer. 1999. "Retail Niche Domination among African American, Jewish, and Korean Entrepreneurs: Competition, Coethnic Advantage and Disadvantage." *American Behavioral Scientist* 42 (9): 1398–1416.

Lee, Jennifer. 2002. *Civility in the City: Blacks, Jews, and Koreans in Urban America.* Cambridge, MA: Harvard University Press.

Light, Ivan, and Edna Bonacich. 1988. *Immigrant Entrepreneurs.* Berkeley: University of California Press.

Marx, Gary T. 1967. *Protest and Prejudice.* New York: Harper and Row.

Merton, Robert K. [1948] 1968. "Self-Fulfilling Prophecy." In Robert K. Merton, *Social Theory and Social Structure.* New York: Free Press.

Min, Pyong G. 1996. *Caught in the Middle: Korean Merchants in America's Multiethnic Cities.* Berkeley: University of California Press.

New York Post. 1990. "Scapegoating New York's Koreans." Editorial. January 25.

New York Times. 1995. "In Nightmare of Anger, Store Becomes Flaming Madhouse" and "Death on 125th Street: A Scene of Carnage." December 9, A1.

Newsweek. 1982. "Asian Americans: A 'Model Minority.'" December 6.

Njeri, Itabari. 1989. "Cultural Conflict." *Los Angeles Times,* November 8.

Noel, Peter. 1981. "Koreans Vie for Harlem Dollars." *New York Amsterdam News,* July 4.

Olzak, Susan, Suzanne Shanahan, and Elizabeth H. McEneaney. 1996. "Poverty, Segregation, and Race Riots." *American Sociological Review* 61:590–613.

Ong, Paul, Gaeyoung Park, and Yasmin Tong. 1994. "The Korean-Black Conflict and the State," In *The New Asian Immigration in Los Angeles and Global Restructuring,* edited by Paul Ong, E. Bonacich, and L. Cheng. Philadelphia: Temple University Press.

Peterson, William. 1966. "Success Story, Japanese-American Style." *New York Times Magazine,* January 9.

Quarantelli, Enrico L., and Russell R. Dynes. 1968. "Looting in Civil Disorders: An Index of Social Change." *American Behavioral Scientist* 11:7–10.

Quillian, Lincoln. 1995. "Prejudice as a Response to Perceived Group Threat: Population Composition and Anti-Immigrant and Racial Prejudice in Europe." *American Sociological Review* 60:586–611.

Schaeffer, Nora C. 1980. "Evaluating Race-of-Interviewer Effects in a National Survey." *Sociological Methods and Research* 8:400–419.

Selznick, Gertrude J., and Stephen Steinberg. 1969. *The Tenacity of Prejudice: Anti-Semitism in Contemporary America.* New York: Harper and Row.

Sheppard, Harold L. 1947. "The Negro Merchant: A Study of Negro Anti-Semitism." *American Journal of Sociology* 53 (2): 96–99.

U.S. Bureau of the Census. 1990. *1990 Census of Population and Housing.* Washington, DC: U.S. Department of Commerce, Bureau of the Census.

U.S. News and World Report. 1966. "Success Story of One Minority in the U.S." December 26.

Waldinger, Roger. 1995. "When the Melting Pot Boils Over: The Irish, Jews, Blacks, and Koreans of New York." In *The Bubbling Cauldron: Race, Ethnicity, and the Urban Crisis,* edited by M. P. Smith and J. R. Feagin, 265–81. Minneapolis: University of Minnesota Press.

Weitzer, Ronald. 1997. "Racial Prejudice among Korean Merchants in African American Neighborhoods." *Sociological Quarterly* 38:587–606.

Yoon, In-Jin. 1997. *On My Own: Korean Businesses and Race Relations in America.* Chicago: University of Chicago Press.

Chapter 8

The "War on the Border"
Criminalizing Immigrants and Militarizing the U.S.-Mexico Border

Sang Hea Kil and Cecilia Menjívar

Criminalizing undocumented immigrants in the U.S.[1] Southwest border region appears to be necessary to solve the problems of drug smuggling and undocumented immigration. However, the escalation of the criminalization process has led to the use of a militaristic model to achieve a "sealed" border. The recent trend of militarization, which allows military equipment and personnel in Border Patrol enforcement, fosters human rights abuses and tragic consequences. As stricter enforcement of border policies pushes the migration path from safer, more urban points of crossing to the harsh, remote deserts and mountains of Arizona, the death toll of immigrants using the more perilous routes reaches record-breaking numbers.

Several studies have detailed the expansion of the militarization strategy by using a wide range of primary and secondary sources, ranging from government documents and media reports to interviews with public officials, INS agents, and nongovernmental organization (NGO) representatives.[2] These studies have been valuable in showing how the material buildup of the U.S. southern border occurred. They have helped document the infrastructure's buildup and the impetus of the military paradigm in fueling expansion despite dismal results. But our intent in this chapter is to explore as well how the militarization of the border shapes racist and violent responses to undocumented border crossing—how public policy, rhetoric, criminalization, and militarization have turned the border into a violent place. An examination of how the processes of militarizing the U.S.-Mexico border and criminalizing undocumented immigrants along it are related to racialization can reveal how the militaristic paradigm, when employed in domestic law enforcement matters, can brutalize both immigrants and the nonimmigrant public, albeit in different ways. Thus such strategy creates a context of violence similar to that experienced in regions of political conflict, even though war has not officially been declared against our neighbors to the south.[3]

To understand the current border strategy not only from the broader public discourse and policy standpoint but also from the viewpoint of immigrants who experience the brunt of this strategy, we use a mixed-methods approach, relying on data culled from academic research, human rights reports from NGOs in Arizona, media reports, interviews with activists, and interviews with Latin American immigrants in Phoenix. Our interviews come from a larger study of immigration to the Phoenix metropolitan area conducted from 1998 to 2001 among different groups of Latin American immigrants.[4] The immigrants' views shed light on how militarized policies continue to affect immigrants even when they are living away from the physical border—a topic that has seldom been researched.[5]

In this chapter we first describe the history of criminalizing immigrants in this region, with a particular focus on military tactics of dealing with undocumented immigration and drug enforcement. Second, we contend that criminalizing immigrants in this way is a type of symbolic racism based on a notion of "us versus the enemy" that brutalizes the public as it encourages hostility toward immigrants who cross the southern border. We analyze how not only the militarized tactics of border enforcement but also the rhetoric of militarization contributes to a social and political climate encouraging violence and social polarization between citizen and noncitizen, white and nonwhite. Third, we describe how this brutalization inspires vigilante and militia-type groups in Arizona to "help" enforce the border. Fourth, through interviews with undocumented immigrants, we highlight how the militarized border and the rhetoric used to discuss it affect these immigrants' already clandestine lives by pushing them further underground into a perilous domain of "legal nonexistence." Finally, we comment on recent developments that further criminalize undocumented immigrants in the post 9/11, Homeland Security era of immigration enforcement and suggest policy changes aimed at reducing human rights abuses against undocumented immigrants and violence at the border.

Criminalizing Immigrants and Militarizing the Border

Some have argued that the border's increased militarization can be attributed to drug enforcement concerns over the supposed criminal nature of immigrants.[6] Timothy Dunn's seminal research focused on the use of military tactics, strategies, equipment, and training on the U.S.-Mexico border by the Immigration and Naturalization Service (INS).[7] Other scholars followed with studies that explained the sharp escalation in Border Patrol budgets and policing that yielded low deterrent effects as a type of public spectacle or theater to show that "something was being done" about undocumented immigration.[8]

Scholars not only have demonstrated that the Border Patrol's plan continues to be ineffective in reducing the numbers of undocumented men, women, and children who cross but also have observed that this strategy encourages human rights abuses by scapegoating undocumented migrants,[9] an attitude that comes from nativist sentiments over the perceived loss of control of the border.[10] Such scapegoating in turn "encourages many to believe that more force is needed to repel the onslaught of illegal migration"[11] and to accept force as a justifiable strategy to restore control. This militarization has created a warlike atmosphere that has contributed to a wide range of abuses, including the use of rape against immigrants; such physical abuse is probably not rare or isolated.[12] Jose Palafox underscores the need for more research on the human rights abuses, especially the rise in deaths, that a militarized border strategy continues to create in the border region.[13]

Economics has also contributed to the militarization of the border and the criminalization of immigrants. The United States' creation of a free-trade zone with Canada and Mexico through such accords as the General Agreement on Tariffs and Trade (GATT) in 1986 and the North American Free Trade Agreement (NAFTA) in 1996 greatly affected the border situation. In effect, the United States would pursue what has been called a "politics of contradiction—simultaneously moving toward integration while insisting on separation."[14] Policies that liberalized trade and the flow of capital between these nations contributed to an increase in the movement of capital, goods, commodities, and information. But these trade agreements effectively decoupled capital from labor: while capital could flow freely, labor could not.

Such shifts in economic policies—together with drug enforcement, immigration, national security, and customs concerns—would create an increasingly hodgepodge-like agency alliance along the U.S.-Mexico border with each subsequent presidential administration. In particular, the Reagan administration was concerned with the terrorist element among the Central American refugees seeking political shelter in the United States from U.S.-sponsored regimes,[15] and this administration would first link immigration and Cold War concerns as a basis for the border buildup. The Bush Sr. administration further developed the massive buildup started by his predecessor and increased the paramilitary nature of the INS with equipment, forces, and training in tandem with an expansion of law enforcement authority.[16]

However, the proclivity for militarizing the border was not a partisan issue, for it was under the Clinton administration that the INS launched an offensive border strategy called "prevention through deterrence." This strategy began with "Operation Hold the Line" (in El Paso, Texas, in 1993) and continued with "Operation Gatekeeper" (in San Diego, California, in 1994), "Operation Safeguard" (in Nogales, Arizona, in 1994), and "Operation Rio Grande" (in the Brownsville corridor that extends from the Lower Rio Grande Valley to Laredo, Texas, in 1997).[17] Walls and stadium-style lighting were placed in these border areas, and Border Patrol staffing was increased dramatically. The goal was to move the migration path away from urban areas into remote (mountain and desert) terrain, to deter people from crossing into the United States, and to make apprehension easier in the remote areas.

Although these efforts did successfully push the migration flow away from urban areas, they did not deter undocumented immigration, except that now immigrants are more likely to hire human smugglers as guides.[18] Nowadays it is not unusual for smugglers who take people across the border to charge $1,000 to $1,500 per person.[19] But instead of focusing public attention on how border policies have created this phenomenon (which mostly harms poor immigrants), the moral panic over *coyote*[20] (smuggler) activities generally emphasizes the greed of the smugglers;[21] compares their tactics to those of drug smuggling in the use of assaults, kidnapping, and extortion;[22] likens human smuggling to a modern form of slavery;[23] accuses *coyotes* of drugging immigrants to make them walk faster;[24] and blames them for unsolved murders of undocumented migrants.[25] Very little debate centers on the immigration and drug policies that have *created* the conditions under which human smuggling proliferates.

Additionally, as Massey, Durand, and Malone have noted, stiffer immigration restrictions may have the unintended consequence of increasing the number of undocumented immigrants in the country.[26] Immigrants are likely to stay longer in the United States because, if they leave, a return/reentry poses a far greater physical danger and monetary cost to them now than before the military buildup at the border.

More importantly, in the fiscal year 2002, the number of immigrant deaths has increased, particularly in Arizona, where 3,217 bodies were discovered.[27] The total number of deaths due to stiffer border policies is unknown, since no official attempt has been made to record them systematically.[28] However, social scientists and human rights groups estimate that more than two thousand people have died in the desert on the U.S. side since a count began in 1994.[29] As a result of militarization, the change in migration patterns (to using Arizona as an alternate border-crossing area, where almost half the border-crossing deaths since 1995 have occurred) has made this region a type of "ground zero."[30]

In response to the rising number of immigrant deaths, the Border Patrol implemented the Border Safety Initiative in conjunction with the Mexican government in 1998 to deploy emergency medical services for migrants, with an emphasis on patrolling the border for rescue purposes.[31] However, these safety initiatives have not stopped the rise in deaths. Such measures only display the benevolent rhetoric of public officials and do not mitigate the lethal consequences of the militarization policy.[32]

Since the tragedy of 9/11, the concern with the "war on terror" has further shaped immigration policy enforcement by focusing even more on threats to national security. These shifts in policy have created a legal gulf for undocumented immigrants crossing the border. The idea that the criminal justice system considers everyone, even undocumented immigrants, to have the right of due process has eventually given way to a militarized construction of undocumented immigrants as an enemy "other" with dubious access to rights.

Symbolic Racism and Brutalization Theory

If the militarized Border Patrol policy has such a high cost in human life, and if it has not deterred people from crossing, why does it still exist and even have plans to expand? Additionally, why have the human rights abuses resulting from a militarized border generated so little public outcry? The answers to these questions are found in the modern and symbolic forms of racism that thrive today. The relationship between militarizing the border and criminalizing immigrants is germane to the study of racism in two ways. First, the use of a military paradigm to plan a border strategy reveals "symbolic racism," an obscure form of racism that naturalizes divisions between races without using overt racist language. Second, militarizing the border is a form of racial brutalization that encourages the public and policy makers to remain complacent about increasing violence and death and even to seek further militarization.

Stuart Hall points out that racism today is mostly "inferential" in the "naturalized representations of events and situations relating to race."[33] As Mark McPhail describes such representations, race and war are both made to seem "natural" manifestations of human civilization,[34] and their rhetoric appeals "1) to the audience's sense of territoriality, 2) to the audience's ethnocentricity, 3) which function to enhance the audience's optimism and 4) which are relevant to war aims."[35] The war metaphor's inferential racism that guides Border Patrol strategies works on the social cognition level, where, in Teun A. van Dijk's formulation, the "exercise of power usually presupposes mind management, involving the influence of knowledge, beliefs, understanding, plans, attitudes, norms and values."[36] There is no declared war between the United States and Mexico, but the territorial boundary between the two countries is talked about and treated like a hostile boundary. As Leo Chavez comments, "The discourse that characterizes the U.S.-Mexico border as a war zone that is under siege, 'invaded,' 'defended,' and 'lost' slips easily between war as a metaphor and practice."[37] This discourse contributes to a mind-set of "us versus the enemy," which serves racist functions in creating boundaries between peoples.

Thus the idea of war, as an armed struggle between two antagonistic nations, grips the national imagination and stimulates racial anxiety within the immigration debate without the need ever to use an open racial slur. The war metaphor acts as a fear-provoking signal, naturalizing racism and justifying war strategies by creating an image of the nation as an innocent victim and an image of undocumented immigrants as an enemy. It enables the public to accept that the border region is "berserk" and thus that more social control and surveillance (to protect the "innocent" body politic) are naturally or commonsensically needed.[38] As Chavez puts it, the "invasion metaphor evokes a sense of crisis related to an attack on the sovereign territory of the nation. Invasion is an act of war, and puts the nation and its people at risk. Exactly what the nation risks by this invasion is not articulated in the image's message."[39] However, evoking ambiguous fears about the border becomes a technique of coercion that politicians and the media craft on the basis of commonsensical assumptions about how to stop an invasion. The assumption that the borders need to be militarized thus allows society to consent to a racialized border policy.[40]

So to speak of war and militarization, to subconsciously ignore race and racism, within the discourse of the U.S.-Mexico border is to give consent to symbolic racism and to allow ethnocentric policies to be implemented. And a militarized discourse of the border demands that action be taken against those who are perceived to deserve it:

> Militarization and criminalization draw upon the rhetoric of legitimation. The imagery of illegal immigrants has been implanted in the public consciousness in ways that instill fear, anger, and resentment among U.S. citizens. They are said to be disposed toward criminal activity, intent on taking much needed jobs from citizen workers, or inclined to bilk the coffers of the state's social welfare system. Thus, they and the coyotes that aid them are said to be a threatening force that must be stopped. Beyond depicting immigrants as an economic threat, rhetoric has increasingly relied upon military terminology that paints the immigrant as an enemy intent on inflicting harm on the American public. This is done by blurring the distinction between undocumented immigration and drug smuggling, by collapsing drug smugglers and the coyotes that smuggle undocumented immigrants in the U.S. under the catchall of an "immigration crisis." As the War on Drugs was coupled with enforcement efforts against undocumented immigration, state officials have shown an increasing penchant for using war terms when discussing border issues.[41]

In effect, the military paradigm brutalizes the public's perception of undocumented immigrants, encouraging an image of them as the "enemy." And given that the "enemy" has a particular racial appearance (being seen as brown), this brutalization allows for racial animus.

Brutalization theory, which developed out of the long debate over capital punishment, posits that when the state metes out punishments on criminals the public morally identifies with the state and imitates it.[42] At central issue is the question over the state's moral message to the public and how the public receives it. Advocates of the death penalty have argued that state executions have a deterrent effect on would-be murderers and communicate to the public that people who murder will be punished likewise. Opponents of the death penalty argue that it encourages violence because the state conveys the moral lesson to its citizenry that deadly violence is an acceptable solution for people who break the law. As William J. Bowers and Glenn L. Pierce write:

> Implicit in the brutalization argument is an alternative identification process, different from the one implied by deterrence theory. The potential murderer will not identify personally with the criminal who is executed, but will instead identify someone who has greatly offended him—someone he hates, fears, or both—with the executed criminal. We might call this the psychology of "villain identification."[43]

In this process of "villain identification," the potential murderer identifies with the state and punishes those he or she loathes as being offending.

In a similar manner, the public can be said to imitate the state with regard to border policy, which allows extralegal violence against immigrants to occur. Thus within a brutalization framework it makes sense that vigilante groups along the border see themselves, not as lawbreakers, but as an additional and helpful "arm" of immigration enforcement and border patrol. The brutalizing effect of the militarized border mentality on the public can be seen in the rise of these vigilante activities along the border. As shown later in this chapter, vigilante groups mimic the government's policy and rhetoric of militarization and patrol the border region armed —many with high-tech equipment, "hunting" for those they perceive as criminals. They are encouraged by the state's example to "do justice" in a similar way. But their targets are not white Europeans who overstay their tourist or work visas; rather, they are people who cross the southern border and thus are assumed to be Mexicans who want to cross into the United States.

Militarized border policies affect not only Mexicans who cross but also other brown peoples from the Americas, as well as entire groups who live in the U.S. Southwest who do not "look" white, regardless of their citizenship status. Using war rhetoric and deploying low-intensity conflict methods to enforce border policies increase social and racial polarization and encourage a climate of abuse and violence toward undocumented immigrants and those who racially or ethnically resemble them.[44] The present border paradigm promotes hate and fear toward, and thus mistreatment of, the people of border communities, who are mostly people of color. The militarization of the border diminishes the human rights and quality of life in these communities, primarily through racial profiling by the Border Patrol, who are looking for drug and immigrant smugglers but who treat as potential criminals brown U.S. citizens. Thus the borderlands become a hostile place for the human rights of both residents and crossers.[45]

The militarized border policy continues to affect immigrants who have successfully crossed the border. Susan Coutin uses the term *legal nonexistence* to describe their situation of being physically present and socially active in civil society but lacking legal recognition.[46] Legally nonexistent persons, Coutin notes, can be seen as potentially subversive in that they are not bound by legal duty.[47] However, legal nonexistence is also a state of subjugation that results in vulnerability. Undocumented immigrants are vulnerable to deportation, confined to low-wage jobs, and denied basic human rights, such as access to decent housing, education, and health care.[48] Placing them outside the legal order in a realm of lawlessness supports extreme actions against them and exempts authorities from obligations toward them; thus the rights of those who are legally nonexistent are ambiguous.[49]

Fueling Vigilante Activity

Human rights groups have noted that the policy of increasing Border Patrol operations in urban areas and thereby redirecting migration flows has affected the geographic strategies of militia-style, vigilante groups. Since Arizona has seen the increase in immigrant traffic, vigilante groups have moved there from California and Texas, bringing weapons, detection technologies, training, and expertise honed in their home states. Currently several vigilante groups are operating in Arizona. For instance, Ranch Rescue, headed by Texan rancher Jack Foote, is an "armed volunteer organization" interested in protecting private landowners' property rights from "criminal trespassers." They claim to have branches in Washington, Oregon, Arkansas, Illinois, Georgia, New Mexico, Arizona, Texas, and California, as well as an international branch. They boast of a membership base composed of Border Patrol agents, military personnel, law enforcement officers, and Soldier of Fortune mercenaries.[50] In 2000, Ranch Rescue circulated a flier in Arizona calling for recruits to "hunt" immigrants and "help keep trespassers from destroying private property."[51]

Another group, the American Border Patrol, moved operations from California (where this organization was called Voices of Citizens Together/ American Patrol and was recognized by the Southern Poverty Law Center as a hate group) to Arizona and began "operations" in 2002 with a focus on high-tech detection equipment installed along the border.[52] Its founder, Glenn Spencer, believes these extra precautions are necessary because the Mexican government purposefully sends undocumented immigrants for a "Reconquista," or the retaking of the Southwest by Mexico. He states that "Mexico, which has been hostile toward the U.S. for over 100 years, is invading us with the intent of conquering the American Southwest. There is no question of this."[53] Since moving his operations to Arizona, Spencer has established his group as a grassroots organization, garnering an incorporated, nonprofit status.[54] Two of the organization's officers are former Border Patrol sector chiefs.[55] Recently, American Border Patrol conducted its first test flight of a radio-controlled, miniature spy plane called "Border Hawk."[56]

Chris Simcox—another former California resident—leads the Civilian Homeland Defense. He openly describes his group as a militia and wants the U.S. government to deputize his members in the interest of national security.[57] Members are openly armed, patrol public lands, and have volunteers apply for concealed weapons permits.[58] A fact card distributed by Civil Homeland Defense claims that the group is a "community service volunteer neighborhood watch group who has answered the call of the President of the USA to report suspicious, illegal activities." The group assumes that "illegal immigration allows terrorists, criminals, people with disease into our country."[59]

However, these organized "import" groups are not alone; there are also less organized local vigilante groups. One notable local vigilante is Roger Barnett, an Arizona rancher who claims to have apprehended nearly ten thousand undocumented immigrants on his twenty-two-thousand-acre property over the past four years.[60] Currently, Roger Barnett and members of his family are being sued by the grassroots nonprofit organization Border Action Network and a local rancher for trespassing on private property and impersonating a police officer.[61]

These are just a few of the vigilante groups that have felt compelled to organize or move to Arizona. They are motivated by the immigration and drug policies that have made this state's border a "war zone," and they thus mimic the government's military border paradigm in rhetoric and strategy. Many of these groups have names similar to those of governmental agencies and wear uniforms that are hard to distinguish from those of the official Border Patrol.[62] Importantly, they see themselves as necessary supplements to the current militarized border effort, which they see as inadequate. They see immigrants as criminals, enemies, and threats to national security. Many have current or past affiliations with national racist hate groups.[63]

Many of these groups use the legal justification of "protection of property" and profess pro-rancher interests to gain public and legal legitimacy in a state with historically libertarian values, although only one vigilante group, the Barnett Family, actually owns ranchland in Arizona. When Arizona Attorney General Terry Goddard was called upon by human rights activists to do something about the vigilante activities, which range from violating Arizona's antimilitia laws to violating state land department leases and impersonating law enforcement officers, he claimed a lack of jurisdictional authority: immigration matters, he says, are the jurisdiction of the U.S. attorney general, and criminal matters are the county attorney's.[64] Thus these vigilante groups, whether intentionally or not, take advantage of a legal vacuum. The toleration of their criminal activities shows how the federal government's militarization rhetoric has created a social and cultural atmosphere in the Southwest border region and particularly Arizona that stirs up racial anxieties based on national security concerns and contributes to an atmosphere of brutalization, violence, and racial hate.[65]

Voices from the Frontlines

Our interviews show that the effects of a militarized border on immigrants' lives are deep and far-reaching. First, the heightened danger and costs of border crossing—costs that are not only monetary but also physical, emotional, and psychological as the business of human smuggling has become more perfidious—have been a major source of stress. Many immigrants cannot afford to risk visits to loved ones even when they would give anything to do so, as when a mother is on her deathbed and a son cannot go say goodbye because coming back to the United States would be almost impossible. And bringing family members into the United States has become increasingly difficult.

Some of our respondents in Phoenix spoke in detail about this. One Salvadoran couple brought two of their three sons at different times in the 1990s and in 2003 decided to bring their third son to Phoenix. Their experience, therefore, offers a comparative glimpse of how the actual border crossing has changed. When they brought Manuel in 1993, according to Manuel and his parents, the trip was "easy" since he was robbed only twice

—once by the Mexican authorities—and it took him one month to get to Phoenix. That trip cost around $1,500, but it was difficult for the parents to come up with an exact amount because the *coyote* kept asking for more money and they had to send additional money to Mexico twice for Manuel to continue the trip. He was abandoned once close to Mexico City, but then he met up with a group and finally made it to Agua Prieta, a town on the border with Arizona, where his father met him.

In 1999 their second son, Eduardo, asked his parents for help to come to the United States because he simply could not earn enough money as a mechanic in El Salvador to support his family. Therefore, the parents contacted a *coyote* who was well known for bringing people quickly and safely and gave him a down payment of $2,000, with $1,000 to be paid upon the safe delivery of Eduardo to Phoenix. Things became complicated and the group was robbed and detained. Finally they made it over to Phoenix, at which point the smuggler demanded another $2,000 instead of the $1,000 agreed upon because, as he explained to the family, the trip had proven more difficult and dangerous than he had calculated. The family refused to pay the additional cash because they had already sent extra money to Mexico—since, as happened in the previous case, they had run out of money in Mexico and needed more to continue the trip. Eduardo's mother ended up threatening the *coyote* with calling the INS because she felt it was outright extortion. The *coyote* immediately accepted the $1,000 and delivered Eduardo to his parents.

In July 2003 the family sent for the last son, Ernesto. This time, the *coyote* was a well-known one who specialized in the elderly and nervous people and was therefore considered "very good." He charged the family $7,000 but offered them a plan in which the money could be paid in three installments. There was no assurance that the trip would be a safe one for Ernesto or when or if he would even make it to Phoenix. As the *coyote* explained to the parents, this time things were extremely dangerous and difficult. For the first time, a *coyote* mentioned the possibility of death, and even though the family paid much more there was more uncertainty about whether the son would actually make it. Now this family will not attempt to make any trips to El Salvador until their "papers are fixed," which could extend their stays for an indefinite period (if they are not deported first).

Another source of stress has been immigrants' inability to turn to and rely upon governmental agencies and resources that ordinarily are meant to protect and serve the public. Robert Bursik Jr. observes that the "new"

Chicago School's most important departure in its approach to immigration and crime has been its emphasis on the external or public networks through which communities potentially obtain political, economic, and social resources from agencies located outside the community.[66] In particular, Bursik cites the work of Zatz and Portillos,[67] who studied Chicano communities long troubled by gang activity. Impoverished ethnic communities were hesitant to ask police for help due to the tense relationship between the two. The doubt stemmed from the general belief that decision makers, including law enforcement agents, could make a difference in the community but had abandoned the area to decline.[68] Similarly, because deportation has become an increasingly serious matter, undocumented immigrants have become more and more reluctant to turn to public resources like the police because they do not trust that the authorities will work on their behalf[69]—a deleterious effect of living in a realm of "legal nonexistence." They now go to great lengths to avoid any contact with the justice system to avoid detection by immigration officials.[70] For instance, Nora, a nineteen-year-old Guatemalan with a second-grade education, simply smiled when asked if she could count on the U.S. police for protection. She explained that she was aware that the police were more helpful in the United States than the police were in Guatemala but that she would not call them in case of need because she was still undocumented and feared deportation. Her fear was so extreme that once she had almost lost her life rather than calling the police. While she was working the night shift at a McDonald's, three men robbed the establishment at gunpoint. The robbers shoved all the employees into a huge freezer but did not lock it. Nora managed to get out, mostly because she got bad migraine headaches in the cold and could not stand being inside the freezer for much longer. Instead of calling the police, however, she grabbed a broomstick, hit one of the men, and knocked him unconscious. She got his gun and threatened the other two men that she would kill their friend if they did not leave. While she was arguing with the men, a manager called the police and the situation was resolved. Only when the police arrived did Nora drop the gun. The managers and the police thanked her but also asked her not to do this again. She added: "At that moment, while I was holding the men, I kept on thinking, What do I do? If I call the police, I'll get deported. Yes, I was nervous [with the gun], but I was even more nervous to have to talk to the police."

The weakness of the ties between the criminal justice system and the undocumented immigrant community is also revealed by domestic dis-

putes. Cándida, a thirty-five-year-old Mexican with a fourth-grade education, had been arguing with her partner, Jorge, a twenty-nine-year-old
Honduran, and he slapped her face twice. She had threatened him that she
would call the police if this ever happened again, but he did not listen.
This time she dialed 911. The police came so quickly that she had not even
put down the receiver when they were already at the door, she said. The
police took the startled Jorge—with no more clothes than a pair of old
shorts and flip-flops—and, to her surprise, turned him over to immigration officials because he was undocumented. He was deported a day later.
Cándida, who is a permanent resident, ended up making all the arrange-
ments for him to return to the United States within twenty-four hours.
She explained, "I didn't know that's what they were going to do. I wouldn't
have called because it was very expensive to bring him back." Cándida
went on to explain, "He didn't speak to me for three days after he got back.
He was very upset at me. But now he knows that I mean business when I
say that I'll call the police."

In spite of Cándida's words, however, she—as well as her Honduran
sister-in-law and other female friends, coworkers, and neighbors who
learned of this incident—now hesitate before calling the police on an abusive partner. They do not want to face the consequences of a partner's
deportation, much less deal with an enraged man who wants the woman
to "pay" for her actions. In the words of Cándida's Honduran sister-in-law,
who was not at all happy with her brother's deportation:

Look what happened. The problem became much worse. She should not
have done that. If I ever do that [call the police on an abusive partner], he
will never forgive me. I'm afraid he'll kill me. My husband [a former soldier
in the Honduran army] has said that already, that he'll torture me if I do
that [smiles a bit]. Cándida thought she'd be protected, but instead the
problem became worse. But now she knows. One learns from the mistakes
of others.

Immigrants also are more afraid to report being abused or cheated by
unscrupulous employers, landlords, and others with whom they do business. When Eduardo felt that he had to do something because his supervisor at work was giving more work to him than to his coworkers and was
simply harassing him, he wanted to write a letter to the company's president, and the second author of this chapter helped him write it in English.
However, after the letter was composed and he signed it and was ready to

take it to work, Eduardo hesitated and thought about it for more than one week. He was equally afraid of losing his job and of being deported. He opted not to give the letter to the president of the company, explaining, "A couple of years ago, in another time, I would have turned it in. But now I'm afraid, you know, with the times now, one has to be so careful. We're walking a tightrope without a net underneath now!"

Another public resource that cannot be accessed is public health agencies. Immigrants often risk their health by treating conditions themselves or letting illnesses go untreated to avoid the risk of deportation. Isabel is a forty-seven-year-old Salvadoran who dropped out in her third year of law school in El Salvador because her family had to flee. They entered the country undocumented, and even though she made a trip back to her country early on, she now feels that she has to stay here because these days she cannot put her life in danger by crossing the border. She is particularly anxious about not having health insurance for her children and tries to avoid as much as possible any contact with health professionals; she has heard that they can contact immigration officials and have her deported. She is terrified by the possibility of being separated from her children if they are deported and at the near-impossibility of trying to make it back into the United States. When asked about her health situation, she said:

> I feel fine now. Insurance? Our insurance company, we call it Our Heavenly Father Company [laughing]. You know why? Because we simply pray to God that we don't get sick or else we wouldn't know what to do. So he keeps us healthy. We try not to go to the doctor, as you know, we cannot expose our [undocumented] situation to everyone. So if anyone gets sick we use our medicines that people bring from Mexico or El Salvador, you know a little penicillin here or there. Stuff like that. But mostly I just try to eat well and once in a while I'll have an aspirin. Do you understand me? We take it one day at a time.

Miguel, for reasons similar to Isabel's, prefers to treat himself at home so that he does not encounter authorities that may report him to immigration. Whenever he or anyone of his family gets sick, he explained, they first try to use some home remedies—like herbal teas, honey, cinnamon, and clove for a cold. If the ailment does not go away, they use Tylenol, Advil, or the like. If that does not work, they call on friends to see what they can recommend or to get their friends' leftover prescription medications that have proven effective. He says that he shares medicine not only because it is a cheaper option for those, like himself, who do not have health insurance but because doing so is "safer" than meeting with any public health professionals.

Even sending children to school may be too great a risk for immigrants to take: it might draw attention to the family's undocumented status. As immigrants' situation becomes increasingly vulnerable, their lives become more clandestine, and many simply strive to become invisible.

Finally, militarizing the legal and physical borders affects how immigrants see each other and how they construct their identities. For instance, after the events of 9/11, a few of the undocumented immigrants in the Phoenix study went out to "99 cents" stores to purchase various-sized U.S. flags and flag images and to display them on their cars, windows, and lawns. Those who worked in fast food restaurants displayed flags even in the kitchens where they flipped hamburgers. For prudential reasons, they wanted at all cost to show their unconditional loyalty to the United States. Manuel, the man mentioned earlier, has thought about the danger one may now incur by "looking" immigrant. In his words:

> Look, you know that I have tried to look and act Mexican all this time, remember? (laughs) If I said I'm Salvadoran, the girls at the disco would look at me different and wouldn't want to dance with me. So I use a hat, my boots, and I speak like a Mexican. But now that may backfire! Just like they shot the poor guy over in Mesa who was wearing a turban because a crazy man thought he was an Arab, now anyone who's not pure white might be suspicious. Now it's probably better *not* to look or sound like a Mexican. Things are backwards!

Conclusion

Before the tragic events of 9/11, as this chapter has highlighted, immigration policy under the INS had already demonstrated an unprecedented coordination between the military and the Border Patrol, a historical trend that also reflects the change in government agencies that handle immigration matters. Before 1940, the Department of Labor handled immigration; later, the Department of Justice handled it under the INS.[71] Prompted by the events of 9/11, the Office of Homeland Security (OHS) now is in charge of immigration issues (the transfer officially occurred on March 1, 2003). With each subsequent transfer of immigration issues to a new department, the criminalization of immigrants has become increasingly severe, with the last department clearly using a military paradigm for creating policy along the border as well as in the interior of the United States. Under the Department of Labor, border-crossing immigrants were seen as surplus or competing labor; then under the INS they were seen as drug smugglers and criminals; and now under the OHS (and with a war mentality) they are seen as potential terrorists.

Two new immigration initiatives are taking shape that could allow military strategies and perspectives to encroach more into the interior of the country. One is federal and the other would affect Arizona specifically but could be a model for other states to follow if passed. The federal initiative is the Clear Law Enforcement for Criminal Alien Removal Act (CLEAR), introduced to the House of Representatives in July 2003 by Representative Charles Norwood (R-Georgia), along with others. If enacted, it would give local law enforcement agencies authority to enforce federal immigration laws by apprehending, detaining, and removing undocumented immigrants. Additionally, the federal government could then penalize states that did not enact statutes that authorize police to enforce federal immigration laws. Finally, CLEAR would require that immigration violators be registered in the database of the National Criminal Information Center. This database, however, would not clearly distinguish for police the difference between a dangerous criminal and an immigrant with an administrative or civil infraction.[72]

In Arizona, a movement to revive the sentiment of Proposition 187 in California is taking shape with the PAN initiative, short for "Protect Arizona Now." It is a "citizens' initiative to require proof of citizenship to register to vote, photo ID to vote, and proof of eligibility for nonfederally mandated public benefits."[73] Much like Proposition 187, which was later deemed unconstitutional in federal court, this initiative seeks to make state and local governments responsible for enforcing federal immigration law.[74] It is premised on the assumption that noncitizens are voting and receiving government benefits to which they are not entitled. This initiative would further discourage undocumented immigrants from seeking medical aid and access to public networks by requiring state and local government workers to check the immigration status of everyone seeking public services. Thus basic education and emergency health care would not be affected, but access to public libraries and Medicaid would be. Moreover, state-supported humanitarian aid, like the thirty-eight water tanks that Human Borders—an interfaith group in Arizona—puts out in the desert to help immigrants who suffer dehydration when crossing, would also cease. "Our worst fear is that this initiative will criminalize compassion," said the Rev. Robin Hoover, Humane Borders director.[75]

Although criminalizing immigrants still affords them rights of due process, the military paradigm, as a guiding model of enforcing immigration and drug laws, erodes the motivation to confer such rights on immigrants. As demonstrated in this chapter, the rhetoric and policy of militarizing the border foster a climate that easily disregards the human rights of undocumented immigrants. This climate is one that brutalizes the public's imagination and encourages a racist assumption that separates these immigrants from American citizens and sees them as "the enemy." Although such racism is more tacit in politicians' and the media's discourse, it is overtly expressed in Arizona's vigilante groups. These groups see themselves in a continuum of the federal government's militarized tactics used to enforce border laws. They identify with the forces of the state and mimic their language, clothing, technology, and strategy. It is this broader context that shapes the spaces of "legal nonexistence" within which undocumented immigrants live ever more clandestine lives, even when they are physically far from the actual border.

Immigration policy and enforcement need to change to reflect the human rights crisis along the border. A "sealed" and controlled border is simply impossible in an increasingly interconnected world, and the economies of sending countries are unfortunately not likely to become prosperous in the near future. This leaves the United States with two choices: legalizing undocumented workers in the United States or continuing with the militarization of border enforcement. The advantages of legalizing the undocumented population are numerous. In general, it would increase national security and reduce crime. First, it would connect now-clandestine immigrants to public networks, making their lives less underground and vulnerable and more secure. Second, it would reduce the exorbitant spending on border containment, allowing more resources to be focused on terrorist interdictions as opposed to the disruption of labor migration into *and* out of the United States. Third, it would put an end to the tragic and needless deaths of undocumented migrants who cross the southern border.[76] Moreover, having labor flows enter and exit through official entry ports would eliminate crime in the border region in numerous ways. In particular, it would discourage vigilante groups and decrease the demand for *coyote* services to transport people, thus reducing the climate of violence in and improving the health of the communities along the border. Finally, by rejecting the militaristic criminalization of immigrants, the brutalizing racism that makes a division between citizen and non-citizen, "us versus them" attitudes would fade, since the public would no longer identify with the state that punishes immigrants who cross the southern border with deadly zeal, as immigrants would no longer be assumed to be the "enemy." This would enable the immigrants to improve their condition and cease to live clandestinely in "legal nonexistence" so that they could live dignified lives as full members of the society to which they contribute in multiple ways.

NOTES

We would like to thank Ramiro Martínez Jr. and Abel Valenzuela Jr., the organizers of the National Consortium on Violence Research conference, "Beyond Racial Dichotomies of Violence: Immigrants, Race and Ethnicity," University of California, Los Angeles, November 6–8, 2003, for inviting us to participate. We also would like to express our gratitude to Richard Rosenfeld, Lisa Rubin, Zeynep Kilic, and Gabriel Kuhn for very helpful comments, to Cecilia Martinez Vasquez for careful editing, and to Mary Fran Draisker for assistance in preparing this manuscript. None bear any responsibility for what we ultimately did.

1. The first author of this chapter prefers to use the terms *U.S. American* or *United States of America* as the adjective and noun to make clear which "United States" or "America" she might be referring to, as there are many different states that might be united in the world as well as many countries in the Americas. For purposes of homogeneity of terms, *U.S.* and *United States* are used but with this caveat.

2. Andreas (2000); Dunn (1996).

3. Crossing the border, though defined as an illegal act, has been characterized by scholars as a "victimless crime" (Schuck 2000), as there are no victims when immigration laws are broken.

4. See Menjívar and Bejarano (2004); Menjívar (2001, 2003); Menjívar et al. (1999).

5. See Heyman (1999).

6. Heyman (1998, 1999); Heyman and Smart (1999).

7. Dunn (1996).

8. Andreas (2000); Brownell (2001).

9. Ortiz (2001).

10. Rodríguez (1997).

11. Nuñez (1999: 1576).

12. Indeed, in a four-month-long investigation, the *Oregonian* newspaper found

that the INS "tolerates racism and sexual abuse in its ranks and has one of the highest rates of misconduct among federal law-enforcement agencies" (Christensen et al. 2000: 1). See Falcón (2001: 144); Christensen et al. (2000).

13. Palafox (1996, 2000, 2001).

14. Massey, Durand, and Malone (2002: 73).

15. As Dunn (1996: 55) notes, a May 1986 report by the INS Investigations Division ("Alien Terrorist and Undesirables: A Contingency Plan") called for the INS, along with other government agencies, to "exclude, apprehend, detain, prosecute, and deport members of targeted groups of nationalities." North African and Middle Eastern countries were used as examples. This is "not surprising, given the Reagan administration's bombing of Libya in 1986." See Dunn (1996).

16. Dunn (1996: 102).

17. Andreas (2000).

18. Reyes, Johnson, and Van Swearingen (2002).

19. Gonzalez (2003).

20. The popularized term *coyote* to refer to immigrant human smugglers is problematic in that it can contribute to "linguistic racism" by suggesting an image of human agents as animalistic, separate, and inferior (and in this case criminal). Due to its usage by the public, the press, and the immigrants themselves, we use it here but note its drawbacks.

21. Associated Press (2003b); Holthouse and Scioscia (2000).

22. Gonzalez (2003); Billeaud (2003).

23. Fiscus (2003).

24. Riley (2003a).

25. Carroll (2003).

26. Massey, Durand, and Malone (2002); Reyes, Johnson, and Van Swearingen (2002).

27. Associated Press (2003c).

28. Eschbach, Hagan, and Rodríguez (1999).

29. Massey (2003).

30. Massey (2003).

31. Eschbach, Hagan, and Rodríguez (2003).

32. See Menjívar and Kil (2002).

33. Hall (1990: 13).

34. McPhail (1994: 40).

35. McPhail (1994: 49).

36. van Dijk (1998: 257).

37. Chavez (2001: 221).

38. Cavender and Bond-Maupin (1993: 311–12).

39. Chavez (2001: 223).

40. See Gramsci (1971).

41. Huspek (2001: 55).

42. Bowers and Pierce (1980).
43. Bowers and Pierce (1980: 456).
44. Dulles (1997).
45. Allen (2003).
46. Coutin (2000).
47. As in the work of Malkki (1995).
48. Menjívar and Kil (2002).
49. Coutin (2000).
50. For example, see the Web site www.ranchrescue.com.
51. Rotstein (2000).
52. Hammer-Tomizuka and Allen (2002).
53. Grigg (1996: 23).
54. Banks (2003).
55. Hammer-Tomizuka and Allen (2002).
56. Associated Press (2003a).
57. Hammer-Tomizuka and Allen (2002).
58. Associated Press (2002).
59. Civil Homeland Defense fact card, Cochise County, Arizona.
60. Riley (2003b).
61. See Border Action Network (2005).
62. See *Donald J. McKenzie v. Roger Barnett, Barbara Barnett, and Donald Barnett,* Case No. CV200400778, filed November 26, 2004.
63. For example, the American Border Patrol and Ranch Rescue.
64. Turf (2003).
65. To be sure, fears of immigrants as invaders or as potential saboteurs of national security are not new to the current era. Even during War World II, Congress gave the Border Patrol additional officers and resources to improve their vigilance of land and water borders. Thus, put in a wider historical frame, the current situation is one more instance of associating immigrants with potential disloyalty to the United States.
66. Bursik (2003).
67. Zatz and Portillos (2000).
68. Zatz and Portillos (2000).
69. Bursik (2003).
70. The following quotes, taken from Menjívar and Bejarano (2004: 135–38), are based on the project in Phoenix mentioned in the data section.
71. Dunn (1996).
72. Wessler (2003).
73. See the Protect Arizona Now Web site: www.pan2004.com/.
74. See Coalición de Derechos Humanos (2003).
75. LoMonaco and Díaz (2003: 1A).
76. Eschbach, Hagan, and Rodríguez (2003: 18).

REFERENCES

Allen, Jennifer. 2003. "Justice on the Line: The Unequal Impacts of the Border Patrol Activities in Arizona Border Communities." November. Retrieved October 27, 2005, from the Border Action Network Web site: www.borderaction.org/PDFs/BAN-Justice.pdf.

Andreas, Peter. 2000. *Border Games: Policing the U.S.-Mexico Divide.* Ithaca: Cornell University Press.

Associated Press. 2002. "Tombstone Militia Will Operate on Public Land, Leader Says." *Associated Press,* December 3. BC cycle, sec. State and Regional.

———. 2003a. "Civilian Border Watch Group Launches Spy Plane." *Associated Press,* May 1, BC cycle, sec. State and Regional.

———. 2003b. "Law Enforcement: Immigrant Extortion Growing Problem." *Associated Press,* July 29, BC cycle, sec. State and Regional.

———. 2003c. "Newspaper Finds Discrepancies in the Number of Border Deaths." *Associated Press,* October 16, sec. State and Regional.

Banks, Leo W. 2003. "Crossing the Line: Tensions Escalate on the Border." *Tucson Weekly,* December 19–25, 14–17.

Billeaud, Jacques. 2003. "Kidnappings Rise as Migrants Smuggling Gets Lucrative." *Associated Press,* January 11, sec. State and Regional.

Border Action Network. 2003. "In Line with National Trend, Arizona Lawsuit Claims Border Vigilantes Threaten Private Property, Public Safety, Human Rights." Press release, December 10. Retrieved from the Border Action Network Web site: www.borderaction.org.

———. 2005. "Civil Lawsuits Pending against Roger, Donald and/or Barbara Barnett." 2005. Retrieved January 13, 2006, from www.borderaction.org/images/3%20lawsuits.pdf.

Bowers, William J., and Glenn Pierce. 1980. "Deterrence or Brutalization?" *Crime and Delinquency* 26: 453–84.

Brownell, Peter B. 2001. "Border Militarization and the Reproduction of Mexican Migrant Labor." *Social Justice* 28 (2): 69–92.

Bursik, Robert J., Jr. 2003. "Rethinking the Chicago School of Criminology in a New Era of Immigration." Paper presented at the National Consortium on Violence Research Conference, "Beyond Racial Dichotomies of Violence: Immigrants, Race, and Ethnicity," University of California, Los Angeles, November 6.

Carroll, Susan. 2003. "Series of Killings Tied to People-Smuggling." *Arizona Republic,* January 6. Retrieved October 27, 2005, from www.azcentral.com/specials/special03/articles/0106executions06.html.

Cavender, Gray, and Lisa Bond-Maupin. 1993. "Fear and Loathing on Reality Television: An Analysis of 'American's Most Wanted' and 'Unsolved Mysteries.'" *Sociological Inquiry* 63 (3): 305–16.

Chavez, Leo R. 2001. *Covering Immigration: Popular Images and the Politics of the Nation.* Berkeley: University of California Press.

Coalición de Derechos Humanos (2003). "Protect Arizona Now Plays on Anti-Immigrant Fervor." July 10. Retrieved January 13, 2006, from www.derechos humanosaz.net/Docs/Protect%20Arizona%20Now%207-10-03.pdf.

Coutin, Susan B. 2000. *Legalizing Moves: Salvadoran Immigrants' Struggle for U.S. Residency.* Ann Arbor: University of Michigan Press.

Christensen, Kim, Richard Read, Julie Sullivan, and Brent Walth. 2000. "Unchecked Power of the INS Shatters American Dream." *Oregonian,* December 10, A1.

Dulles, John F. 1997. *Federal Immigration Law Enforcement in the Southwest: Civil Rights' Impacts on Border Communities.* Washington, DC: U.S. Commission on Civil Rights.

Dunn, Timothy. 1996. *The Militarization of the U.S.-Mexico Border, 1978–1992: Low Intensity Conflict Doctrine Comes Home.* Center for Mexican American Studies. Austin: University of Texas Press.

Eschbach, Karl, Jacqueline Hagan, and Nestor Rodríguez. 1999. "Death at the Border." *International Migration Review* 33 (2): 430–54.

———. 2003. "Deaths during Undocumented Migration: Trends and Policy Implications in the New Era of Homeland Security." Paper presented at the 26th Annual National Legal Conference on Immigration and Refugee Policy, Washington, DC, April.

Falcón, Sylvanna M. 2001. "Rape as a Weapon of War: Advancing Human Rights for Women at the U.S.-Mexico Border." *Social Justice* 28 (2): 31–50.

Fiscus, Chris. 2003. "Arizona a Hub for Human Trafficking." *Arizona Republic,* October 11. Retrieved October 27, 2005, from www.walnet.org/csis/news/usa_2003/arizrep-031010.html.

Gonzalez, Daniel. 2003. "Gangs Are Menacing 'Coyotes,' Immigrants." *Arizona Republic,* August 17. Retrieved October 27, 2005, from www.azcentral.com/specials/special03/articles/0817immigrant-bajadores17.html.

Gramsci, Antonio. 1971. *Prison Notebooks.* New York: International Publishers.

Grigg, William Norman. 1996. "Race and Revolution." *New American,* August 19. Retrieved August 19, 2005, from www.thenewamerican.com/tna/1996/vo12no17/vo12no17_revolution.htm.

Hall, Stuart. 1990. "The Whites of Their Eyes: Racist Ideologies and the Media." In *The Media Reader,* edited by M. Alvarado and J. O. Thompson, 7–23. London: BFI Publishing.

Hammer-Tomizuka, Zoe, and Jennifer Allen. 2002. "Hate or Heroism: Vigilantes on the Arizona-Mexico Border." December. Retrieved October 27, 2005, from the Border Action Network Web site: www.borderaction.org/PDFs/BAN-Vigilante %20Report.pdf.

Heyman, Josiah M. 1998. "State Effects on Labor Exploitation: The INS and Undocumented Immigrants at the Mexico-United States Border." *Critique of Anthropology* 18:157–80.

——. 1999. "The United States Surveillance over Mexican Lives at the Border: Snapshots of an Emerging Regime." *Human Organization* 58 (4):430–38.

Heyman, Josiah M., and Alan Smart. 1999. "States and Illegal Practices: An Overview." In *States and Illegal Practices*, edited by J. M. Heyman, 285–314. Oxford: Berg.

Holthouse, David, and Amanda Scioscia. 2000. "Phoenix or Busted: The Valley Is Now the Prime Way Station for Ruthless Smugglers Engaged in Lucrative Trafficking of Human Cargo—Illegal Immigrants." *New Times,* April 6. Retrieved October 27, 2005, from www.phoenixnewtimes.com/issues/2000-04-06/feature .html.

Huspek, Michael. 2001. "Production of State, Capital, and Citizenry: The Case of Operation Gatekeeper." *Social Justice* 28 (2): 51–68.

LoMonaco, Claudine, and Elvia Díaz. 2003. "Bid to Bar Immigrant Services under Fire: Determining Who Is Illegal Would Be Troublesome, Critics of Initiative Say." *Tucson Citizen,* July 9, 1A.

Malkki, Liisa H. 1995. *Purity and Exile: Violence, Memory, and National Cosmology among Hutu Refugees in Tanzania.* Chicago: University of Chicago Press.

Massey, Douglas S. 2003. "Beyond Smoke and Mirrors: Paradoxes of U.S. Immigration Policy." *Points of Migration* (Princeton University, Center for Migration and Development), August. Retrieved October 27, 2005, from http://cmd.princeton .edu/files/POM-August2003.pdf.

Massey, Douglas S., Jorge Durand, and Nolan J. Malone. 2002. *Beyond Smoke and Mirrors: Mexican Immigration in an Era of Economic Integration.* New York: Russell Sage Foundation.

McPhail, Mark L. 1994. *The Rhetoric of Racism.* Lanham, MD: University Press of America.

Menjívar, Cecilia. 2001. "Latino Immigrants and Their Perceptions of Religious Institutions: Cubans, Salvadorans, and Guatemalans in Phoenix, AZ." *Migraciones Internacionales* 1 (1): 65–88.

——. 2003. "Religion and Immigration in Comparative Perspective: Salvadorans in Catholic and Evangelical Communities in San Francisco, Phoenix, and Washington D.C." *Sociology of Religion* 64 (1): 21–45.

Menjívar, Cecilia, and Cynthia L. Bejarano. 2004. "Latino Immigrants' Perception of Crime and Police Authorities in the United States: A Case Study from the Phoenix Metropolitan Area." *Ethnic and Racial Studies* 24 (1): 120–48.

Menjívar, Cecilia, and Sang Kil. 2002. "Exclusionary Language in Official Discourse on Immigrant-Related Issues." *Social Justice* 29 (1–2): 160–76.

Menjívar, Cecilia, et al. 1999. "Contemporary Latino Migration to the Phoenix Metropolitan Area." Report presented to the Center for Urban Inquiry, Arizona State University.

Nuñez, Michael J. 1999. "Violence at our Border: Rights and Status of Immigrant Victims of Hate Crimes and Violence along the Border between the United States and Mexico." *Hastings Law Journal* 43 (6): 1573–1605.

Ortiz, Victor. 2001. "The Unbearable Ambiguity of the Border." *Social Justice* 28 (2): 96–112.

Palafox, Jose. 1996. "Militarizing the Border." *Covert Action Quarterly* 56 (Spring): 14–19.

———. 2000. "Opening up Borderland Studies: A Review of U.S.-Mexico Border Militarization Discourse." *Social Justice* 27 (3): 56–72.

———. 2001. "Introduction to the Gatekeeper's State: Immigration and Boundary Policing in an Era of Globalization." *Social Justice* 28 (2): 1–16.

Reyes, Belinda I., Hans P. Johnson, and Richard Van Swearingen. 2002. *Holding the Line? The Effect of the Recent Border Build-up on Unauthorized Immigration*. San Francisco: Public Policy Institute of California.

Riley, Michael. 2003a. "A Grim Gamble: Mexican Immigrants Bet Their Lives They Can Make It across the U.S. Border through the Blazing Arizona Desert; Poverty Drives Them; Hope Lures Them; But in Ever Greater Numbers, the Desert Is Killing Them." *Denver Post*, October 19.

———. 2003b. "Vigilantes Go on Patrol for Migrants." *Denver Post*, October 20.

Rodríguez, Néstor P. 1997. "The Social Construction of the U.S.-Mexico Border." In *Immigrants Out! The New Nativism and the Anti-Immigrant Impulse in the United States*, edited by J. F. Perea, 223–43. New York: New York University Press.

Rotstein, Arthur H. 2000. "Vigilante Recruiting Brochure Aimed at Deterring Illegal Crossers Sparks Protest." *Associated Press State and Local Wire*, April 26.

Schuck, Peter. 2000. "Law and the Study of Migration." In *Migration Theory: Talking across Disciplines*, edited by C. Brettell and J. H. Hollified, 187–204. New York: Routledge.

Turf, Luke. 2003. "Activists Hope to Take down Vigilantes." *Tucson Citizen*, December 2. Retrieved October 27, 2005, from www.tucsoncitizen.com/index.php?page=border_news&story_id=120203c1_vigilantes&toolbar=print_story.

van Dijk, Teun A. 1998. "How 'They' Hit the Headlines: Ethnic Minorities in the Press." In *Discourse and Discrimination*, edited by G. Smitherman-Donaldson and T. A. van Dijk, 221–62. Detroit: Wayne State University Press.

Wessler, Stephen. 2003. "The Fractured American Dream: The Destructive Impact of U.S. Antiterrorism Policy on Muslim, Latino, and Other Immigrants and Refugees Two Years after September 11, 2001." Center for the Prevention of Hate Violence Report, University of Southern Maine, Portland, ME. Retrieved October 27, 2005, from www.cphv.usm.maine.edu/FracturedAmericanDream.pdf.

Zatz, Marjorie S., and Edwardo L. Portillos. 2000. "Voices from the Barrio: Chicano/a Gangs, Families, and Communities." *Criminology* 38:369–401.

Chapter 9

New Immigrants and Day Labor
The Potential for Violence

Abel Valenzuela Jr.

Every morning in most major cities, thousands of men gather at open-air, street curb hiring sites in a seemingly chaotic and frenzied search for employment. Securing temporary work daily on a street corner is frantic; as moving cars come to a halt, men eagerly surround them, aggressively drawing attention to themselves in the hopes of being selected for a day of hard work. These men vigorously compete with each other for jobs with employers who drive by in search of cheap labor.

By most accounts, searching for work on a daily basis in a public and visible space such as a busy street, sidewalk, storefront, or empty parking lot is a desperate and potentially dangerous undertaking. Day laborers encounter violence primarily from other day laborers, police, and their employers, and to a lesser extent from merchants and local residents. Many are undocumented immigrants who have risked being robbed, assaulted, raped, or murdered in attempting to enter the United States and who, once here, may encounter violence or harassment from the Immigration and Naturalization Service (INS; now known as the CIS or Citizenship and Immigration Service) as well.

Day labor is difficult, and almost all day laborers are poor and are unable to make ends meet. Because consistent work is difficult to obtain at these hiring sites, competition among day laborers is fierce and aggressive and can flare up into violence. Employer-worker relations are also fraught with tension. Often wages are not fixed and are instead negotiated at the hiring site or the work site. Work opportunities fluctuate from day to day. Employers often assume correctly that most of the laborers are recent arrivals and illegal. As a result of these and other circumstances, the potential for employer abuse or violence is great. And because day laborers do not have a standard or regularized relationship with their employer(s), because most of them do not have documents, and because most are unfamiliar with their legal, human, workplace, and civil rights, many of the abuses committed against them may go unreported.

For employers, hiring day labor is a risk. The legal sanctions for hiring an unauthorized worker from the street are unclear. Hiring a day laborer is like playing the "worker lottery"; unless one hires the same worker regularly, one really doesn't know if the hire will produce good or skilled work. Employers have few telltale signs of a day laborer's work ethic or experience—traits that all employers prefer to know prior to hiring someone. As a result, the potential for unfair expectations, shoddy work, and misunderstandings, aggravated by the inability of many new immigrants to communicate adequately in English, can result in disagreements, particularly related to wages and partial or no payment for completed work. Because most employment of day laborers is in the primarily male construction industry, where deadlines are often overrun, costs are high, and pressures to keep the bottom line are great, the potential for abuse and violence increases as contractors and workers buckle under pressure or conflict over wages, work effort, deadlines, and other workplace issues. When conflicts are not resolved and a contractor or a day laborer feels harmed, one or the other may resort to violence. For day laborers, who are mostly poor, male, desperate, and with little to lose, not being paid for a day's work is a serious matter. In a sense, violent crime becomes a workplace dispute mechanism for them because it is one of the few viable social control options that they possess.[1] This is especially the case with undocumented immigrants, who may be reluctant to draw attention to themselves by calling in the police or other formal social control agencies.

Despite the difficulty in finding daily work in this market and the potential for abuse and violence, day labor has increased rapidly and is visible throughout the United States.[2] Given the desperate nature of this employment exchange, the vulnerability of the workers, and the potential for conflict and abuse, a simple question emerges: To what extent is searching for and working day labor violent? This chapter answers this question by cataloging different instances of violence either experienced or witnessed by day laborers in Los Angeles. The chapter also provides a context for understanding violence in day labor work and life. The chapter is divided into four sections: (1) a brief theoretical overview of work and violence, (2) a discussion of the data and methods used to collect the empirical evidence for this chapter, (3) a presentation of the findings into three broad categories, and (4) a concluding discussion.

Work and Violence

Newspapers and TV and radio programs have contained numerous accounts of violence and day labor.[3] The violent acts range from drive-by shootings to assaults and thefts. The accounts usually chronicle violence at the hiring site or nearby, at a local store, hotel, or residence.[4] Day laborers are particularly vulnerable to theft because most do not have bank accounts where they can deposit their earnings. Opening a bank account usually requires the provision of an individual taxpayer identification number, which most day laborers do not possess. As a result, they are usually paid in cash for their work, and unless they need to make a payment the cash is on their person. This and their reluctance to call the police because of their unfamiliarity with U.S. institutions or their lack of legal documents make them easy targets.[5]

Day laborers are also exposed to violence at hiring sites that are controversial or particularly volatile as a result of community conflict. For example, in Farmingville, a suburban outpost on Long Island, day laborers have been the target of daily protests, shouting matches, police harassment, a firebombing of a day laborer's home, and an incident where a couple of day laborers were severely assaulted by two white supremacists.[6] In Jacksonville, Florida, a string of sixty-two armed robberies on day laborers left two dead during a recent violent span.[7] There are undoubtedly other unreported incidents of this type in other parts of the country.

Finally, while not analyzed in this chapter, death as a result of occupational hazard is high among day laborers, particularly Mexican immigrants, who take difficult and dangerous jobs. An investigation by the Associated Press[8] reported that hazardous jobs that lure Mexican workers to the United States are "killing them in a worsening epidemic that claims a victim a day." In the South and West, a Mexican worker is four times more likely to die than the average U.S.-born worker and nearly twice as likely as the rest of the immigrant population to die at work. The factors most associated with these deaths are improper training or safety equipment and inability to communicate an objection if workers know no English or are in the United States without documents. Finally, the work culture and safety expectations from workers' country of origin may not discourage risk taking.[9] These factors seem to affect deaths that occur outside the job setting and have implications for violent crime.

A combination of several factors make day laborers particularly vulnerable to violence; these include communication barriers, immigration status, fear of reporting crimes, cash-only employment, and naiveté or newness to a new country. In addition, their searching for work in public spaces that are high-crime areas and in communities where feelings run high against immigrants increases the probability that violence will occur against them. Contextualizing violence and day labor in academic research is difficult because only popular accounts (e.g., newspapers, radio, television) of violence in this industry exist. Indeed, the intersection between day labor and violence is so unique that no published academic article was found on this issue, despite several bodies of work that look at occupational violence and workplace violence. Below, I briefly discuss this literature and suggest parallels to how day labor and violence should be contextualized in this body of literature.

Violence at work has largely remained outside the discourse of occupational safety and health except for instances of workplace homicide such as postal workers shooting their co-workers and supervisors. Part of the problem of the dearth of scholarship on this topic has been the lack of an accepted or uniform definition of occupational violence. In 2002, several organizations (International Labor Organization, International Council of Nurses, World Health Organization, and Public Services International) collaborated on a definition that serves as a point of departure for organizing past and future work on this topic: "[i]ncidents where staff are abused, threatened or assaulted in circumstances related to their work, including commuting to and from work, involving an explicit or implicit challenge to their safety, well-being or health."[10] According to Mayhew, this definition can include verbal abuse, threats, assaults, homicide, "behaviors that create an environment of fear" stalking, bullying, and activities that lead to stress or avoidance behavior in the recipient.[11] In a different article, Mayhew sorts occupational violence into three useful categories: external, client initiated, and internal.[12] An additional category, structural violence, reveals yet another dimension of the problem.[13]

External Violence

Persons perpetrate external violence from outside the firm or business, as in the case of armed hold-ups. This type of occupational violence is the most frequent, and work sectors or occupations at the highest risk are banks, post offices, gambling outlets, armored vehicles, taxis, the retail trade, drive-through sales outlets (fast food), liquor stores, and auto service stations. As noted earlier, a good portion of violence on day labor is committed by outside actors. These might be rogue gangs or individuals attempting to rob workers who are presumed to have cash, hate groups trying to harass and intimidate immigrants, or merchants and residents who fear the effect of day labor hiring sites on their businesses or neighborhood property values. In addition, because day laborers often work alone or in small groups at a work site, including at a home or a faraway location, their probability for victimization increases.

In the United States, workers in the following occupations are at greatest risk of external violence: taxi drivers, security guards, police, prostitutes, and convenience store workers.[14] Heskitt and Warshaw and Messite identify four risk factors for businesses that increase the probability for external violence: (1) exchanging money with customers, (2) having few workers on site, (3) conducting business in the evening or at night, and (4) having fact-to-face contact with customers/clients.[15] Taxi drivers are at high risk because, like day laborers, they work alone and carry cash.

Client-Initiated Violence

Clients were the primary perpetrators of violence against day laborers. In general, the jobs with the highest risk of "client-initiated" violence in the United States, the United Kingdom, and Australia are police, security personnel and prison guards, firefighters, teachers, and welfare, health care, and social security workers. The main underlying risk factor appears to be the extent of face-to-face contact with higher-risk clients, such as young male clients who have been affected by alcohol or clients who use illicit drugs, particularly cocaine or multiple drugs. Long waiting periods for service, workplaces with insufficient staff resources, and overcrowded facilities further contribute to this problem.

Day laborers perform services for a wide variety of people, mostly construction contractors, who may be young or old, experienced or inexperienced, and, one would imagine, may have problems with drugs, alcohol, or a combination of both. Often day laborers are hired by contractors to cut labor costs or to make up for a shortage of workers. As a result, pressure to complete a task on time or under budget (i.e., with fewer workers) leads to increases in stress, which may lead to conflict. Additionally, day laborers tend to have face-to-face contact with those for whom they perform services.

Internal Violence

Internal violence occurs between employees within an organization, such as a supervisor's bullying of an employee or threats among coworkers. The underlying risk factors are individual and local characteristics; demographic factors that have been reported to be associated with perpetrators of a range of violent offences in the workplace include being male, young, from a poorer area or group, and affected by alcohol or other substances. Clearly, these characteristics occupy a central place in day labor demographics. Day laborers are overwhelmingly poor, young adults (mean age is thirty-three), and male.[16] As a result, violence among day laborers is more likely to occur given these demographics and well-founded research associated with these underlying risk factors.

Structural Violence

Clearly, the violence related to day labor falls under the larger rubric of structural violence as described in the sociological and criminological literature.[17] The fact that most day laborers are undocumented and have few equal opportunities in this country for gainful employment and fair treatment places them at a structural disadvantage that exposes them to an increased risk of incidents of violence in the workplace, as well as an increased risk of dying from hazardous conditions on the job. The connection between exposure to workplace hazards and employee race/ethnicity and nativity status has been well documented, and this chapter expands such long-standing concerns to include as well violence perpetrated by day laborers whose access to legal forms of social control is limited.[18] Below, I discuss how some day laborers respond to unfair treatment, abuse, nonpayment of wages, or a particularly violent encounter by perpetrating violence against their abusers or other day laborers. These acts by day laborers are consistent with Black's classic notion of crime as a form of social control.[19]

Data and Methods

Day labor, while highly visible and often depicted by the popular press, is relatively unknown in the academic literature.[20] To address this gap and to contribute to the discourse on nonstandard employment, which includes part-time work, temp agencies, contract company employment, short-term and contingent work, and independent contracting,[21] I began researching the day labor industry in Los Angeles. This market is fluid and dispersed across a wide geographic swath, and the participants, while visible to the public eye, do not necessarily want to be identified as such, given that the market is primarily informal, "underground," or illegal. As a result, a study of day labor requires a multimethod approach to best capture the nuances and particulars of a labor market not well documented in the social science literature. I developed a four-part multimethod study that included (1) a randomly administered survey of 487 workers at eighty-seven different hiring sites in Los Angeles and Orange County, (2) ten case studies of hiring sites, (3) twenty-nine in-depth interviews of employers, and (4) forty-six in-depth interviews of workers. This chapter overwhelmingly relies on the last data collection component—the in-depth interviews of day laborers.

The day laborers who were interviewed were all recruited from the hiring sites where we had previously surveyed. The interviews were done after the survey had been completed, during the spring, summer, and fall of 1999. Each interview was completed in Spanish and audio-recorded. And each respondent who successfully finished the interview was given $80—the equivalent of a good day's wage. Depending on the mood of respondents and their willingness to "open up," interviews lasted between four and eight hours. An interview protocol was used, and respondents were encouraged to expand and allowed to deviate somewhat from the specific goals of the questionnaire, which included learning about their immigration to the United States, their work and family history, the abuses they experienced in their search for and work in day labor, how they made ends meet, their health, and their educational background. The interviews were conducted near the site, often inside a coffee shop, on a park bench, or in the interviewer's car.

Recruitment was mostly snowball and nonrandom, though we took particular effort to interview a variety of day laborers—legal and unauthorized, young and old, and experienced and inexperienced. At a few official hiring sites, we would select some of the respondents for our in-depth interviews through a lottery to maintain fairness among the day laborers there. The official hiring sites also helped us identify potential respondents who were in this country legally. As a result, we didn't have to undertake the very difficult and awkward task of trying to identify "legal" respondents among the many unauthorized workers. The participants were guaranteed anonymity and were promised that their names would not be used in the write-up of their interviews. All the interviews were translated to English and transcribed. Each interview was coded according to key words, topics, and subtopics and was analyzed through the use of NUD*IST, a text-based software analysis program. For this chapter, I extracted several hundred pages of text having to do with violence and using key search words such as *robbery, theft, death, murder, fights, beatings, police, INS, residents, merchants, gangs, cholos,* and *threats.* The text was then reviewed and coded for instances of violence either experienced or witnessed.

The study sample of day laborers was predominantly unauthorized (60 percent), came from Mexico (67 percent), and had no or fewer than six years of education (39 percent). In addition, most of the respondents (55 percent) were married, and a good number had lived in the United States for many years (29 percent for over eleven years).

Findings on Violence and Day Labor

The forty-six in-depth interviews of day laborers contained accounts of 106 incidents of experienced or witnessed violence in which day laborers were victims or perpetrators. Of these, 84 were related to undocumented day laborers, and the rest (22) were related to day laborers with documents.

The majority of violent acts committed against day laborers was performed by their employers. Police violence toward day laborers was also mentioned frequently, as was gang or *cholo* violence in the form of gang beatings or robberies. There were a few isolated instances of merchant, resident, and INS violent acts directed at day laborers. Finally, day laborers had experienced violence at the hands of a variety of individuals, mostly *coyotes* (human smugglers)[22] and Mexican soldiers, during their journey into the United States without documents.

As perpetrators, day laborers engaged in acts of violence against their fellow workers—usually in their search for work and over miscellaneous issues related to their employment or lack thereof. In attempts to salvage a hard day's labor or to secure the terms of their wage negotiation, they also engaged in violence in the form of fights, job sabotage, or theft against their employers.

Violence, whether as a victim or a perpetrator, was clearly a significant component in the lives of these workers. While day laborers had a higher incidence rate as victims of violence (58 percent), they nevertheless committed a large proportion (42 percent) of violent acts, mostly against other day laborers (87 percent). Below, I more carefully analyze the violence data culled from the forty-six in-depth interviews of day laborers by looking at violence in the context of three broad categories of day laborers' lives and work: (1) their immigration to the United States, (2) their search for work, and (3) the work itself. All of these were to some degree fraught with violence.

Violence en Route to the United States

Many immigrants are not fully prepared for or aware of the extreme difficulties that await them as they attempt illegal entry into the United States. They may travel thousand of miles, enduring inclement weather, scarce resources, hunger and thirst, and inadequate shelter. Also they are often at the mercy of *coyotes*, who charge exorbitant rates to deliver immigrants into the United States. No guarantees are made for safe passage, and many immigrants speak of repeated attempts to cross. *Coyotes* are clearly in a position to exploit their clients and do so with impunity and violence. They may hold recent arrivals captive until the cost of smuggling them is paid by a family member or by themselves through servitude or other means. Attempts to cross can fail not only because of capture by immigration officials but also because of violent incidents with the Mexican police, robbers, other *coyotes*, other would-be crossers, and vigilantes who patrol the Arizona border in search of "illegals" to apprehend. Members of these organizations depict themselves as "civilian border patrol agents determined to stop the immigration flow that routinely, and easily, seeps past federal authorities."[23] Many of these men are untrained and carry firearms, increasing the potential for violence. In response to the announcement by the Minutemen of their intention to patrol the Arizona border, Robert C. Bonner, the U.S. Customs and Border Protection Commissioner of the Department of Homeland Security, stated, "Any time there are firearms and you're out in the middle of no man's land in difficult terrain, it's a dangerous setting."

Several of the day laborers we interviewed mentioned that their trek to the United States had been difficult and sometimes violent. I include some of their stories here because crossing the border is such a central part of their lived experience as immigrants, as day laborers, and as a community of undocumented workers.

Rudy, a twenty-five-year-old undocumented immigrant from Guatemala, made his way to the United States like most Latino immigrants without documents—through Mexico. After several tries, he finally entered the United States in 1994. He left his only child behind, under the care of the child's mother, Rudy's live-in girlfriend. Though he had the equivalent of fourteen years of education, economic opportunities in Guatemala proved few. Because he needed to care for his child and the child's mother, he decided to immigrate to the United States, where, he was told, job opportunities were plentiful and where even standing on the street led to employment.

After several failed attempts at crossing the border through Tijuana, he tried his luck through Nogales, in the Mexican state of Sonora, where he was finally able to secure a more or less reliable *coyote* to transport him over. On his failed journeys, he encountered not only Mexican soldiers who accosted him but also robbers who assaulted him and several other crossers on subsequent trips. All told, his travel to the United States involved a beating and the theft of his watch, ring, and other personal belongings. He was angry and felt hopeless. When asked if his money had been taken by the robbers, he responded:

> *Rudy*: Everyone's and everything. We had suitcases, and they took everything. I had my graduation ring, watch, and everything was taken there: money, chains, everything.
>
> *Interviewer*: With guns?
>
> *Rudy*: Yes, with guns. There were only two of them. During that time we were very close to crossing. There were about thirty-five of us. And I was the only one who was hit because I got very upset because there were so many men with us and we couldn't do anything. I was the only one who got hit. They hit me behind the head with the pistol so that I wouldn't do anything. There were a lot of men who were trying to cross and we

couldn't do anything. They took our clothes off, men and women completely, so they could take everything.

Rudy's encounter is typical of the violence that illegal immigrants face as they make their way toward the United States. Women who are trying to cross the border face the additional threat of sexual assault. Ernesto Soto, a thirty-three-year-old immigrant from Mexico who was making his way to the United States, describes a rape in recounting how *coyotes* mistreated one couple they had agreed to smuggle to the United States:

They treat you very badly. They don't give you any food. They treat you very badly. They behave very badly. . . . I don't know why. I would imagine they [*coyotes*] suffered just as we did. But they're earning money. Well, this man didn't have enough money for his passage and so he left his wife with the *coyotes* while he went to look for his relatives for money. And they were raping the woman. And that woman had a cut on her arm because they had cut her. They had threatened her and told her that if she said anything they would kill her or her husband. I imagine that she tried to defend herself because her hands were cut.

Not all immigrants experience the same difficulties; some experience few problems in their travels. But journalists' reports, academic studies on illegal immigration, and the interviews conducted for this study recount many violent incidents attendant on traveling to the United States without documents.

Violence during the Search for Work

The daily search for work in public spaces is the most regular part of day labor work. Every day, often for many hours, thousands of day laborers across the country attempt to secure employment from passersby, contractors in pick-up trucks, homeowners attempting do-it-yourself projects, and others. Throughout the morning, when the search for day labor is usually undertaken and is at its most competitive, day laborers encounter a myriad of employers, other workers similarly searching for work, merchants angry about scruffy unkempt men at their storefront or parking lot, police officers being pressured by local residents and elected officials to do "something" about day laborers, and more recently in-your-face protests by anti-immigrant individuals and organizations. As a result, the possibility of conflict or harassment is great.

For the most part, day laborers try to avoid conflict at any cost. For them, any attention, other than on their availability and work ethic, is avoided to prevent their possible incarceration, loss of wages (from not securing employment), and deportation. In addition, many day laborers are new arrivals and have little knowledge of the legal system and immigration laws. They cannot afford to get in trouble with the law, injure themselves, or face deportation.

FIGHTS BETWEEN DAY LABORERS

On average, day laborers secure employment three days in a seven-day workweek. Some weeks are even slower, and sometimes several weeks can go by without any employment. On any given day, at most hiring sites, including those that are regulated, the vast majority of workers do not obtain work. Searching unsuccessfully for temporary employment begins to take its toll, especially when there are other mouths to feed or a sick child to attend to, when rent is due, and when other obligations are left unfulfilled. As a result, competition for the few available jobs is particularly keen and can be volatile.

Pablo, a seasoned day laborer from El Salvador, spoke of the fierce competition between several workers over a possible job opportunity and an ensuing altercation.

> When the boss comes, there is pushing. I got here first, no, you got here first. . . . You have to respect me. . . . When I am negotiating, you push in to give another price. . . . That is why he takes you and he does not take me.
>
> Well, they [workers] were all on top of the car, and the *gabacho* [Anglo] had already said, "Ok, you and you." And there's still a whole bunch of stubborn men, pulling at each other and everything. And on one of those occasions, I was just trying to negotiate with the Anglo and then they began hitting me from behind. So that's when the punches began.

Non-job-related fights also occur, mostly because of a misunderstanding, owed money, or some other seemingly inconsequential or petty reason. In most instances a non-job-related altercation comes about because one or both parties are drunk. Martin, thirty-seven, talks about how day laborers fight among themselves after they have been drinking: "They start getting along and then they start drinking, and like that, they come to the point of throwing blows, and, well . . ."

In response to complaints by merchants and local residents, police often patrol day labor hiring sites. In some municipalities, soliciting day labor work on public grounds is illegal, and police will sometimes try to enforce this ban. Other municipalities may have an arrangement with the police to "encourage" day laborers in the surrounding neighborhood to search for work at the official city-sponsored site. As a result, police attempt to move workers gathered on different, nearby blocks to the official hiring sites. Finally, some cities may simply ignore day labor in their city boundaries, prompting overzealous police enforcement to "clean up" the streets or to attempt to rid the city of day laborers. Such policing usually results in harassment, First Amendment violations, and altercations that can be violent and harmful to workers.

In one particularly ironic incident, an employer who also happened to be a police officer threatened a day laborer with his weapon because he did not like the work that the day laborer had performed. As Martin, a day laborer of six years, describes the incident, "Once an employer who was a police officer took me to work for him, and he didn't like the work that I did, and he didn't pay me, and when I complained, he took out his gun on me. I could tell he wanted to hit me."

Merchants who fear a decline in their business and residents who fear a decline in their property values as a result of day labor activity nearby will sometimes mistreat day laborers and in a few occasions will lash out violently. An organizer with a local civil rights agency recounts a town forum to discuss conflict-reducing strategies at hiring sites: "On one occasion, I was with a bunch of neighbors and business owners yelling at each other . . . , saying, 'Let's get rid of the day laborers,' and one of them said that the next time he saw those 'fat bastards' he was going to take out his gun and he was going to kill them." Reactions such as these are not surprising considering the emotional reactions that illegal immigration seems to elicit, including an increase in hate crimes toward immigrants, the growth of vigilantism in rural border areas to ward off illegal immigration, and the "in-your-face" protests at different hiring sites that are becoming commonplace.

In addition to drawing organized harassment from anti-immigrant groups, day laborers may be the target of isolated random acts of violence by passersby. Because the search for day labor is ubiquitous, many passersby come into close proximity or contact with workers on many corners. In some public spaces as many as seventy-five to a hundred men might be searching for work during the morning hours. Many workers often linger well into the afternoon to meet the demand of the few employers who are still looking for hired help. As a result, you often see groups of men throughout the day milling around a public hiring site in the hopes of securing employment. The combination of tired, desperate, unemployed, hungry, and impatient men looking for work results in aggressive actions to draw attention to themselves and potential employers. They will dart in and out of traffic, move from the sidewalk to the street and back, huddle around a parked car pointing to themselves and yelling, "Pick me, pick me," gather inside a pickup truck's bed, jump inside a car, or undertake other similar acts. These aggressive search strategies, while for the most part harmless, might seem odd and annoying to many passersby, resulting in awkward moments, outright hostility, or even violent action.

The random acts of hostility and violence toward workers searching for employment range from being yelled at, including being told to "go back where you come from" and racial epithets, to having rotten eggs, ice cream, bags of water or urine, and other objects thrown at them. Being injured by a thrown rock or other object can be painful and result in lost employment opportunities. Samuel, a day laborer from Mexico describes a typical day at a hiring site.

> What I like the least is when they don't treat you like they should. Or the attacks on immigrants—people drive by yelling, "Wetbacks! Go back to your country! Go back to Mexico!"
>
> A lot of times neighbors will pass by and insult us throw rocks at us, eggs, and what-not to intimidate us to leave. There is also a group of people that pass by and well, have anti-immigrant sentiments, a lot of prejudice.... They pass by making racist comments like "You're a wetback." Sometimes they throw rotten eggs or ice cream or hurl verbal insults of all types.

Passersby who act out their feelings may undertake actions that are mean-spirited and even violent. Day laborers are left with little option other than to ignore these harmful actions or to secure employment.

Violence at Work

Most workers lucky enough to secure employment will find no problems in securing a fair wage, undertaking an honest day's work, and receiving adequate breaks, water, and instructions on safety equipment and particular jobs. Most employers are honest and fair. They fully realize that hiring day laborers will provide them with a nice break from having to pay market wages for non–day labor workers and that their profit margin is likely to increase over the long run if they continue to use day labor. Contractors also appreciate the flexibility and ease in hiring a temporary worker—it helps them meet their completion deadline, make the transition from one job to another, and cover their crew shortfall when a permanent worker calls in sick or when more personnel are needed. As a result, they treat day laborers with respect, pay them fairly, return them to the hiring site after work, and generally appreciate their existence.

Not all employers, however, are fair and benevolent toward day laborers from the streets. They have figured out that most day laborers are in this country without documents, that most are unable to communicate well in English, and that most are extremely shy and scared of being deported and as a result are unlikely to cause trouble, complain, or defend themselves from unscrupulous contractors. Most day laborers are vulnerable and can provide ill-intentioned employers with easy opportunities to engage in exploitation, abuse, and violence.

EMPLOYERS' VIOLENCE AGAINST DAY LABORERS

Employers will sometimes act violently against day laborers, mostly to circumvent payment for work partially completed or because they take issue with the work of a particular day laborer. Day laborers often discuss nonpayment of wages or being paid below an agreed amount as a form of violence, albeit economic. In most instances, violence directed by employers against day laborers is the result of a wage dispute or a conflict over work expectations. Below, Manuel, a day laborer of three years, describes abuse from a particular employer over poor payment for work completed.

I had an experience when I got here with a boss who took me to work. At the end of the job, after eight hours, he tells me, "You know what? Here is $20, and go help yourself. I'm going to help you and give you $20." I told him, "Hey, but $20 is very little." He took out a weapon and told me to leave. Since I did not know how to get around in the city, I got lost. I got home very late with less than half of the money because I had to spend it. It was sad, it was a bad experience. They take you to work and they do not pay you, and then they threaten you with a gun when you complain.

Misunderstandings between contractor and worker over workplace instructions, sometimes arising from day laborers' poor command of English, sometimes erupt in violence. Rudy, a day laborer from Guatemala, describes how a simple misunderstanding resulting from multiple instructions from two different contractors from the same company led to an unfortunate altercation.

> We were placing bricks. They told my friend to place them in a specific way, and then another came and told him to place them differently. And my friend asked them whom he should listen to, the man who was talking to him or the other one. And that upset the man he was talking to. And they hit my friend. They beat him, they threw him down . . . and that was when they wanted to hit me.

Sometimes employers, perhaps feeling the pressure of making a contractual deadline that could result in thousands of dollars of lost revenues, turn to desperate measures to complete a job quickly. Workers described instances in which employers would pressure them to continue working by yelling at them, getting in their face and intimidating, and pushing them around, or used violence and coercion to compel day laborers to work harder or to work for longer hours. Often they have underestimated the time needed to finish the job or the ability of the day laborer that they hired. Employers are quick to forget that there is no sure way of knowing the quality of the particular worker they are hiring off the streets. As a result, when they hire a day laborer and realize that he has little or no experience in a particular trade, they get angry and take out their frustration on the worker. Sometimes they beat a worker, as in an incident recalled by Rene, a day laborer of two years:

> I have seen some workers beaten. Only recently a young man started to work and he went to work with some Hawaiians, and since the guy didn't have the capacity of doing the work that he was contracted for, they beat him. They beat him and beat him, and they still came back to the corner and beat someone else. And they didn't pay him.

Some employers become violent to rid themselves of an injured worker. One worker retells an experience in which he was injured while on the job and the employer, rather than pay for care for him, asked him to leave at gunpoint.

> On one occasion I went to work with three others, and what happened was that I fell and could not get up, and the boss came out and he did not want to call the ambulance because he would have to pay, and so he took out a gun and pointed it and said, "Get out of my house," and so the other men got scared and he told them also, "You leave as well." And so the others began to leave, but I could not get up easily, and so one of my co-workers helped me to my feet and took me to the hospital.

Employers of day laborers clearly know that they are in an unfair power relation and sometimes take advantage by violently abusing their hired help. They may become violent for seemingly random reasons, including just being nasty. Day laborers, some who feel very fortunate to have secured employment for the day, find themselves in a terrible situation that makes them feel even more hopeless and desperate. Not knowing their legal rights and what to do about an abusive employer, some of them lash out in the only manner they see fit, through violence of their own.

DAY LABORERS' RESPONSES TO EMPLOYERS' ABUSE
AND VIOLENCE

Day laborers, like all workers, are human beings with quirks, dysfunctional behaviors, personal problems, and an ability to defend themselves. However, because most of them do not have proper documents to be in this country legally, they are less likely than other workers to challenge an unscrupulous employer, to engage in a fist fight after being pushed around or bullied, or to instigate a fight in response to a wage abuse or nonpayment. The fear of deportation is great, especially since the cost of getting back into this country is so high. Losing a day's wage is preferable to the cost of deportation and reentry, not to mention the opportunity cost of not being able to search for employment until one is able to return to the United States and search for work again.

But a day laborer can only take so much abuse and pain at the hands of a terrible employer. Being desperate for work, unable to feed oneself or one's family, and feeling the indignity of working a full day and then encountering an employer who does not wish to pay the agreed-upon wage or who attempts to pay a wage lower than was negotiated is enough to tip most human beings into violent action. Some day laborers defend themselves from violent or abusive employers by retaliating with violence, theft, or other forms of criminal behavior.[24] Pablo, a day laborer from El Salvador, told how an employer attempted to forestall payment after three days of work had been completed.

> He asked us to come back for another day of work and that he would pay us then. We said no, that we had agreed to get paid after the first day and that we had already worked for him for three days and he owed us. He laughed at us and then said, "Too bad, then, I won't pay you at all." The other day laborers and I then quickly gathered some of his expensive equipment and started walking away with it. We basically had a standoff and I thought we would have to fight him, but in the end he paid us, but only because we threatened to take his equipment or fight him for our wages.

Juan, thirty-two, tells of an employer who frequently bothered him at the work site, almost initiating a fight with him for no reason, until Juan was provoked to violence by the employer's assault on his person. The employer, apparently bothered by the Spanish music playing on Juan's portable radio, kept pulling out the cord from the electric outlet.

> And then I connected it [the cord] again. Then later he goes and pulls it again. Then later he goes and pulls it again. He tells me that if I keep on plugging it in he'll kill me. When it wasn't one thing, it was another, but he always bothered us. And once I was getting things in the big company refrigerator and he came and took a box without warning and hit me. I knew he had done it on purpose, and I was so angry that . . . there was a plastic tubing, and the truth is that I took it and hit him across the head. I said, "That's it. It's been several times that you've done this, but no more."

I have also heard of day laborers sabotaging or damaging a work site after not being paid or because of unfair treatment. Day laborers do not stand by passively in the face of abuse, but they do seem to respond only when provoked by very serious or repeated victimization.

Conclusion

Coming to the United States, searching for day labor, and working in this industry are difficult undertakings fraught with unforeseen dangers, abuses, and sometimes violence. Nevertheless, thousands of day laborers toil daily in temporary jobs, many more search for these jobs every day, and almost all day laborers have either experienced violent acts against themselves or witnessed such acts against their counterparts, whether this occurs while they are immigrating to the United States, searching for work in public spaces, or working day labor.

Even before entering the United States and looking for work in public spaces, would-be day laborers are likely to experience or witness violence in their travels to this country. Entering this country clandestinely is highly dangerous and difficult. Attempts to cross into the United States may involve violent incidents with robbers, *coyotes,* other would-be crossers, border vigilantes, or police from Mexico.

The search for day labor also involves a risk of violence. Day laborers are routinely harassed by gangs and individuals who yell at them, threaten them, or throw dangerous objects at them and may go so far as to assault them. Day laborers also fight among themselves for the scarce jobs that become available or for seemingly petty and personal reasons.

Finally, violence in the workplace can erupt because contractors are trying to avoid paying workers or fulfilling their contractual agreements, are dissatisfied with the help they hired, or are simply being bullies. Day laborers, for the most part, avoid conflict and encounters that lead to violence. However, there comes a point when desperation, angst, and frustration boil over and day laborers are provoked to act, sometimes violently.

To best comprehend violence in the day labor industry, three primary factors need to be considered: (1) day laborers' demographic and worker characteristics, (2) risk factors associated with workplace violence, and (3) the unique characteristics of day labor and its propensity to dole out work in the construction industry. As mentioned earlier, the overwhelming majority of day laborers are vulnerable to violence and other types of workplace abuses because they have second-class status by virtue of their illegal immigration status and their poor command of the English language. These factors alone largely explain why immigrants are likely to encounter abuse and exploitation in their search for work and while working day labor; they also explain why so many abusive acts committed against day laborers go unreported. Other factors are day laborers' recency of arrival (a full third have been in this country for less than one year), their low levels of education, and their inability to make wage claims and obtain other forms of government redress. Employers, merchants, residents, police, and others who wish to inflict harm, obtain an economic edge, or intimidate day laborers into leaving a neighborhood (or leaving the country) know that they can take advantage of the vulnerable position of these workers and get away with committing crimes against them.

In addition, several features of individuals and businesses that have been identified by researchers as heightening the likelihood of workplace violence are characteristic of day laborers and the day labor industry.[25] For example, almost all day laborers are young, male, and trying to survive under harsh economic conditions—factors that increase their tendency to resort to violence if things don't go their way. Risk factors of their business include the exchange of cash for work, the presence of few workers at the site, and, typically, face-to-face contact with clients. Client or employer characteristics may also help explain the incidence of violence in day labor. Employers who are young and male and businesses that are understaffed or under deadline are more likely to be associated with violence, and the construction industry in which so many day laborers are employed tends to fit this description. And given that violence between workers is higher among those who are young, male, poor, and affected by alcohol or other substances, the tendency of day laborers themselves to fit this description adds to the risk.

For many day laborers, then, violence in their work lives began on their trek to this country and, unfortunately, continues in this country—as they search for work, as they perform work and, after the workday, as they make their way home and fall prey to thieves and others. In their attempt to make a better life for themselves, this particular group of hardworking immigrants is finding that their road to economic security can be filled with violent hazards.

NOTES

I thank Dontraneil Clayborne and Jennifer Tran, students at the University of California, Los Angeles, for their assistance in analyzing the data on which this chapter is based.

1. See Black (1983).

2. In Los Angeles alone more than one hundred hiring sites exist, representing

approximately eighteen thousand to twenty thousand workers (Valenzuela 1999). In New York, where day labor can be traced back to the custom of hiring dock workers (stevedores) by telling them to "shape up," forming a half-circle so that they could be selected for work that day, contemporary hiring or "shape-up" sites number more than fifty (Valenzuela and Melendez, 2003). Finally, on the basis of our research for the National Day Labor Survey, more than four hundred formal and informal hiring sites exist throughout the United States (Valenzuela, 2005).

3. See, for example, O'Toole (2004); Associated Press (2004); Healy (2004); Moser (2004); Weathersbee (2004).

4. Van Derbeken (2005); Garcia (2004).

5. O'Toole (2004); Jones (2004); Associated Press (2004).

6. Castillo (2005); Gootman (2002); Associated Press State and Local Wire (2004); Healy (2004).

7. Weathersbee (2004); O'Toole (2004); Jones (2004).

8. Pritchard (2004).

9. Pritchard (2004).

10. Di Martino (2002).

11. Mayhew (2002).

12. Mayhew (2003: 32).

13. Chasin (2004).

14. Jenkins (1996).

15. Heskitt (1996: 16); Warshaw and Messite (1996).

16. See Valenzuela (2002).

17. Chasin (2004).

18. Chasin (2004).

19. Black (1983).

20. See Valenzuela (2003) for a review of the literature on day labor.

21. See Kalleberg (2000).

22. *Coyotes* are mostly men (however, some women undertake this task) who clandestinely transport immigrants across the U.S.-Mexico border for a fee.

23. Jordan (2005).

24. Black (1983).

25. Heskitt (1996: 16); Warshaw and Messite (1996).

REFERENCES

Associated Press. 2004. "Attack Raises Racism Worries: Georgia Teens Accused of Beating Man." *Columbia Daily Tribune,* May 11.

Associated Press State and Local Wire. 2004. "Pennsylvania Man Arraigned on Charges He Robbed Day Laborers." August 4.

Black, Donald. 1983. "Crime as Social Control." *American Sociological Review* 48 (February): 34–45.

Castillo, A. Alfonso. 2005. "Justice for Beaten Day Laborers." *Newsday* (New York), February 12.

Chasin, H. Barbara. 2004. *Inequality and Violence in the United States: Casualties of Capitalism.* Amherst, NY: Humanity Books.

Di Martino, V. 2002. *Joint Programme on Workplace Violence in the Health Sector: Synthesis Report.* Informal Technical Consultation Draft Document. Geneva: International Labour Organization, International Council of Nurses, World Health Organization, and Public Services International.

Garcia, Ernie. 2004. "Cash-Carrying Illegals Fall Prey to Crime." *Journal News* (New York), March 21.

Gootman, Elissa. 2002. "2nd Man Gets 25-Year Term for Beating Mexican Day Laborers." *New York Times,* January 10.

Healy, Patrick. 2004. "Latest Crimes against Migrants on Long Island Have a Familiar Ring." *New York Times,* July 27.

Heskitt, S. 1996. *Workplace Violence: Before, During, and After.* Boston: Butterworth-Heinemann.

Jenkins, L. 1996. *Violence in the Workplace: Risk Factors and Prevention Strategies.* Washington, DC: National Institute for Occupational Safety and Health.

Jones, Tiani. 2004. "Hispanic Day Laborers Targeted by Thieves." *First Coast News* (Jacksonville, FL), November 10.

Jordan, J. Lara. 2005. "Minutemen to Patrol Arizona Border." Associated Press, February 21.

Kalleberg, Arne L. 2000. "Nonstandard Employment Relations: Part-Time, Temporary, and Contract Work." *Annual Review of Sociology* 26:341–65.

Mayhew, C. 2002. "Occupational Violence in Industrialized Countries: Types, Incidence Patterns, and 'at Risk' Groups of Workers." In *Violence at Work: Causes, Patterns and Prevention,* edited by M. Gill, B. Fisher, and V. Bowie, 21–40. Cullomption: Willan.

———. 2003. "Occupational Violence: A Neglected Occupational Safety and Health Issue?" *Policy and Practice in Health and Safety* 1 (1): 31–58.

Moser, Bob. 2004. "The Battle of 'Georgiafornia.'" *Southern Poverty Law Center, Intelligence Report,* no. 116 (Winter).

O'Toole, Cathleen. 2004. "Latin Community Targeted." *First Coast News* (Jacksonville, Florida), November 10.

Pritchard, Justin. 2004. "Mexican-Born Workers More Likely to Die on Job: Risky Work, Compliant Attitude and Language Barrier Contribute to the Trend, AP Study Shows." *Associated Press,* March 14.

Valenzuela, Abel, Jr. 1999. "Day Laborers in Southern California: Preliminary Findings from the Day Labor Survey." Working Paper (Technical Report) 99-04.

Center for the Study of Urban Poverty, Institute for Social Science Research, University of California, Los Angeles.

———. 2002. "Working on the Margins in Metropolitan Los Angeles: Immigrants in Day Labor Work." *Migraciones Internacionales* 1 (2): 5–28.

———. 2003. "Day-Labor Work." *Annual Review of Sociology* 29 (1): 307–33.

———. 2005. "Final Narrative Report: National Day Labor Study." Rockefeller and Ford Foundations, Center for the Study of Urban Poverty, University of California, Los Angeles (May 3).

Valenzuela, Abel, Jr., and Edwin Melendez. 2003. "Day Labor in New York: Findings from the NYDL Survey." Technical Report 03-01. Center for the Study of Urban Poverty, Institute for Social Science Research, University of California, Los Angeles, California and Community Development Research Center, Milano Graduate School of Management and Urban Policy, New School University, New York.

Van Derbeken, Jaxon. 2005. "2 Recent Immigrants Die in Drive-by Shooting in Mission." *San Francisco Chronicle*, January 25.

Warshaw, L., and J. Messite. 1996. "Workplace Violence: Preventive and Interventive Strategies." *Journal of Occupational and Environmental Medicine* 38 (10): 993–1005.

Weathersbee, Tonyaa. 2004. "Leads Needed to Stop Wave of Violence against Laborers." *Florida Times-Union*, November 29.

Chapter 10

Multiple Disadvantages and Crime among Black Immigrants

Exploring Haitian Violence in Miami's Communities

Amie L. Nielsen and Ramiro Martinez Jr.

"We have a criminal element that has nothing to do with the vast majority of law-abiding Haitian-American citizens who are making significant contributions to this community." This statement was made by a high-ranking Miami Police Department official to the *Miami Herald* and rephrased to one of the authors in the late 1990s. It seemed to acknowledge both that violent gang activity was rapidly increasing in the northeastern Miami community of Little Haiti and that the problem was relatively rare and involved a small segment of residents in the poor but hardworking neighborhood. This statement also reflected a transformation researchers were documenting at that time. Specifically, as the children of the first wave of Haitian immigrants matured, a growing number were engaging in crime and violence rather than adapting to work in a struggling local economy. At the same time, neighborhood residents were enduring high levels of homicide, whether it was gang related or not[1] and were encountering negative stereotypes about Haitians.

However, as the high-ranking police official suggests, most Haitians were negotiating the difficult terrain they faced in the impoverished community by attending school and working at least one job while avoiding becoming victims of, much less engaging in, street violence. Also, many residents realized that absorption into mainstream society was a difficult and complex process for the new black immigrants as they navigated life within and beyond the Miami neighborhood of Little Haiti. Few immigrant groups have had to overcome the racial, economic, and political obstacles (explained in more detail below) to attaining the "American dream" that are confronted by Haitians in the United States.[2] Despite the wide recognition of such difficulties, the issue of whether the multiple disadvantages faced by many Haitian immigrants have led to high levels of involvement in violence is relatively unexamined.

Our specific interests in examining nonlethal violence among Haitians stem from our collaborative efforts on racial/ethnic differences in homicide. In a series of published articles and book chapters, written jointly and with others, we have argued that immigrant groups, Latino and Afro-Caribbean in general and Mariel Cubans and Haitians specifically, have been consistently ignored in violent crime studies. The relatively few existing studies have usually demonstrated that homicides among immigrant groups were lower than expected given high levels of economic disadvantage.[3] We found that at various points in the late 1980s Haitians had lower homicide rates than the Miami city total and than African Americans[4] but that Haitians were more likely to be homicide victims than other Afro-Caribbean groups.[5] Last, we found that Haitians are rarely overinvolved as either victims or offenders in the types of homicide that concern the public (e.g., those involving strangers or robberies).[6] In sum, we did not find a high degree of Haitian involvement in homicide or homicide types. However, these studies covered an earlier time (1980–90) and examined some of the first Haitian arrivals, or at least those who arrived as young adults. As discussed below, segmented assimilation perspectives suggest that Haitians and especially their children may have faced another set of obstacles—downward mobility—since then.[7]

This chapter updates the first studies on Haitians and violence for a number of compelling reasons. Many Haitians encounter obstacles and difficulties that most ethnic minorities routinely avoid.[8] Not only are they born abroad, but they are also black, and they converse in a language—French Creole—rarely used by others in the United States. Further, the Centers for Disease Control and the popular media have singled them out and labeled them as public health threats (e.g., AIDS prone and drug abusers), and they have faced a harsh reception due to prejudice and discrimination from the government: U.S. Coast Guard interception of boats of Haitian refugees before their entry into U.S. waters, a disproportionately high rate of incarceration in the Immigration and Naturalization Service's Krome Detention Center on the edge of the Everglades in far west Miami, and one of the highest rejection rates of political asylum requests for any national group. These distinctions have separated Haitians[9] from other immigrant and ethnic group members and proved formidable obstacles to adaptation and assimilation. Haitians have undergone a great deal of adversity to enter and reside in the United States. Yet little is known about how, or if, they respond to the crime-generating conditions found in similarly situated immigrant or nonimmigrant black communities.

In light of this we follow the writings of other race and crime scholars by extending earlier research on the relatively rare crime of homicide to examine aggravated assault and armed robbery for this theoretically important Haitian population.[10] Because of the potential influence on immigrant life experiences of living in a neighborhood dominated by co-ethnics, we also compare Haitian violence patterns within and outside the confines of Little Haiti. This is important because failing to do so may result in misleading conclusions about the race and crime relationship. Our chapter suggests that race and crime studies should acknowledge the growth of black immigrant groups and immigrant crime.[11] Indeed, researchers should move beyond studying just whites and blacks, as well as Latinos, whenever possible. We examine Haitian nonlethal victimization rates and the varying community contexts in which these occur, including Miami's Haitian neighborhood of Little Haiti and adjacent primarily African American and Caribbean Latino communities. This enables us to examine the contexts—economic and racial/ethnic/immigrant—of Haitian victimization.

Finally, the study of Haitian crime beyond the confines of Little Haiti is important. Not only does it illuminate within-race variations in crime, but it also offers the opportunity for investigating the impact of nativity, ethnic communities, and economic conditions for understanding crime. In this regard, the study of Haitians challenges scholarship on race and crime. Because they are "black," Haitians confront bias and bigotry similar to that faced by African Americans. Yet they are distinct from African Americans because of language, cultural background, and immigration experiences. These social forces and multiple disadvantages, combined with residence in highly segregated black and immigrant areas[12] and areas with poor economic conditions, suggest that Haitians should have high levels of violent crime victimization. Yet research has established that immigrant groups, regardless of race, have lower crime involvement than native minority populations.[13] Along with other immigrant groups, including those from the Caribbean, Haitians may be less crime involved than expected despite their isolation and disadvantage.

Below, we address three questions that contribute to the nascent Haitian violent crime literature: How do Haitians fare relative to African Americans or Caribbean Latinos? Are black immigrants more or less crime involved (as assessed by victimization) inside or outside Little Haiti? To what extent are there variations in Haitian violence victimization across communities that differ in terms of economic conditions and racial/ethnic/immigrant compositions? By addressing these issues, this chapter moves beyond the traditional ecological perspective that characterizes much macro criminological research, and it represents one of the first attempts to compare violence within the Haitian population in distinct local communities.

To understand Haitian violence, we draw on three prominent theoretical approaches rooted in the violence and immigration literatures: segmented assimilation theory, social disorganization theory, and the immigration revitalization perspective. Before extending this discussion, however, we provide a brief history of Miami's immigrant/racial/ethnic groups, with an emphasis on Haitians.

The Research Context: Haitians in Miami

Miami, Florida, has been transformed since the 1960s largely because of immigration.[14] While the city is often associated with Cubans, other Latino groups and Haitians arrived in appreciable numbers in the early 1980s, making Miami the gateway for immigrants from the Caribbean and from Central and South America. The area has been cited both as an example of a successful ethnic enclave with regard to its Cuban population and as a key setting where segmented assimilation may occur, particularly for Haitians.[15] Thus the city represents a particularly important site for examining many social phenomena, including violence, for "as immigration from Latin America continues, the situation in Miami is likely to foretell changes and challenges throughout the United States."[16]

Haitians began immigrating in substantial numbers to other areas of the United States, especially the Northeast, in the late 1950s and 1960s following political turmoil in Haiti. Subsequent Haitian immigrants, including those who moved to Miami beginning around 1980, tended to be less well off than earlier arrivals. Although often still fleeing the political situation, these initial Haitian immigrants in Miami were considered by the U.S. government to be economic refugees rather than political refugees, an important distinction that led the United States to try to keep Haitians from entering the country. However, the treatment of Haitians, particularly in 1980, when contrasted with the admission of Mariel Cubans to the United States, was viewed by many as racist, and this led to efforts to help this group enter and remain in the country.[17] Although Haitians had some preexisting contact with the United States and some agencies assisted them in settling in the Miami area, for the most part their entry and adjustment were difficult.

Many Haitians and other migrants from the Caribbean possess relatively limited education and skill levels compared to natives.[18] Stereotypes concerning cleanliness, the carrying of diseases (tuberculosis, HIV), and drug use provided additional obstacles for Haitians to overcome upon arriving in the United States and trying to find jobs.[19] The stigma associated with being Haitian limited the ability of some members of this group to obtain legitimate jobs in the local community, especially in the early 1980s. Language barriers were also important, as French Creole is a language not spoken by many non-Haitians. As time passed, however, many adult Haitians were able to gain access to legitimate employment, albeit typically in low-skill and low-paying jobs. Others became involved in the "informal" sector and performed off-the-books jobs for cash. While a small number of Haitians are professionals or middle class, the socioeconomic conditions of Haitians in Miami overall are "dismal."[20] Additionally, except for members of the middle class, Haitians are residentially concentrated in "the poorest ghetto areas[, which] is not surprising, given the unwelcome official reception and their own modest backgrounds."[21]

Theoretical Approaches

The multiple disadvantages Haitians continue to face in Miami provide a unique opportunity to explore theories of crime and violence. We draw upon segmented assimilation theory, social disorganization theory, and the immigrant revitalization perspective to help us conceptualize the potential relevance of studying Haitians and Haitian violence. Each provides a different view of the role of immigrants with regard to crime.

Segmented Assimilation Theory

According to this perspective, "social capital," or the ability to gain access to resources by virtue of membership in social networks and social structure, is a key element in explaining the achievements or difficulties faced by immigrant groups. Some immigrant communities are very poor, but they may be able to assist co-ethnics in adapting to the new area while buffering deleterious factors typically associated with crime (e.g., extreme disadvantage). Segmented assimilation also describes processes through which the second generation may become assimilated into different race and class groups (e.g., inner-city black vs. immigrant ethnic enclave) rather than only into the American (mainstream) middle class.[22]

Haitians are a group that may be particularly at risk for segmented assimilation, especially downward mobility into the urban underclass. Although Little Haiti is an important neighborhood for many Haitians, as an impoverished community with few jobs it does not offer the economic advantages that some other ethnic communities do. As noted above, Haitians have had a difficult time becoming incorporated into the local economy. Additionally, the west side of Little Haiti is adjacent to a sizable African American community (Liberty City) that has been and is now largely disenfranchised.[23] Altogether, these conditions—modes of incorporation, race, lack of economic mobility due to the nature of Miami's economy, and inner-city residential location—provide a situation that increases the possibility that second-generation Haitians (and those who immigrated when very young) may assimilate into a street-oriented and largely impoverished African American culture.[24] Such assimilation includes perceived and actual discrimination based on race, a devaluing of education, and an oppositional culture, increasing the likelihood of downward socioeconomic mobility.[25]

Such assimilation also has potentially important consequences for violence.[26] In Philadelphia, Anderson demonstrates that a phenomenon similar to an oppositional culture, what he terms a "code of the street," emerges that serves to promote violence in impoverished and disorganized African American communities.[27] Such a code of the street specifies the use of violence for many reasons, including demonstrating masculinity, defending oneself, and gaining and maintaining respect as well as acquiring goods or money. A number of scholars argue that similar processes occur in other locations and can involve different racial/ethnic groups.[28] From this perspective, Haitians living in or navigating on the fringes of Liberty City and Overtown, two predominantly African American and disadvantaged communities, may be at especially high risk of violence involvement.

Social Disorganization Theory

The original focus of this line of inquiry was to illustrate the role that social conditions played in shaping crime-inducing contexts in immigrant communities in urban Chicago in the early and middle twentieth century. According to this perspective, economic disadvantage, population instability, and racial/ethnic heterogeneity were structural conditions that served to undermine community social control, or the ability of communities to exert social control over the behavior of neighborhood residents or visitors.[29] Such disorganized communities had high rates of juvenile delinquency and other social problems over time, regardless of which racial/ethnic/immigrant groups lived in the areas. Indeed, Shaw and McKay argued that the higher levels of delinquency among (European) immigrant groups and blacks in Chicago were due to the neighborhoods and their accompanying conditions into which the groups moved and resided. Such findings led these scholars to conclude that it was characteristics of communities, rather than racial/ethnic/immigrant groups per se, that were associated with high delinquency and crime rates.[30] From this perspective, higher levels of violence should be found especially in those areas with the highest levels of economic disadvantage and other negative community conditions, which historically included immigration as a social process that weakened community social bonds because of increased population instability (turnover) and increased racial/ethnic heterogeneity.

Immigrant Revitalization

A third theoretical perspective suggests that immigrants may help to revitalize the communities into which they move. That is, according to this perspective recent immigration does not disrupt social ties and undermine community social controls in the manner predicted by social disorganization theory.[31] Instead, immigrants may encourage new types of social organization and strengthen neighborhood institutions and social ties. Because they do so, areas with higher levels of immigration may be able to negate the criminogenic conditions (e.g., economic disadvantage) of communities into which immigrants often first move. Thus immigrants may help to stabilize communities and to reduce rates of crime.[32] If the immigrant revitalization perspective is correct, we should expect to see lower levels of violence involvement for Haitians in Little Haiti and in other communities where there are high levels of recent immigrants (Allapattah and Wynwood) than in neighborhoods such as Liberty City and Overtown, where there are few recent immigrants.

Miami offers a unique opportunity to consider the relative merits of these three theoretical perspectives through an examination of Haitian violence victimization in the local communities in which Haitians have settled. All of these areas have relatively sizable populations of Haitians, although they differ in their sizes and proportions of residents. They also vary in the racial/ethnic/immigrant compositions of other residents and in their economic conditions. This enables us to consider Haitian victimization in a variety of local contexts.

Ethnic Communities

Our study of Miami's Haitian communities allows us to provide empirical evidence on the characteristics of local communities where Haitians reside and where they are largely victimized. Here we examine locally recognized neighborhoods within the city of Miami. We focus on those that are particularly relevant for Haitians, including communities with large numbers of Haitian residents and those with smaller numbers but adjacent to Little Haiti. Little Haiti itself is of central relevance, but it is surrounded by neighborhoods that vary tremendously in racial/ethnic composition and economic conditions. Most are areas in which large proportions of members of other ethnic groups live and are recognized as such (e.g., Puerto Ricans in Wynwood) rather than locations that necessarily include many businesses that employ co-ethnics. Little Haiti includes both a sizable Haitian population and small businesses owned by co-ethnics, while two of the predominantly African American neighborhoods (Overtown and Liberty City) now are recognized more as local black ghettos. We discuss each of these "ethnic communities" below. Figure 10.1 shows the locations of these communities in the northern part of the city of Miami.

Little Haiti was established in the late 1970s and early 1980s. Based on support from a number of organizations and from middle-class Haitians in New York and other U.S. urban areas, the new community of Little Haiti included small businesses and agencies to serve Haitians.[33] Some of

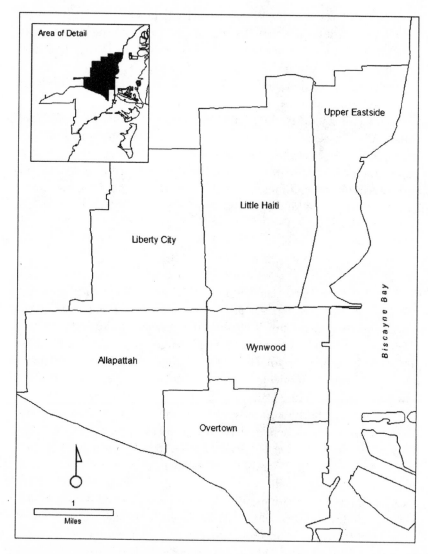

Fig. 10.1. Miami's Ethnic Communities

the newly arrived Haitians settled in and around Little Haiti. Most Haitians lived near other co-ethnics or with or near African Americans. Little Haiti itself tends to be populated by poorer Haitians, with middle-class Haitians living elsewhere even if they own businesses in the neighborhood. The community itself may be characterized as "weak" economically and politically.[34] Indeed, because it lacks financially successful businesses and an employment opportunity structure for the incorporation of other co-ethnics, Stepick indicates that Little Haiti, as of the mid-1990s, did not qualify as an ethnic enclave.[35]

In the city of Miami, there are two predominantly African American communities. These two neighborhoods, Overtown and Liberty City, are now extremely impoverished, and businesses and related job opportunities are few and far between. However, both neighborhoods originally included many businesses and some well-to-do residents. Overtown was established early in Miami's history, while Liberty City developed more recently (1930s to 1940s).[36]

Two other communities studied are predominantly Caribbean Latino areas, Wynwood and Allapattah. While not technically an immigrant group, the Puerto Rican population in Miami is large. Puerto Ricans began moving to the Miami area in the 1950s,[37] and by 1990 more than twelve thousand members of this group lived in the city. About one-fifth of this population resides in Wynwood,[38] the primary neighborhood known locally for its relatively sizable Puerto Rican community. However, other Latinos, including Hondurans, Colombians, Dominicans, Nicaraguans, and Cubans (newer arrivals including Balseros ["rafters"] and Mariel Cubans) reside here as well.[39] And the area is also home to relatively sizable numbers of Haitians. Similarly, although a primarily Latino area, Allapattah has a relatively large Haitian population. In Allapattah the largest ethnic groups are Cubans (including Balseros and Mariels) and other Latinos from the Caribbean and Central America (especially Dominicans, Nicaraguans, and Hondurans) as well as Puerto Ricans.[40] This area is next to the Miami International Airport and adjacent to both Liberty City and Little Haiti.

The last area considered is the regentrified Upper Eastside community. This is a waterfront and relatively affluent neighborhood forming the northeastern tip of Miami that is located along Biscayne Bay just north of the downtown area. The area is adjacent to Little Haiti and Wynwood. It is the most ethnically diverse community considered in this chapter and includes a sizable proportion of whites and a relatively large Haitian population.

The emphasis on examining community variations in Haitian violence and the characteristics of such areas is a unique contribution of this chapter to the race/ethnic/immigrant crime literature. We consider our data next.

The Current Study and Methods

The data used in this study come from two sources. The information for the community characteristics is derived from the 1990 U.S. Census.[41] The violence data are based on aggravated assault and robbery victimizations that occurred in 1996 and 1997 in the city of Miami, Florida, and were reported to the Miami Police Department (MPD). Haitian victims were determined through two procedures: checking self-reported identity in the MPD reports and using a French Creole surname dictionary. The location of each reported victim incident was linked to the census tract in which it occurred, and the number of victims for each tract was computed. The communities examined in this study are each based on two or more census tracts and reflect boundaries recognized by city agencies as well as our knowledge of the local context.

We examined Haitian victimization involving the two most common forms of violence—aggravated assaults and robberies. The numbers of victims of each offense in 1996 and 1997 were averaged for the two years. We calculated victimization rates per thousand Haitians based on the number of victims divided by the number of Haitian residents per tract and multiplied by one thousand. In the results presented, the rates are based on average rates per thousand for the local community areas. A similar approach was used to calculate white, African American, and Latino violence victimization rates.

We focused on the six local communities in Miami displayed in figure 10.1 in which the vast majority of the city's Haitians reside and are victims of violence.[42] Each community is composed of multiple census tracts.[43] The communities combined contain about 40 percent of the city's population and 97 percent of the city's Haitian population. To examine the economic and racial/ethnic/immigrant compositions of each of the communities, we relied on several measures from the 1990 census. The economic measures included the percentage of the population living below the poverty line, the percentage of adults twenty-five and older who did not complete high school, and the percentage of employed persons (sixteen and older) working in low-skill jobs. All are relevant for consideration of social capital and segmented assimilation. Additionally, we examined the following measures of racial/ethnic and immigrant composition: the percentage of the population that was Haitian, the percentage of the population that was African American, and the percentage of immigrants that arrived in the 1980s.

Results

We first consider the economic characteristics and racial/ethnic/immigrant composition of the six communities of interest. This enables us to begin to address the question of the extent to which there are variations in Haitian violence victimization rates across communities that differ in terms of economic conditions and racial/ethnic/immigrant compositions. Figure 10.2 shows the economic characteristics of each of the six communities. Overall, Little Haiti is among the most disadvantaged areas according to the three measures we examine. While Overtown has the highest levels of poverty (49 percent), Little Haiti, Liberty City, and Wynwood each follow closely behind with about 45 percent of their populations living in poverty. "Only" one-third of Allapattah's residents are impoverished, while the Upper Eastside has the lowest levels at just under one-quarter of residents in poverty.

On the percentage of high school dropouts, an important measure of social capital, Little Haiti fares the worst among the communities. Two-thirds of the area's residents did not complete high school. This is also the

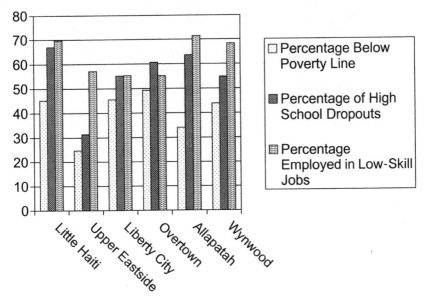

Fig. 10.2. Economic Characteristics in Miami Communities (Minimum of Fifty Haitian Residents per Tract). *Source*: U.S. Census (1990a, 1990b).

case for just over 60 percent of adults living in Allapattah and Overtown. In Liberty City and Wynwood, more than half of adults did not finish high school, while this is true of about one-third of residents of the Upper Eastside. Given the high proportions of adults who did not complete high school, it is not surprising that most of Little Haiti's and Allapattah's employed populations are working in low-skill jobs. Most (68 percent) of Wynwood's working adults are also employed in low-skill jobs. For the other three areas, over half of employed adults are working in low-skill jobs. Given the Upper Eastside's relatively low percentage of adults who did not complete high school, it is somewhat surprising that levels of low-skill employment are nearly as high as in the other areas and in some cases are slightly higher.

Figure 10.3 shows the racial/ethnic/immigrant compositions of the six communities. Not surprisingly, Little Haiti has the largest percentage of Haitian residents at 44 percent. About one-quarter of the Upper Eastside's residents are Haitian, while this is so for about 5 to 10 percent of the populations of the other four areas. African Americans constitute just under 40 percent of the population of Little Haiti. Both Liberty City and Overtown are predominantly African American communities. African Americans constitute between 14 and 20 percent of residents in the Upper Eastside, Allapattah, and Wynwood. Although not shown, both of the latter two areas have majority Latino populations. With regard to percentage of recent immigrants, about one-third of Allapattah's (32.6 percent) and Little Haiti's (31.7 percent) residents moved to the United States between 1980 and 1990; the Upper Eastside and Wynwood follow closely behind. The percentage of recent immigrants in Liberty City and Overtown is much smaller.

In sum, the economic characteristics of the areas suggest that Little Haiti is at least as disadvantaged as the other areas. This is especially the case in comparison to Liberty City and Overtown, the two recognized very disadvantaged and predominantly African American communities in Miami. The Upper Eastside is the most advantaged, relatively speaking, particularly with regard to poverty and high school noncompletion. If immigrants are disorganizing areas, Little Haiti in particular, given its high levels of immigrants and disadvantaged economic status, should have the highest rates of Haitian violence victimization. Alternatively, if Haitians residing in economically disadvantaged, predominantly African American areas are experiencing downward mobility and acceptance of norms of such poor communities, including an oppositional culture, arguments

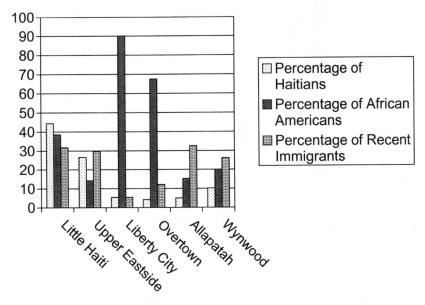

Fig. 10.3. Ethnic Composition of Miami Communities (Minimum of Fifty Haitian Residents per Tract). *Source*: U.S. Census (1990a, 1990b).

consistent with segmented assimilation, we should expect Haitian victimization rates to be higher in areas such as Liberty City and Overtown. Before we consider these issues, however, we address the question of how Haitians fare relative to African Americans or Caribbean Latinos. Figure 10.4 enables us to examine this issue.

Figure 10.4 shows Haitian, white, African American, Latino, and total violence rates for the six communities (combined) under consideration.[44] These results show that Haitians have lower aggravated assault and robbery victimization rates than do the other groups. Aggravated assault rates are highest for African Americans and whites, followed by Latinos. Overall, robbery rates are much higher for whites than for the other groups. Latinos and African Americans have relatively similar robbery rates.

While we see that Haitians overall have the lowest violent crime rates compared to other groups, we now address whether this black immigrant group is more or less crime involved (as assessed by victimization) inside or outside Little Haiti. Figure 10.5 enables us to examine this issue. As the figure shows, Haitian violence victimization rates are highest in Overtown and Liberty City. In Overtown, aggravated assault rates are about 43 per

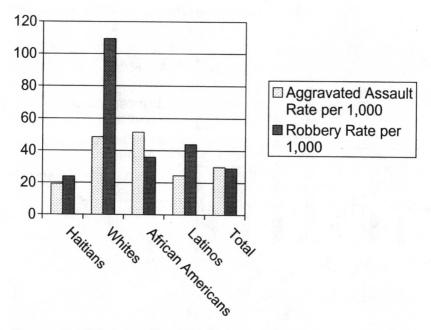

Fig. 10.4. Race/Ethnic-Specific Violence Victimization Rates (per 1,000) (Minimum of Fifty Group-Specific Residents per Tract)

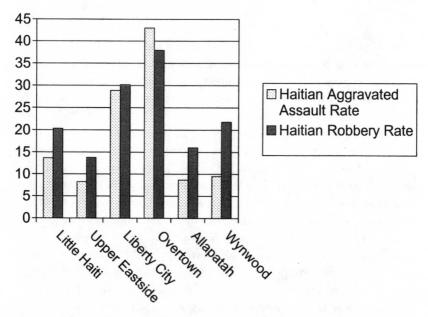

Fig. 10.5. Haitian Violence Rates (per 1,000) in Miami Communities (Minimum of Fifty Haitian Residents per Tract). *Source*: U.S. Census (1990a, 1990b).

1,000 Haitians, while robbery rates are about 38 per 1,000 Haitian residents. In Liberty City, there are about 30 victims per 1,000 Haitian residents for both aggravated assault and robbery. Little Haiti has a slightly higher aggravated assault rate than the three remaining areas, at 13.7 per 1,000 Haitian residents. This is followed by Wynwood, Allapattah, and the Upper Eastside. For robbery, both Wynwood (21.8) and Little Haiti (20.3) have similar rates per 1,000 residents. Rates per thousand Haitian residents are somewhat lower in the Upper Eastside and Allapattah. Haitian rates vary across communities, yet they are never as high as might be expected given residence in disadvantaged communities.

Conclusion

In this chapter we examined Haitian violence victimization across Miami communities. To our knowledge, this is one of the first studies to focus on Haitian violence at the local level. Although descriptive, it enables initial exploration into the community contexts associated with aggravated assault and robbery victimizations of Haitians. It also provides an opportunity to explore whether living in the primary Haitian "ethnic neighborhood" in Miami—Little Haiti—offers protective effects from victimization, an argument consistent with the immigrant revitalization perspective,[45] or represents a disorganized area marked by especially high victimization rates. Additionally, it allows an opportunity to explore the possibility of downward mobility and acceptance of a "code of the street" or "oppositional culture" for Haitians living in primarily impoverished African American communities, an argument consistent with the segmented assimilation perspective.[46]

Our results are more in line with the immigrant revitalization perspective and to a lesser extent with segmented assimilation perspectives. Despite being among the most disadvantaged areas considered, Little Haiti had Haitian violence victimization rates similar to those in Wynwood but slightly higher than those in Allapattah and the Upper Eastside. Notably, the aggravated assault rates and robbery rates in Overtown were two to three times higher than those in Little Haiti, and those in Liberty City were about twice as high as those found in Little Haiti. That is, Haitians were victimized at much higher rates in predominantly African American and very disadvantaged areas than in Little Haiti, despite its equivalent or even higher levels of disadvantage. Although we are examining victimization rather than offending, these results suggest that Haitians in very disadvantaged African American neighborhoods are at least exposed to high levels of violence, findings consistent with segmented assimilation arguments.

Additionally, our results suggest that Little Haiti (and the adjacent Latino and immigrant communities) may offer a buffer from victimization. At a minimum, Little Haiti does not have substantially higher victimization rates than largely Caribbean Latino areas (Allapattah, Wynwood, and Upper Eastside), and its rates are much lower than in African American communities. These findings are consistent with the immigrant revitalization perspective.[47]

Nevertheless, some support for social disorganization theory is also evidenced with regard to poverty. That is, two of the most impoverished areas (Overtown and Liberty City) had the highest violence rates, while the least impoverished community (the Upper Eastside) had correspondingly low Haitian violence rates. Still, poverty and other economic conditions were as severe in Little Haiti and Wynwood as in Overtown and Liberty City, and these areas had lower rates of Haitian violence victimization.

In sum, this exploratory study suggests that Haitian nonlethal violence victimization rates are lower than might be expected in Little Haiti, and for Haitians overall relative to other ethnic groups, given the socioeconomic conditions and manner of reception to which this group has been subject. Despite the multiple disadvantages Haitians have experienced, their rates of violence are low overall. Although we address victimization rather than offending, such findings are in contrast to the widely publicized "criminal immigrant" stereotype found in the media, echoed by some politicians but disputed by others, such as the police department official quoted at the beginning of this chapter.

Clearly, however, many questions remain for future research, including, for example, whether similar predictors influence Haitian violence in Miami as those in other cities with sizable Haitian communities, such as Boston or New York City. More importantly, we encourage other crime scholars to acknowledge and examine the impact of black immigrants from all parts of the Caribbean and Africa. The increasingly diverse population of the United States requires us to think more about the impact of immigration, more about newcomers, and more about how immigrants influence routine types of violence in poor but "law-abiding" communities like Little Haiti.

NOTES

We would like to especially thank Robert Crutchfield, Robert Bursik Jr., and Richard Rosenfeld, as well as the other participants of the National Consortium on Violence Research conference "Beyond Racial Dichotomies of Violence: Immigrants, Race, and Ethnicity," at the University of California, Los Angeles, November 6–8, 2003, for their helpful comments on an earlier version of this chapter. Alex Stepick and Matthew T. Lee provided valuable comments on a later version of the chapter, and we thank them as well.

1. For example, Miami's black homicide offender rate in 1995 was almost 60 per 100,000 (Martinez 2002: 98). Levels among black youths and young adults were even higher (Martinez 2002: 129). While these rates are not community specific, the vast majority of these homicides occurred in or around Little Haiti.

2. Stepick (1998).

3. See Martinez and Lee (1998). The percentage of Haitian homicide victims was in line with their percentage of city population.

4. Martinez and Lee (2000b: 513).

5. Martinez and Lee (2000a).

6. See Martinez, Nielsen, and Lee (2003); Martinez, Lee, and Nielsen (2001).

7. Portes and Zhou (1993); Zhou (1997).

8. Stepick et al. (2001).

9. For more background, see Stepick et al. (2001).

10. For studies that examine race-specific nonlethal violence at the community level, see, for example, McNulty (2001); Nielsen, Martinez, and Lee (2005); Woolredge and Thistlethwaite (2003).

11. According to Logan and Deane (2003), just over 68 percent of all Afro-Caribbeans are foreign born.

12. Logan and Deane (2003).

13. Lee and Martinez (2002); Martinez (2000).

14. Portes and Stepick (1993); Waldinger (2001b).

15. Stepick (1998); Stepick et al. (2003).

16. Stepick et al. (2003: 25); but see Waldinger (2001a).

17. Stepick (1998).

18. Stepick (1998); Waldinger and Lee (2001).

19. Portes and Stepick (1985); Stepick (1998).

20. Stepick (1992: 67; 1998).

21. Portes and Stepick (1993: 56).

22. Portes and Rumbaut (2003).

23. See Dunn (1997); Portes and Stepick (1993); Stepick (1998). As Zhou ([2001: 291], but see Stepick 1998) notes concerning the greater Miami area, especially in contrast to other major centers of immigration, "[T]he stark decline in second-

and third-generation [college attendance] rates in Miami is likely a reflection of the problems encountered by blacks in this relatively poor southern metropolis."

24. Portes and Zhou (1993).

25. Portes and Zhou (1993); Stepick (1998); Stepick et al. (2003); Waters (1994); Zhou (1997).

26. Martinez, Lee, and Nielsen (2004).

27. Anderson (1999).

28. Baumer et al. (2003); Kubrin and Weitzer (2003); see also Sampson and Wilson (1995).

29. Shaw and McKay ([1942] 1969).

30. See also Sampson and Wilson (1995).

31. Shaw and McKay ([1942] 1969).

32. Lee, Martinez, and Rosenfeld (2001); Lee (2003).

33. Portes and Stepick (1993); Stepick (1992, 1998).

34. Portes and Stepick (1993).

35. Stepick (1998).

36. Dunn (1997); Portes and Stepick (1993).

37. Dunn (1997).

38. U.S. Bureau of the Census (1990a).

39. U.S. Bureau of the Census (1990b).

40. U.S. Bureau of the Census (1990b).

41. U.S. Bureau of the Census (1990b).

42. There are tracts that have no Haitian residents but that have Haitian victims, as there are also tracts that have a few Haitian residents and no victims. Nonetheless, the vast majority of victimizations occurred in the communities under consideration.

43. We established a fifty–Haitian resident minimum for inclusion in the study (to help stabilize the victimization rates). That led to the exclusion of one tract each from the original Liberty City and Allapattah areas. The tracts constituting the communities average, at a minimum, more than 143 Haitians per tract (Overtown) up to in excess of 2,100 persons (Little Haiti). Little Haiti is composed of seven tracts, Liberty City has six tracts, the Upper Eastside has three tracts, and Overtown, Allapattah, and Wynwood each have four tracts.

44. For each group, a minimum threshold of fifty residents per tract was established. Similar cross-group comparisons are found for the entire city and within the individual communities, with two exceptions involving Haitians (robbery rates are slightly higher for Haitians than for Latinos in Allapattah and in Overtown).

45. Lee, Martinez, and Rosenfeld (2001); Lee (2003).

46. Portes and Zhou (1993); Stepick et al. (2003); Waters (1994).

47. Lee, Martinez, and Rosenfeld (2001); Lee (2003).

REFERENCES

Anderson, Elijah. 1999. *Code of the Street: Decency, Violence, and the Moral Life of the Inner City.* New York: W. W. Norton.

Baumer, Eric, Julie Horney, Richard Felson, and Janet L. Lauritsen. 2003. "Neighborhood Disadvantage and the Nature of Violence." *Criminology* 41:39–72.

Dunn, Marvin. 1997. *Black Miami in the Twentieth Century.* Gainesville: University Press of Florida.

Kubrin, Charis E., and Ronald Weitzer. 2003. "Retaliatory Homicide: Concentrated Disadvantage and Neighborhood Culture." *Social Problems* 50:157–80.

Lee, Matthew T. 2003. *Crime on the Border: Immigration and Homicide in Urban Communities.* New York: LFB Scholarly Publishing.

Lee, Matthew T., and Ramiro Martinez Jr. 2002. "Social Disorganization Revisited: Mapping the Recent Immigration and Black Homicide Relationship in Northern Miami." *Sociological Focus* 35:363–80.

Lee, Matthew T., Ramiro Martinez Jr., and Richard Rosenfeld. 2001. "Does Immigration Increase Homicide? Negative Evidence from Three Border Cities." *Sociological Quarterly* 42:559–80.

Logan, John R., and Glenn Deane. 2003. *Black Diversity in Metropolitan America.* Albany: Lewis Mumford Center for Comparative Urban and Regional Research, University at Albany.

Martinez, Ramiro, Jr. 2000. "Immigration and Urban Violence: The Link between Immigrant Latinos and Types of Homicide." *Social Science Quarterly* 81:363–74.

———. 2002. "Moving beyond Black and White Violence: African American, Haitian, and Latino Homicides in Miami." In *Violent Crime: Assessing Race and Ethnic Differences,* edited by Darnell F. Hawkins, 22–43. Cambridge: Cambridge University Press.

Martinez, Ramiro, Jr., and Matthew T. Lee. 1998. "Immigration and the Ethnic Distribution of Homicide." *Homicide Studies* 2:291–304.

———. 2000a. "Comparing the Context of Immigrant Homicides in Miami: Haitians, Jamaicans, and Mariels, 1980–1990." *International Migration Review* 34: 793–811.

———. 2000b. "On Immigration and Crime." In *The Nature of Crime: Continuity and Change,* vol. 1, *Criminal Justice 2000,* edited by G. LaFree, 485–524. Washington, DC: National Institute of Justice.

Martinez, Ramiro, Jr., Matthew T. Lee, and Amie L. Nielsen. 2001. "Revisiting the Scarface Legacy: The Victim/Offender Relationship and Mariel Homicides in Miami." *Hispanic Journal of Behavioral Sciences* 23:37–56.

———. 2004. "Segmented Assimilation, Local Context and Determinants of Drug Violence in Miami and San Diego: Does Ethnicity and Immigration Matter?" *International Migration Review* 38:131–57.

Martinez, Ramiro, Jr., Amie L. Nielsen, and Matthew T. Lee. 2003. "Latinos, Immigration and Homicide: A Reconsideration of the Mariel Legacy." *Social Science Quarterly* 84:397–411.

McNulty, Thomas L. 2001. "Assessing the Race-Violence Relationship at the Macro Level: The Assumption of Racial Invariance and the Problem of Restricted Distributions." *Criminology* 39:467–90.

Nielsen, Amie L., Ramiro Martinez Jr., and Matthew T. Lee. 2005. "Alcohol, Ethnicity, and Violence: The Role of Alcohol Availability and Other Community Factors for Latino and Black Non-Lethal Violence." *Sociological Quarterly* 46:479–502.

Portes, Alejandro, and Rubén G. Rumbaut. 2001. *Legacies: The Story of the Immigrant Second Generation.* New York: Russell Sage Foundation.

Portes, Alejandro, and Alex Stepick. 1985. "Unwelcome Immigrants: The Labor Market Experiences of 1980 (Mariel) Cuban and Haitian Refugees in South Florida." *American Sociological Review* 50:493–514.

———. 1993. *City on the Edge: The Transformation of Miami.* Berkeley: University of California Press.

Portes, Alejandro, and Min Zhou. 1993. "The Second Generation: Segmented Assimilation and Its Variants." *Annals of the American Academy of Political and Social Science* 530:74–96.

Sampson, Robert J., and William J. Wilson. 1995. "Toward a Theory of Race, Crime, and Urban Inequality." In *Crime and Inequality,* edited by J. Hagan and R. D. Peterson, 37–54. Stanford: Stanford University Press.

Shaw, Clifford R., and Henry D. McKay. [1942] 1969. *Juvenile Delinquency and Urban Areas.* Rev. ed. Chicago: University of Chicago Press.

Stepick, Alex. 1992. "The Refugees Nobody Wants: Haitians in Miami." In *Miami Now! Immigration, Ethnicity, and Social Change,* edited by G. J. Grenier and Alex Stepick, 57–82. Gainesville: University of Florida Press.

———. 1998. *Pride against Prejudice: Haitians in the United States.* Boston: Allyn and Bacon.

Stepick, Alex, Guillermo Grenier, Max Castro, and Marvin Dunn. 2003. *This Land Is Our Land: Immigrants and Power in Miami.* Berkeley: University of California Press.

Stepick, Alex, Carol Dutton Stepick, Emmanuel Eugene, Deborah Teed, and Yves Labissiere. 2001. "Shifting Identities and Intergenerational Conflict: Growing up Haitian in Miami." In *Ethnicities: Children of Immigrants in America,* edited by Rubén G. Rumbaut and Alejandro Portes, 229–66. Berkeley: University of California Press.

U.S. Bureau of the Census. 1990a. *1990 Census of Population and Housing.* Summary Tape File 1. Washington, DC: U.S. Bureau of the Census.

U.S. Bureau of the Census. 1990b. *1990 Census of Population and Housing.* Summary Tape File 3a. Washington, DC: U.S. Bureau of the Census.

Waldinger, Roger. 2001a. "Conclusion: Immigration and the Remaking of Urban America." In *Strangers at the Gates: New Immigrants in Urban America,* edited by Roger Waldinger, 308–30. Berkeley: University of California Press.

———. 2001b. "Strangers at the Gates." In *Strangers at the Gates: New Immigrants in Urban America,* edited by Roger Waldinger, 1–29. Berkeley: University of California Press.

Waldinger, Roger, and Jennifer Lee. 2001. "New Immigrants in Urban America." In *Strangers at the Gates: New Immigrants in Urban America,* edited by Roger Waldinger, 30–79. Berkeley: University of California Press.

Waters, Mary C. 1994. "Ethnic and Racial Identities of Second-Generation Black Immigrants in New York City." *International Migration Review* 28:795–820.

Woolredge, John, and Amy Thistlethwaite. 2003. "Neighborhood Structure and Race-Specific Rates of Intimate Assault." *Criminology* 41:393–422.

Zhou, Min. 1997. "Growing Up American: The Challenge Confronting Immigrant Children and Children of Immigrants." *Annual Review of Sociology* 23:63–95.

———. 2001. "Progress, Decline, Stagnation? The New Second Generation Comes of Age." In *Strangers at the Gates: New Immigrants in Urban America,* edited by Roger Waldinger, 272–307. Berkeley: University of California Press.

About the Contributors

Avraham Astor is a sociology graduate student at the University of Michigan.

Carl L. Bankston III is Associate Professor of Sociology at Tulane University and coauthor (with Min Zhou) of *Growing Up American: How Vietnamese Children Adapt to Life in the United States.*

Robert J. Bursik Jr. is Curators Professor of Criminology and Criminal Justice at the University of Missouri–St. Louis and coauthor of *Neighborhoods and Crime: The Dimensions of Effective Community Control.*

Roberto G. Gonzales is a sociology graduate student at the University of California, Irvine.

Sang Hea Kil is a graduate student in the School of Justice and Social Inquiry at Arizona State University.

Golnaz Komaie is a sociology graduate student at the University of California, Irvine.

Jennifer Lee is Associate Professor of Sociology at the University of California, Irvine. She is author of *Civility in the City: Blacks, Jews, and Koreans in Urban America* and co-editor (with Min Zhou) of *Asian American Youth: Culture, Identity, and Ethnicity.*

Matthew T. Lee is Assistant Professor of Sociology at the University of Akron and author of *Crime on the Border: Immigration and Homicide in Urban Communities.*

Ramiro Martinez Jr. is Associate Professor of Criminal Justice and Public Health at Florida International University and the author of *Latino Homicide: Immigration, Violence, and Community.*

Cecilia Menjívar is Associate Professor of Sociology at Arizona State University and author of *Fragmented Ties: Salvadoran Immigrant Networks in America.*

Jeffrey D. Morenoff is Associate Professor of Sociology at the University of Michigan.

Charlie V. Morgan is a sociology graduate student at the University of California, Irvine.

Amie L. Nielsen is Associate Professor of Sociology at the University of Miami.

Rubén G. Rumbaut is Professor of Sociology and Co-director of the Center for Research on Immigration, Population and Public Policy at the University of California, Irvine. He is co-editor of *On the Frontier of Adulthood: Theory, Research, and Public Policy and Ethnicities: Children of Immigrants in America.*

Rosaura Tafoya-Estrada is a sociology graduate student at the University of California, Irvine.

Abel Valenzuela Jr. is Associate Professor of Chicana/o Studies and Urban Planning at the University of California, Los Angeles, and co-editor of *Prismatic Metropolis: Inequality in Los Angeles.*

Min Zhou is Professor of Sociology and Chair of Asian American Studies at the University of California, Los Angeles. She is co-editor (with Jennifer Lee) of *Asian American Youth: Culture, Identity, and Ethnicity* and coauthor (with Carl L. Bankston III) of *Growing Up American: How Vietnamese Children Adapt to Life in the United States.*

Index